Transnational Theatre Histories

Transnational Theatre Histories illuminates vectors of cultural exchange, migration, appropriation, and circulation that long predate the more recent trends of neoliberal globalization. Books in the series document and theorize the emergence of theatre, opera, dance, and performance against backgrounds such as imperial expansion, technological development, modernity, industrialization, colonization, diplomacy, and cultural self-determination. Proposals are invited on topics such as: theatrical trade routes; public spheres through cross-cultural contact; the role of multi-ethnic metropolitan centers and port cities; modernization and modernity experienced in transnational contexts; new materialism: objects moving across borders and regions; migration and recombination of aesthetics and forms; colonization and decolonization as transnational projects; performance histories of cross- or inter-cultural contact; festivals, exchanges, partnerships, collaborations, and co-productions; diplomacy, state and extra-governmental involvement, support, or subversion; historical perspectives on capital, finance, and administration; processes of linguistic and institutional translation; translocality, glocality, transregional and omnilocal vectors; developing new forms of collaborative authorship.

More information about this series at
https://link.springer.com/bookseries/14397

Urmimala Sarkar Munsi

Uday Shankar and His Transcultural Experimentations

Dancing Modernity

palgrave
macmillan

Urmimala Sarkar Munsi
School of Arts and Aesthetics
Jawaharlal Nehru University
New Delhi, Delhi, India

Transnational Theatre Histories
ISBN 978-3-030-93223-7 ISBN 978-3-030-93224-4 (eBook)
https://doi.org/10.1007/978-3-030-93224-4

This Palgrave Macmillan imprint is published by the registered company Springer Nature Switzerland AG
The registered company address is: Gewerbestrasse 11, 6330 Cham, Switzerland

To the memory of
Uday and Amala Shankar
Sri P. Raghavan
and
Uday Shankar India Culture Centre—Kolkata

Preface

The book does not want to be a hagiography. It is also not intended to be a biography. My research interest on this topic has been long, personal, and also academic. It has its roots in my prolonged engagement with Uday Shankar's dance as a student/troupe member/faculty of Uday Shankar India Culture Centre, Kolkata (a dance institution started by him and his wife Amala Shankar). It is an endeavour at creating a historiography, while engaging in a corporeal and academic conversation with a dance culture that has influenced and socialised me.

The book proposes to present a specific experience of modernity within the context of Indian dance by looking at the transcultural journey of Indian dancer/choreographer Uday Shankar (1900b–1977d). His popularity in Europe and America as an Oriental male dancer in the first half of twentieth century, brought him the worldwide recognition as the Ambassador of Indian culture. Shankar's dance style has an uneasy relationship with the broader history of Indian dance. While a lot of the writing on him concentrates on his physical appeal, stage presence and his becoming known through his multiple collaborative ventures with significant cultural persona in the west, no detailed analysis exists of his dance techniques/choreography. His artistic journey is extraordinary and this book cannot claim to cover all details. Looking for his dance amidst his eventful life spent as a artist, a migrant and a celebrity choreographer, this book makes an attempt to understand his contribution in the emergence of modernity in Indian dance.

The essential fieldwork and archival research were funded by a grant for Overseas Fieldwork Visit, under the scheme 'University with Potential for Excellence' (UPE II), funded by the University Grants Commission through the UPE II Project (2017) of the Jawaharlal Nehru University. The project was made possible also through a Visiting Fellowship at the Theaterwissenschaftliche Sammlung, University of Cologne in the summer of 2017.

New Delhi, India
September 2021

Urmimala Sarkar Munsi

Acknowledgements

I have learnt to dance/perform, travel, walk, talk, think, and dare from Smt. Amala Shankar. Her generous sharing of the histories she lived and danced through with her husband/mentor Uday Shankar pushed me to write this book. I acknowledge my Kathakali Guru P. Raghavan and the musicians at Uday Shankar India Culture Centre—Rabin Das, Soumen De and Souren Ghosh for making dance come alive in our lives with movements and rhythms.

I am grateful to Uday Shankar's disciple, late Narendra Sharma for his interview on life at the Uday Shankar India Culture Centre, Almora, and his son Bharat Sharma for sharing rare insights and excellent photographs from Narendra Sharma Archives. I thank Polly Guha and Bisakha Sarkar, past students of Uday Shankar for sharing their memories and experiences with me. Encouragement of Amala Shankar's students, my seniors, and friends at the Uday Shankar India Culture Centre, Kolkata, especially Mamata Shankar and Tanushree Shankar, Anomita Goswami, Bhaswati Ghosh, Bipasha Gupta Roy, Nandita Khan, Indrani Mitra, Mousumi De, Saswati Thakur, Aditi Sinha, and Piali Ray made it possible for me to take on this extremely subjective research. Special thanks go out to Chandroday Ghosh for having generously shared many insights and documents over the years.

I remain grateful to my parents, Sunil and Vidya Munsi whose academic rigour and habitual archiving have provided me with rare insights, references, reviews, souvenirs, and programme brochures of

Uday and Amala Shankar. My son Aditya Sarkar has been a patient and hyper-critical reader without whom this project would not have taken off. My sisters, Manasi and Namrata Kanuga have encouraged my obsession with this book, never losing hope through the endless delays in finishing the manuscript. I am thankful to Semanti Basu, without whose help the final work on the manuscript would not have been possible.

The Archival pilgrimage to collect the familiar and yet unknown materials on Uday and Amala Shankar began with my stay at the Jacob's Pillow Archive—made special by Mr. Norton Owen; My visits to the Boston Public Library in Boston, the Dartington Hall Archives housed currently at the Devon Heritage Centre, Exeter, the British Library, London, the Cologne and Berlin Dance Archives, and the Theaterwissenschaftliche Sammlung of the University of Cologne have added immeasurable archival material to make my research an exciting one. I thank Dr. Priyanka Basu for the help in finding rare material at the British Library.

I am thankful to Prof. Ira Bhaskar and Prof. Bishnupriya Dutt for having facilitated the elaborate processes for getting funding supports for my research. I would like to extend my special thanks to Prof. Peter Marx, for having extended his support through a Fellowship at the Theaterwissenschaftliche Sammlung of the University of Cologne for my archival research in Germany. I also would like to extend my appreciation for the support extended by the Series editors Professors Tracy C. Davis (Northwestern University), Christopher B. Balme (LMU Munich), Catherine M. Cole (University of Washington), for the Palgrave series 'Transnational Theatre Histories'. The book could not have found a more contextual affiliation.

I am grateful to Harsha Vinay, Director, Alice Boner Institute, Varanasi, and Dr. Johannes Beltz. Deputy Director, Curator of South and Southeast Asian Art, Museum Reitberg, Zurich, for making available invaluable material from the Legacy Alice Boner archives.

Finally, this book is an outcome of many years of teaching, conversations, workshops, performances, and publications at the School of Arts and Aesthetics in Jawaharlal University, New Delhi. I can not thank this fantastic space of discourse and the students thereof enough!

Praise for *Uday Shankar and His Transcultural Experimentations*

"A sustained study of Uday Shankar's work and his influence in the field of modern Indian performance practice is long overdue. Urmimala Sarkar Munsi's monograph, Dancing Modernity: Uday Shankar and his Transcultural Experimentations, is therefore both timely and pertinent. Urmimala has been a student at the Uday Shankar India Culture Centre, Kolkata and this positionality brings a particular intensity to her work. Via Shankar's life and practice, she annotates the effects of dance that travels across continents, and the translation and repurposing of both the grammars of dance and the artist's persona that this necessitates. This book will no doubt be of interest to scholars and practitioners alike, for it reflects on performance practices as they are being fashioned today."

—Anuradha Kapur, *Former Director of National School of Drama*

Contents

List of Figures

CHAPTER 1

Introduction: Uday Shankar and Indian Dance History

Questions asked about what is Indian about modern Indian dance are on a par with questions on what is Indian about modern Indian painting. These questions should be asked. (Vatsyayan 1995: 490)

Writing History as an Insider

Shortly after Uday and Amala Shankar opened their school, the Uday Shankar India Culture Centre (henceforth mentioned as USICC) in 1965 in South Kolkata (erstwhile Calcutta), I met Uday and Amala Shankar at my uncle's chamber—I was all of seven years old. My uncle was an eye surgeon and they were his favourite patients, visiting for an eye check-up. I was an only child, living in a joint family but there was nobody else of my age in the extended family structure that I was a part of. I joined the USICC in 1966. With a sense of wonder I remember being called to his chamber by my uncle and being introduced to the illustrious couple—whose significance I understood much later. After my mother and I were introduced to them, I was asked by Uday Shankar if I liked dancing. Sitting on his lap I had nodded vigorously. The next question came from Amala Shankar directed towards me and my mother: 'Would she like to come to our school?' That day unknowingly I, with my mother, chose a path that I have walked with much joy till now.

U. Sarkar Munsi, *Uday Shankar and His Transcultural Experimentations*, Transnational Theatre Histories,
https://doi.org/10.1007/978-3-030-93224-4_1

By the time I became a student of USICC, Shankar was a disillusioned pedagogue. He had lost his dream institution in Almora (see Chapter 4), he had lost money in making his film that did not do well at the box office, in spite of being lauded by many critics (see Chapter 5), and he was disappointed at the way the nation had treated a world renowned artist of his calibre. It was Amala Shankar, who was principally running the school. It shaped my universe—an universe that was part of my vocabulary, that was in constant dialogue with my dance, shaping it or being shaped by it. We learnt the basics of Bharatanatyam, Kathakali, and Manipuri along with the improvisational dance form that was called Creative Dance in a class conducted by Smt. Amala Shankar. (Later the Bharatanatyam class was replaced by Kathak.) By the time we did our diploma examinations, our bodies had acquired a huge movement repertoire, they had become repositories of a range of kinaesthetic combinations—linear as well as square movements, rigid as well as soft torso movements, jumps, stomps, flat or soft steps, and so on. These bodies could do jumps and walks and gestures from different styles and were given the freedom to improvise on those forms of basic knowledge that were perfected through rigorous practice and unrelenting diligence. We could transform or interpret alphabets, numbers, emotions, painted lines, architectural drawings, and any image to dance movements with ease.

The creative dance teaching introduced and energised empathetic spaces for innovation, reaction, dialogues between bodies, and experiencing music, rhythms, ideas, props, and boundless imaginations. These spaces also produced a common will in all of us, to create and share the embodied ecology, to achieve together through contributory and compound labour—an outcome, that belonged to no one in particular, but was an achievement that everyone was congratulated or critiqued together for. It created a space of comfort, shared effort, and dancing dreams. When I look back, Susan Leigh Foster's words reflect the outcome precisely,

> The dance constructs this new ground through its practice of remembering, sowing the past into the present in order that it might be regrown. On this ground the ability of one person to feel with another must also be cultivated. The possibility for fellow-feeling exists as a prior given, yet all individuals participating in the dance must continually dedicate themselves to making it happen. (Foster 2011: 186)

The class learnt together the difference between presence and representation—two basic elements to be taken care of in the idea of performing. The classes in enactment and movement practices also led us through the process of a seamless way to go travel between these two ways of being in a performance moment, i.e. being present and taking on the responsibility of being in the moment; and portraying or representing texts, character roles, music, words, ideas. Added to these two primary ways to get into a dance space, were the introduction to a range of ways to enjoy dancing. The 'five distinct theories of why dance sparks this sense of enthusiasm' (Foster 2019: 34) suggested by Foster in her book *Valuing Dance: Commodities and Gifts in Motion* 'account for dance's energizing capacity', i.e. (1) dance as play; (2) dance as synchrony; (3) dance as bodily becoming; (4) dance as virtual power; and (5) dance as mobilisation (ibid.), sum up the important takeaways from our training. These five theories speak for the basic structure of the not so well worked out, but evidently the basic ground rules) that were used to draw us into dance through simultaneous use of grammatic embodiment and improvisation—through a range of processes—connected either to either presence or representation or both. As Foster also says, there is no way to put these theories in a hierarchy of importance or group a few of them together as possible processes to energise the dancing bodies in our classes. I would rather read them as the motives for the pedagogy that made it possible for Uday Shankar to create a pedagogic structure for the modern dance that we were learning in the institution.

At USICC Kolkata, we were given references of rich performance practices from different regions of India in class, and often were told about the importance of dancing the 'Indian' dance. On the other hand all of us were encouraged and in fact most often accompanied Mashima (Amala Shankar) to see performances from visiting dance troupes from all over the world. With these choreographers and dancers from all over the world visiting us at the school and holding workshops, the world of dance and the imagination of faraway dance spaces took wings in our minds. We only saw Uncle (as we called Shankar) occasionally, but we were encouraged to see rehearsals and classes of the older students. We heard the stories of the tours and we began dreaming of becoming dancers. Within a year of being a part of the institution, I absolutely adored dancing, with all its baggage, such as the pain of achieving perfection in the classical dance classes, the fear of lack of perfection, the loss of free time during weekends and holidays. I can go on endlessly about the class on creative dance.

It is what taught me to observe human and non-human elements around me and also created a mind and body that made it imperative for me to experience the world through and as literally and metaphorically a 'moving' space. These tools also made me an anthropologist much before I trained to become one.

From Archives and Memories to Discourse

The classes of Amala Shankar, Guru P. Raghavan, and the musicians associated with the USICC, Kolkata, such as Rabin Das and Soumen De, have also contributed to gathering a great deal of anecdotal information about Shankar's aesthetic and imaginative experiments. We learnt many of Shankar's choreographies much later, after he had passed away in 1977, also after finishing our training in Kathakali, Manipuri, and Kathak. For us, his dance was never about grammars, but an embodied knowledge system, a way of viewing and living life. The USICC, Kolkata, modelled itself according to its first version in Almora. The pedagogy that developed emphasised an extremely complex relationship of love/criticality (reflexivity)—where one learns to be able to criticise one's own creations, to try and create something tangibly 'new' out of 'old' ideas, as well as dances. On one hand, it increases the students' abilities to observe intensely and concentrate and embody the movements that they are asked to 'follow'. They are trained to remember music and beats and the ability to recreate exactly what they see being performed in class or rehearsal. But on the other hand, they are trained to imagine and improvise, with or without music or text, movement sequences that they can repeat over and over again, for others to follow and memorise. Learning to be constructively reflexive for self and others is part of that culture and that knowledge system. It also ideally points towards a world of knowledge-sharing beyond hierarchy.

But of course, those utopic ideals are as fragile in this particular niche environment as they are everywhere else in the world, and hence it took a while to gather the courage to face my own subjectivity and position within this particular knowledge system that I have loved and grown up in. Actually quite late in life, after I moved to Delhi to start teaching at the School of Arts and Aesthetics in Jawaharlal Nehru University, I first realised that not everyone liked or even understood what Shankar's style was. The knowledge about Shankar's dance was negligible, full of misinformation, and misrepresentations coming out of a huge bias for classical dances and an unsurmountable disdain for anything that was not sanctified by the state and its official knowledge banks as the real historical/classical culture—such as the classical dances in the list of the Ministry of Culture of the Government of India. Anything outside that list was synthetic, fusion, popular, imitative, influenced by the West, and so on and so forth. These dancers were seen as appropriators, imposters without proper training, selling themselves and their art to the West, borrowing from the so-called classical dances to create their own repertoires. All of a sudden it dawned on me that I had spent my life learning some dance that actually was being refused a name by the country where its practitioner was born.

I did not have an answer for people who asked me, 'Oh so you are a dancer? What form did you learn? Bharatanatyam?' When I dared to say anything, it would sound like a mumbled apology about having learned 'creative dance taught at USICC, Kolkata, along with classical styles such as…'. By the time I uttered the word 'creative', the brows were up. If I was lucky to finish the sentence, and there was no smirk or complete confusion all over the face of the listener, I would venture further to elaborate on the technique classes and how I loved the dance institution. But that chance came very few times in my life. By the time I was a teenager, I had understood that I was learning an idea, of making dance and was capable of creating new patterns of moving. I knew by then that I had been taught to go on experimenting, in thinking of my dancing body in minor details, such as small negotiations between control and commitment, stability and destabilising, observing and remembering not only how people move or stop or run or walk on roads, but also how they look far and squint to focus on something when they read small letters or how people suppress their emotions or expand on them by moving their hands or bodily movements. That was not enough either. I knew that in classes of creative dance, my teacher might ask me to drag out any of these memories and by the end of the class that memory might have become a full-fledged moment segment with all my friends following and perfecting it. In these difficult teen years, where I was negotiating the emotions of growing up as the only girl-child with middle-class communist parents who were both engaged in journalistic and academic activities, my dance school and the imaginative as well as collective universe it provided to all of us as students went far beyond what any school space could provide. My strength and vulnerability was reflected in many of my cohorts from the USICC, Kolkata.

So what did I say when I was asked what style of dance I had learnt? The first few times I was defiant, I said I was from the USICC. Almost in all cases, there was either a smirk or a question mark on the face of the person who tried hard in both cases to hide either the dismissiveness that they felt or the ignorance they had about this style. This new understanding of his status or rather the lack of it, made me realise though that in spite of all these negativities, Shankar was definitely a national figure, because the international dance community had long since recognised him as the ambassador of Indian dance to the world way back in the early 1930s. Here I was in the city of Delhi, where exhibitions and festivals celebrating all classical dances happen round the year; after the centenary year's tokenistic celebrations, Uday Shankar rests in undisturbed peace, forgotten and under-documented. The smirk that irked me when I had mentioned him along with the prominent names in dance history in India in one of my public talks, reappear on the faces of many prominent speakers on Indian modernity as well as dance. Dance writers were happier to talk about his work in terms of his stagecraft, and, of course, his excellent physique and handsome presence on stage. The writings, therefore, remained conspicuous in terms of their silence on his dance-making process.

In spite of a fairly busy publishing history, my choice to stay away from actually writing a book on Uday Shankar has surprised many of my close associates, both within the world of dance and dance studies. Apart from short articles contributed here and there, and three chapters in books edited or written by me, I have cautiously stayed away. But now it feels like a compulsion of sorts, hence now is the moment. As a social anthropologist I am aware of the uncritical acceptance that may colour my writing. Acknowledging all such misgivings, I attempt to place Shankar's dance, his dance-making process, and his legacy, if any, in a socio-political as well as a complex historical context in this book. To do so, I have drawn on a range of methodologies: ranging from reconnecting auto-ethnographical data to archival analysis, while working consistently with interviews of fellow dancers from the USICC, Kolkata, as well as the dancers who have worked with Uday Shankar after he settled in Kolkata after having made the film *Kalpana*.

Framing Uday Shankar—The Dancer, Choreographer, Dreamer

Renowned Indian dancer Uday Shankar was born on 8 December 1900, in Udaipur. He was the eldest of seven sons born to Shyam Shankar Chowdhuri and Hemangini Devi. As the foreign minister of the state of Jhalawar, Shyam Shankar was an ambitious person and was involved in various intellectual and cultural activities, while Shankar was growing up. He was also a frequent traveller and in 1920 he accompanied the king of the princely state of Jhalawar, Bhawani Singh to London. Hemangini had already been virtually separated from her husband even before that, and was looking after the sons alone with the help of her own family. Uday Shankar was brought up in the opulence of the Royal Palace, while spending time at his maternal grandfather's home intermittently in the village of Nasrathpur.

This was the time in pre-independence India when the young generation of learners from India had started to travel to foreign universities in post-First-World-War Europe. Vilayat[1] (Bilet in Bengali), a word which represented an undistinguished imaginary foreign land representing the 'West', had become desirable to the young and upper class people whose families could somehow afford to send them abroad to fulfil their dreams. In most cases, of course, these dreams were also those of their family members, who aspired for a modern education for their offspring. The desire to go abroad was often not clearly structured, other than somehow reaching a land where modern dreams could materialise. Shankar's opportunity to go to London to study art and become a dancer is one such story. Shankar had left home for Bombay to study at the Sir J. J. School of Arts in 1917, and eventually for London to study at the Royal College of Arts in 1920. Shyam's initial reason for calling Uday to London in 1920 was to use his artistic training for the variety shows Shyam presented in the city. The first one of them was 'The Great Moghul's Chamber of Dreams', at the Royal Opera House, Covent Garden. Shankar helped his father with the staging of that performance.

Going through training in modern art under British art educator William Rothenstein and experiencing British museums, archives, and libraries added to his exposure to modern art education. Coming in

[1] Usually meaning a foreign land, the word was/is used in India specifically with reference to Europe or Britain.

contact with the Russian Ballerina Anna Pavlova, and getting a chance to explore somewhat untrained ideas of choreography with a ballerina of her stature, consolidated his place in the history of modernist negotiations within the world of art in general and dance in particular.

Most evaluations of Shankar's work, attribute most of his fame to some orientalist fascination of the Western audience of the late colonial times—for a handsome, good-looking, brown (but not revoltingly so), but altogether a charming man—who at the age of twenty-three came in contact with some very significant people in the art world of the colonial masters. His willingness to be influenced by Western dances, bodies, performance discipline, and presentational rigour is also seen by many as reflective of his impressionistic nature, and his lack of respect for his own culture. He is seen to be an eager adventurer as well for leaving the Royal College of Arts even after he won a prize acknowledging his extraordinary talent as a visual artist. His first experiment with choreography for Pavlova is viewed as more of a tableau than a dance, reaffirming the idea of the orient for the Western audience. This complex history is explained by Priya Srinivasan's words 'I argue that a re-examination of the inception of modern dance in Oriental dance reveals the labour of transnational dancing women and men from India that has been rendered invisible thus calling the "national" and modernist project of American dance into question' (Srinivasan 2007: 9). These words help situate Shankar in the West in a prologue to his organised dance endeavours. In her essay on Ruth St. Denis' composition of *Radha* in 1906, Srinivasan establishes through archival explorations and newspaper reports of this performance that portrayed her as a genius, did not see it as a result of her seeing some *Nautch* girls from Kolkata perform in a spectacle named *Durbar of Delhi* in Coney Island, UK in 1904. Unlike what is popularly believed to have originated from St. Denis' brilliant research and imagination on the dancing girls from India, St. Denis was appropriating the nameless dancers from a colonised country. Srinivasan argues:

> Even though modern and post modern dance historians fail to remember the Nautch women and Indian men whose labour enabled St. Denis' creation of Radha (1906), the first elaborate piece she premiered after seeing the exhibitions in the Coney Island 'spectacle,' I argue that St. Denis' white female body in performance highlights and makes visible their kinesthetic legacies. The labour of Nautch dancing women thus

haunts American dance histories through the very basic dance principles of movement; spiral turns and whirls. (Srinivasan 2007: 8)

This trend of appropriation of dance and performance from the East continued with various ways of authentication produced by St. Denis (by painting her body brown and dancing surrounded by Indian men) and many other dancers. In fact, Anna Pavlova seemed to be doing the same thing when she invited Shankar to work with her. Shankar's writings and interviews often include gratitude for Anna Pavlova for inviting him to choreograph and dance with her. Shankar saw this hierarchical collaborative process clearly as an achievement and he remained grateful for the public visibility or 'adjacency'[2] that his role as the dance partner/authenticator of Pavlova allowed him.

Shankar's journey also foregrounds the trope of orientalism that plagued the world of Indian art and culture. The emergence of orientalist stereotypes, I argue, is not to be blamed only on the colonisers, but also on the self-orientalising processes, consolidated by many artists, dancers, and musicians who wanted to secure and hold a special place in the emerging global cultural negotiations. This book aims to understand the journey of an individual who shapes himself as a skilled performer/entertainer/choreographer through this time in multiple locations in different countries, consciously or unconsciously existing and surviving in diverse transcultural artistic atmospheres.

Specifically of interest is the fact that he existed unintentionally alongside people considered to be the pioneers of modernity in India such as Rabindranath Tagore[3] and Abanindranath Tagore.[4] He also was present

[2] 'Wish for adjacency' is a term used by Srinivasan in her personal interview (dated 27 August 2021) to explain the wish and hope in many colonised people of colour to be seen alongside the white colonisers.

[3] Rabindranath Tagore's contribution to the institutionalised teaching and experimentation with a variety of dance forms along with his initiative in modern education, brough a consciousness of multiple forms of dance practice co-existing in India and other south and south East Asian countries. His experimentations with balletic representation of his texts in the form of what he named as 'dance drama' stand out a historical predecessor to the later work done by Uday Shankar with creative dance. Tagore is recognised as the Nobel Laureate from Bengal, known worldwide as the poet, writer, painter, and music composer who shaped Modernism in early twentieth-century India.

[4] Abanindranath Tagore established the 'Indian Society of Oriental Art' and also founded the Bengal school of art. He is seen as one of the first modern Indian painters.

in the same geographies at the same time as famous modern dancers such as Martha Graham and Mary Wigman. But Uday Shankar never claimed to be a modern dancer. But he danced as Shiva and also represented the industrial labouring body covered in sweat and dirt in a factory setting. His most productive time was within the last twenty-five years of the colonial era. But his (probably deliberate) staying away from active political engagement either in the cultural planning for India, and/or in its nationalist discourses, need to be connected to his expressions that were articulated through his choreographic language in some of his presentations and his film *Kalpana*.

This book is provoked by the curiosity about the role of such an individual in establishing a transcultural and translocational connection between worlds that were still disconnected through cultural biases and colonial histories. Shankar's institution-building efforts, his projection of the newly emerging urban India, and his concern regarding the vanishing of cultural practices, create a sharp contrast to the post-independence policies of the Indian government. Those policies virtually erased Uday Shankar's presence and contribution to dance by denying it legitimacy through the systematic erasure of any space for modernity in Indian cultural practices. A sharp binary between the classical forms of dances[5] and the folk/community performances, pushed out Shankar's efforts as something foreign, of fusion-like quality, and lacking skill. That phase of policy creation also took charge of the writing of history of Indian dances, through deliberate exclusions of the intruders in the specific context of dance traditions such as those of Rabindranath Tagore and Uday Shankar.

Kapila Vatsyayan describes the intention of creating classical dances as a contemporary idea. She writes in her book *Indian Classical Dance*:

> The classical dance styles of contemporary India are largely reconstructions of fragments of [these] antiquity. On one level they have great antiquity

[5] There are eight classical dances in India. The country's cultural policies helped to create a space of advantage for some genres of dance—where tradition, history, and cultural heritage added legitimacy to the 'Classical' dances as inherited from pre-colonial antiquity. A well-established model has since then been created for other such constructed forms to aspire to get recognition as a classical dance. And since the early 1950s, this list has grown with time. All it has taken for the new inclusions in the current list of eight classical dances is for a form to run through the examination and scrutiny of a government appointed team of experts and to confirm the essential characteristics for it to become classical.

which links them to the past, on another level they are contemporary and recent, performed outside the traditional milieu and context, each time performing the past, but are not the past. (Vatsyayan 1997: 8)

The period of recognition and reconstruction of regional dance forms and their local histories coincides with Shankar's increasing awareness of the diversity in dance forms in India. His experiencing of dance forms (later recognised as Manipuri, Bharatanatyam, and Kathakali forms of classical dances) from Manipur, Tamil Nadu, and Kerala, respectively, in the early 1930s led to their becoming Shankar's favourite dance forms that later were used by him to develop the body vocabulary for institutional dance pedagogy.

My reading of the history of colonialism with that of the emergence of the category of classical dances sees Uday Shankar's struggle for recognition within the dance community as not born or located within the dance community in India at all. Rather, it is the result of being caught in an in-between space within a tug-of-war between the pre-colonial, colonial, and postcolonial Indian cultural identities and trying to balance tradition and modernity in thinking and dancing simultaneously. Explaining this phenomenon in the larger context of modern Indian history, Sumit Sarkar writes:

> Much of what has come to be widely assumed as 'traditional' in Indian society does seem to have come into existence in the colonial era. The processes of 'construction' or 'invention', however, were more complicated than a mere imposition of alien colonial-Western categories on a helpless, passive, and undifferentiated mass of the colonised.... (Sarkar 2015: 22–23)

Shankar's dance was shunned by the cultural planners as not Indian enough for having originated in a process of transcultural negotiation and through a shifting translocational experience. This was at a time when being linked to the emerging idea of the independent nation and having a strong claim to the Indian national identity was crucial for any artist. Throughout his life, Shankar tried very hard to be accepted within this elite group of 'Indians'. Intermittently he succeeded as well, to be shunned again soon after. The uneasy story of these alliances and break-ups are written through the chapters that identify elements of modernity, his auto-exoticised and self-orientalising creations, his institution-building effort and its failure, and his experimental dabbling in multimedia performances that were arguably the first of their kind within the dance ecology of India.

Until his death in 1977, Shankar collected many tags, some complimentary and some derogatory. One undeniably complimentary tag was that of a 'cultural ambassador' of India. The other ones—not always used in a complimentary manner—were those of 'world traveller', 'entertainer', and 'oriental dancer'.

Framing Shankar as the Intruder in Indian Dance History

Shankar's dance was a product of his negotiations with and in the world and his personal experiences—often evolving out of his instinctive aesthetic understanding. The deep engagement and fascination with human physical forms as a visual artist is consistently reflected in his understanding of human figures—used by him both in his art practice and his dance. In spite of the structure of his pedagogy and the reflection of his innovative teaching in the work of his students and the troupe productions, the Indian critics went all out to destroy Shankar's work repeatedly. In her chapter on Shankar in *New Directions in Indian Dance*, Kapila Vatsyayan criticised Shankar's dance and choreographic works, emphasising the (undisciplined) free flow of movements and the grammarless-ness of his dance. praised many artists who respected the classicisation process in Indian dance as their respect for cultural roots within traditional life of India. She said, 'Their art was shaped and chiselled in accordance with their discoveries of the tradition, lying mouldy, dusty, but genuine…. The significant fact was their strict adherence to the classical pattern of relating movement to the metric cycle (tala), and the literary word (sahitya)' (Vatsyayan 2003: 21). She felt Uday Shankar did not know or follow the classical pattern, and in his work 'The distinction between nritta and abhinaya was broken. It was movement of the human form for its own sake, primary and independent of the tala or the poetic line' (Vatsyayan 2003: 22).

In a recent book by Prarthana Purkayastha, *Indian Modern Dance, Feminism and Transnationalism*, a brief chapter on Shankar elaborates his position as the floating entity between the East and the West. Purkayastha expresses concern that 'there have been few attempts at critical analyses and evaluation of Shankar's body of choreographic work made in

India at the height of anti-colonial sentiment in the 1940s' (Purkayastha 2014: 51). Her writing foregrounds a socio-cultural analysis of Shankar's journey till *Kalpana* and provokes a curiosity in the readers, wanting to understand what actually was the base for Shankar's pedagogical process. Purkayastha writes, 'Shankar can be positioned as an outsider within the framework of South Asian cultural nationalism: a floating figure who travelled between two worlds, the Euro-American and the Asian, without ever wholly belonging to either one' (Purkayastha 2014: 58).

Pushing Purakayastha's argument further, I find Shankar as an intruder in the emerging cultural understanding in his own country, who refused to accept the position of an outsider. Shankar's work in *Kalpana* unfortunately remains the only noteworthy access to Shankar's dance (some other examples being a few very short film clips of his duets with Simkie) and many people analyse the dances and movements recorded in *Kalpana* as his dance repertoire. The creative endeavours of Shankar and the performance and pedagogic analysis attempted in this book hope to complicate the idea of the 'floating' identity in Purkayastha's writing.

One of the informative books is *His Dance, His Life: A Portrait of Uday Shankar* (1983). It is a biographical narrative, rich in archival documents, letters, photographs, and details of Uday Shankar's life and dance, written by Mohan Khokar. His personal interview of Shankar and their close association in the last seven years of Shankar's life has made the book one of the best sources of information.

A recently published book containing memoirs of Amala Shankar in Bengali, *Shankarnama: Smritichitre Amala Shankar* (2019), by Bishakha Ghosh, carries a lot of unpublished letters and some archival collections of Amala Shankar. The documents and interviews that were earlier serialised in a Bengali periodical are informative but tend to turn into a spicy inside story. One gets very little about Shankar's dance techniques in this writing.

One of the systematic descriptions of Shankar's early career is "Uday Shankar: The Early Years, 1900–1938" by Ruth Abrahams (Abrahams 2007: 363–426) whose thorough archival work helps us understand the dancer's journey. She mapped Shankar's progress as a dancer/choreographer and public figure to present a social history of his achievements. To describe Shankar's contribution, Abrahams quoted Coomaraswamy's essay 'Uday Shankar's Indian Dancing' (1937) where he mentioned Shankar's dance to be a useful 'technique to give expression to Indian themes that enable Americans to hear the instrumental music of India for the first time' (Abrahams 2007: 365).

Joan Erdman, who had spent a long time researching on Shankar and co-writing Zohra Segal's biography *Stages: The Art and Adventures of Zohra Segal* (1997), spent a long time with Amala Shankar and the rest of the Shankar family, and published some important articles that contributed to an active reclamation of Shankar's position within the realms of dance history in India. A number of essays by her have been helpful for my research. She has quoted extensively from Mohan Khokar's biographical work on Shankar (1983), besides referring to her interviews with members of Shankar's family, and his troupe members. Both Abrahams' and Erdman's research are detailed documentations of highlights in Shankar's life and career. About Shankar's dance Erdman wrote:

> As in the translation of literary texts, a translation of performance is for a particular time (one's own) and audience (whether literary, artistic, scholarly, immigrant, elite, public, national, or international). Shankar's translations, like those of the Russian novelists in the 19th century, have significantly affected the genre to this day. Developing a perspective on the times in which Shankar presented his programs is essential to understanding how he was able to translate and, at the same time, act as catalyst to the renaissance in Indian classical dance. (Erdman 1987: 69)

Erdman's work is a rigorous exercise of analysing the process of translation and the product that emerges out of it. It leads to a detailed understanding of Shankar's sensibilities, exposure, awareness, and understanding of the spaces for arts presentation in the West. She ends her essay on Shankar's translations of his dance for the West with, 'Recognized as India's first modern dance, Shankar's translations for the west become both a success in their own time and a significant reference for contemporary attempts in modern and ethnic dance production' (Erdman 1987: 84). As a follow-up, Zohra Segal's autobiography, *Close-up: memories of a life on Stage and Screen* (2010) helps to substantiate her views on Shankar's pedagogy, success, and failures, further in an unimitable manner.

Erdman's work stands out as one of the most important academic contributions that helps in placing Shankar's dance productions in a Western context. One of the basic question it helps us formulate is regarding the ways in which a performance text, whether of music, dance, or dance theatre can be translated and why does it have to be seen as a translation at all? For me, this question creates an opportunity for a historiographic exercise to understand the scope of the word 'translation' when the work has not intentionally been recognised as a translation by the choreographer himself. Shankar's strategies and skills of presentation used during the late 1920s and the whole of the 1930s do not appear to be claimed as translations. According to Erdman, depending on the genre that it presents, a performance text is 'an image memory', or 'a sound memory', or 'a movement memory' that can be 'fully restated only in images, sounds, and movement' (Erdman 1987: 67). Taking off from this observation, Shankar's work may be read in the context of the period between the two world wars, with colonisation still in its dominant phase, when the onus of being seen, accepted, and acknowledged by the Europeans and Americans is seen commonly in many performers and their works. It is also seen as something one has to do to get an entry into the world of privilege. For a choreographer such as Shankar to feel the same way and to have to take up the responsibility of translating is often an expectation, a chance given to lesser cultures who are seen as seeking to expand their audience and market rather than expressing their creativity. At the same time, creative and expansive urges among the Western experimenters in oriental dance of the same time is seen as people searching for a newer vocabulary.

This book acknowledges the available publications and looks at Shankar as a product of the transcultural and translocational crosscurrents[6] between the Orient and the Western world of dance. It investigates Shankar's role as a cultural mediator (between the East and the West) as well as a popular intruder (as he was caught in the middle of the push and pull of both the worlds trying to construct his own 'new' terrain in dance). It is an effort to address the layered history in which Shankar becomes the agent of an intercultural conversation. In that historical interchange, the simple flow of acculturative overpowering by the coloniser of the colonised needs to be complicated by acknowledging the counterflow

[6] The recent readings that I have used to hone my understanding of the words/theoretical paradigms around the negotiations of Shankar across geographical and cultural boundaries, i.e. the use of the words 'transcultural' and 'translocational'—create a subject-specific domain for this book, while being strongly referential to their own their histories of prior use.

of influence on the coloniser by the colonised as well. In this context, one may refer to the writings of Carl Weber in his essay in *Interculturalism and Performance* who suggested the pairing up of the anthropological term 'acculturation' with 'transculturation' to acknowledge the transactional/exchange process in operation between two cultures, even when one of them is dominant over the other more oppressed or (in this case) colonised one. Weber says:

> If the reader will accept the term 'acculturation' along with the presently more popular 'transculturation', he or she gains the options of using each term in a specific way. The latter would signify a genuine effort to 'transculture' (as in 'transcend' and 'transform') both the foreign and the indigenous tradition, or specific elements from them, the former an effort to 'acculture' (as in 'acquire' and 'acclimate') a foreign culture or aspects of it. The complimenting of 'transculturation' with the term 'acculturation' will help in analysing the phenomenon to be signified by the two terms and the problems they represent. (Weber 1991: 31)

Shankar's travel to the imperial "mother country" (Robins 2008: 245) and his identity as a student, underwent changes after he left his studies and began searching for different ways to survive as a migrant, first in England and then Paris, striving to find the best way to utilise the artistic practice that he was passionate about. His non-Western negotiations necessitated 'sustaining of plural cultural identities and different loyalties over the desire to identify and achieve specific equality status as a fixed minority in any particular state' (Robins 2008: 247). He further explained,

> Migrants are seen, not as moving between containing societies, but rather as operating across transnational social spaces - spaces with a multipolar geographic orientation, rather than one limited exclusively to a single coherent geographic space. (Robins 2008: 248)

Robins problematised the term culture 'as a unitary and bounded entity' that is conceived in such individual cases as a representative one responsible for asserting and establishing the image of the nation. He wrote, 'It is thought normal for people to live in one culture at a time, for example; to speak one language; to adhere to one polity. It is a principle that defies the actual complexity of peoples cultures and identities' (Robins 2008: 250).

At the same time, Shankar's beginning years in Europe, in my opinion, can never be understood without taking into account his status as that of a migrant, where many decisions were made on the basis of no or very limited options. Thus, transcultural negotiations in his case were often the outcome of the only way of survival, or an acute anxiety to remain and survive (both as a human as well as an artist) in the West. The terms 'transnational' as well as 'translocational' are therefore ways to locate that particular migrant sensibility. The process of re-searching during the archival work, created an urgency to create a space where the in-between world of Shankar's dance could be accessed and laid out as a map. This was necessary to complicate his everyday negotiations with the bodily markers of his corporeal experience through the specific in-between identity in and outside of the realms of dance while traversing the two worlds geographically as well.

In this book I also would like to propose an alternate historiography about a subject that has only gone beyond it's hagiographic space through the 'scholarly writings' mostly of people from the Western world, for whom, the migrant figure of Shankar remains forever a subject to be read through his reception in the world that he was trying so hard to belong to. This methodological choice is energised by Rustom Bharucha's contribution to the related arguments posited in his essay 'Politics of Culturalisms in an Age of Globalisation: Discrimination, Discontent and Dialogue' (1999). His article helps to legitimise my own readings of a truly in-between aspiration of Shankar to bring the East to the West together. Shankar's subjecthood is born out of his creative imagination that took his dance beyond what Bharucha described as 'reflections on the political and economic inequities of north–south cultural transaction' (Bharucha 1999: 477).

While reading the archives, all efforts at dance-making, troupe formation, working with international presenters of the top order, establishing temporary households in distant lands, appeared to be based on creating new 'homes' and deliberately choosing a migrant status to facilitate the idea of a performing artist readily available accessible and willing to travel. These translocational negotiations are seen as choices that were made with certain time and space-specific requirements in terms of resources and privileges. As a migrant by choice, Shankar was empowered by a freedom to move beyond the bondage of the references of his original location, if and when he wanted. For me the idea of the 'translocational' is a presence across: (1) political borders, whereby identification of the 'original' place (nation) of birth continues to be present in the cultural, economic, and social identification in the newer spaces inhabited; (2) a presence that is established through networks and relationships across geographies, whereby there is noticeably significant leap and formalisation in economic, cultural, and social exchanges and contracts with cross-border contacts; and (3) a move towards larger temporal as well as socio-cultural investments in the transnational locations across borders.

Any analysis of Shankar's work would depend largely on placing him, his dance, as well as his associates in his dance journey, in a historiographical text. In such a text, the intermingling dance history of the East and the West, the colonised and the colonisers, have to come together to make sense of each of the distinct stages in Shankar's dance trajectory. At the same time as Shankar's European sojourn, the dance world in and outside India also was quite interestingly registering many life-changing occurrences. In India, the all-pervasive discourse of the time was on and around dance as the art of the fallen. The general social stigma against the temple dancers in the southern parts of India, known as devadasi, was being addressed by imposing different manners of social control. The dancing women were legally identified as the pollutant human elements. A series of debates led to the introduction of legal acts to stop such performances which got finalised in the year 1947. The dancing and singing practices of the disenfranchised devadasi community[7] became available for urban elite women performers such as Rukmini Devi Arundale to appropriate. Dance motifs, movements, and content were reworked and reformed to suit the sensibilities of the changing urban patrons, learners, and audiences. These changes were supported by the invention of a classicism that is mentioned above by Vatsyayan. In that shift of the rights to perform—from traditional lower caste devadasi performers to urban elite women dancers—all changes and new aestheticisations[8] were normalised as 'authentic' and 'genuine' as Bharatanatyam was established as a classical Indian dance form. There is no record of what Shankar actually thought of such acts of social reform as a male member of Brahminic descent, though his support of Balasaraswati, a Bharatanatyam dancer of extraordinary artistic capabilities belonging to a traditional devadasi family, is

[7] A large number of significant academic research exists on this particularly important issue, that continues to have contemporary resonance. See Soneji (2012), Uma Chakravarti (1996), Meduri (1996), and Amrit Srinivasan (1985).

[8] Please see Meduri (1996) and Chakravarti (1996).

well known. Thus, without any active resistance to the marginalisation of devadasi women, he established his support to the traditional performers from within the community of temple performers, who were forcibly being denied their art practice and occupation at the same time.

At the same time his admiration for Tagore is well known. He proudly displayed and talked about the letter Tagore wrote to him to request him to lead the way for Indian dancers to find a new path of glory. One also sees his confusing alliance with the same nation-builders he was often critiquing. Later in the chapters it will become clearer that in his plan to build an institution, Shankar was also making a commitment to create knowledge and consciousness about traditional culture and philosophy among young citizens through art. His programme notes clearly tell us about his choice to take on the responsibility to develop his and his students' 'Indian'ness through studies and embodied practices. It also explains his self-appointed role in reviving and popularising Indian performing arts traditions.

Methodological Issues

In order to make an honest attempt at staying away from a biographical or hagiographical writing, I have strived to organise the material available on Shankar around important themes, mostly following the temporal order of history. I propose through the chapters that Shankar could successfully turn the influence and control of the West through different stages of his dance career into a counter-mechanism whereby he made a specific place for himself and Indian dance in the aesthetic paradigm set by the colonisers.

In the introductory chapter 'Uday Shankar and Indian Dance History', Shankar is located in an intermingling dance history of the East and the West, the colonised and the colonisers, and the discourse on and around the dancing body and the acceptability of the dancer. In this chapter I use my subjective position as an erstwhile prominent student, troupe member, and an administrator of Uday Shankar India Culture Centre, Kolkata to engage with the history of Shankar's negotiation with dance. The second chapter 'Modern Dance? Placing Shankar's Transculturality in Colonial South Asia' analyses Shankar's urge of creating an innovative dance technique, breaking away from power structures of hereditary dance learning, performing, and teaching. The investigation of his dance language as well as the creation, presentation of, and reception to Shankar's dance as a creative experiment is read through his tranlocational and transcultural negotiations. The chapter also tries to place Shankar within the history of the nationalist impulse of the artists that resisted being recognised as 'modern' during their lifetime. In the third chapter, 'Dancing Oriental Masculinity: and His Experiments in Modern Dance', I see his dance as his negotiation with his self-perception, his creativity, as well as his reception by his audience at home and in the world as an oriental male subject within the colonial understanding of Indian culture. This chapter talks of his transcultural conversations, his auto-exoticisation, and his journey with important fellow travellers who have played very distinct parts in the way the 'work' of developing his dance began and grew over the years. The fourth chapter, 'An Attempt at Creating a Modern Institution', concentrates on two important institutions that played crucial parts in the shaping of how Shankar is remembered after his passing—the Dartington Hall—the United Kingdom-based institution that trusted Shankar's ideas, and his institution, the USICC, which they helped him build in Almora. Shankar's brief experiments in institution-building are discussed to highlight the transcultural essence of Shankar's imagination around dance and its future. In the fifth chapter, 'Beyond the Proscenium with Dance, Magic, and Film', the seldom mentioned and even less analysed creative projects of his shadow plays, his experiments with dance and magic in *Shankarscope*, and his only film *Kalpana* are discussed in detail. I have chosen to use my auto-ethnographic accounts of performing in restaged performances and the shadow play *Mahamanav* under Amala Shankar, along with the interviews of performers from *Shankarscope*, in absence of written documentation of both these experiments. In the same chapter, *Kalpana* is seen as a proof and a witness of Shankar's awareness of the important moment of a landmark shift for India from a colony to an independent nation, through the time of its making. Chapter 6, 'The Illusive Legacy', is reflective of the illusive and somewhat ungraspable legacy of Shankar. It tries to document the sporadic experimental efforts while searching for some of the more tangible remnants of his legacy that remain as an inherited embodied experience among many dancers of today.

Archival Investigation as a Pilgrimage

I have long since wanted to see all the material that was available in the archives to make sense of what was being used as the archive on Shankar over the years. A grant from the Jawaharlal Nehru University under the UPE II scheme and a Fellowship at the Theaterwissenschaftliche Sammlung at the University of Cologne, Germany, made it possible for me to do my long-drawn archival work through six months in 2017. I see this journey as my pilgrimage across significant dance archives across the world. It started with the British Library in London (that houses the music recordings of Shankar's original productions, autobiographies, and biographies of many of the people significant in different parts of Shankar's translocational existence). My next destination was the Archives of Dartington Hall (now in Exeter at the Devon Heritage Centre) that yielded extensive records of Shankar's Institution in Almora and all the negotiations around its creation and closure. The fortnightly newsletters known as the 'USIC Centre Bulletin' on stencilled pages is the source of many details in this book to discuss the effort, extent, and excitement of the activities of the USICC, Almora. The Jacob's Pillow Archives, Boston has provided surprising photographs and publicity material related to Shankar's extensive tours of the United States, the first of which was in the early 1930s. Most exciting discoveries have come from my archival research at the Theaterwissenschaftliche Sammlung, and German Dance Archives Cologne, which connected me to the historical photographs of Zohra Sehgal as a student at the Wigman School, Dresden, in 1931; Shankar's troupe photographed with Wigman at the Wigman School; and publicity material of dance seasons presented by Sol Hurok where Wigman and Shankar performed with their troupes along with Ruth St. Denis and Ted Shawn in the same season. The archive of Alice Boner at the Rietberg Museum, Zurich helped me in understanding the roots that began Shankar's journey as a dancer.

Some of the material, zealously archived by my mother, since my admission at USICC Kolkata, has also helped me. My biggest archive was my experiential and embodied memory of having spent the long time from December 1966 (when I became a student) till June 2006 (as an active troupe member) and beyond, associated with the USICC, Kolkata, and around my teacher Smt. Amala Shankar. The great discovery in this process was that the records of his life do exist, but they are held often in private collections of people who have no idea or inclination to share them with the generations of dancers who are growing up without even knowing Uday Shankar's name, while these small documents that are part of his huge achievements get destroyed or remain unknown over time.

In this research, audience reception plays an important part. looking at Shankar's reception at home and in the world has strengthened my conviction about the requirement of a rewriting of dance histories. The press coverage as well as critical reviews of Shankar from India and abroad have been important in reading the perception of an artist, who struggled hard to traverse both the worlds with equal ease. Sieving through the archived reviews one finds that Shankar was accustomed to the highest accolades by critics from different parts of the world as well as frequent dismissals by many from India. Mohan Khokar mentions that in the southern part of India, the place where the first organised endeavour of classicisation became successful in the form of recognition for orthodox dance styles (created out of already existing performance traditions and community knowledge) such as Bharatanatyam and Kathakali as classical dance forms of India, Shankar was severely criticised. He quotes G.K. Sheshagiri from one of his published reviews of Shankar's dance as 'a typical example of the present day decadence in one of our arts due mainly to the deterioration in our taste' (Khokar 1983: 79). He also mentions a dictionary of musicians and dancers published from Tanjore that gave Uday Shankar a 10-word entry: 'Unorthodox. Performs Lasya type only. Unfit physically to perform Tandewa' (Khokar 1983: 79). Words such as 'unorthodox' were used as evaluative markers, while 'unfit physically' was an outright dismissal. For Shankar the Indian critics' principle critique was aimed at his daring to dance without any training. He was also never quite forgiven for his unauthorised and daring entry (as a trespasser or intruder) into the world of the sacred and coveted 'Indian' dance.

The writings and descriptions of Mohan Khokar,[9] Narendra Sharma,[10] Amala and Ravi Shankar,[11] Zohra Sehgal,[12] Boshi Sen,[13] and the newsletter from the USICC, Almora, edited by Rajendra Shankar,[14] have helped me to understand the archives. Aided by secondary materials and my personal memory, I have taken off on an exciting journey of rediscovering Uday Shankar. This attempted historiographic analysis then, reveals him as a multifaceted artist who imagined many new developments in Indian dance-making, much before others, as is evident from the material that became available through archives, collective and individual embodied memory, and Amala Shankar's anecdotes, and later documentations in governmental and personal archives.

While writing this book I have been aware that dance is an intensely personal and corporeal experience. Even when the dance process is collective, the experience remains individual, depending on the meaning-making processes within one's own corporeal system. It takes people on journeys that are completely subjective, which also change as experiences outside the dance realms continue to mould, change, and reorganise the

[9] Mohan Khokar's personal archives and his connections with the USICC, Almora, have provided the material for many researches on Shankar. His book, *His Dance, His Life* remains one of the best documentations of Uday Shankar's works.

[10] Narendra Sharma's insights in his interview printed in the Seagull Theatre Quarterly are different from that of many others such as Mohan Khokar as they come from two simultaneous positions that Sharma occupies in his reflections. He is at once in the past and the present, in his position as an admiring student, as well as in the time much after those days of studentship are over when he is speaking as an experienced dance-teacher-choreographer.

[11] Amala Shankar, in her many conversations with us would refer to the structure of classes, the creative energy of the space, and the performance tours, constructing a picture of the dance company that spent the winter touring. Ravi Shankar's writings published often in his different interviews and his recently published Biography by Craske (2020).

[12] Zohra Sehgal, in her autobiography, and her recorded audio interview with Kapila Vatsyayan, talked about the syllabus that she helped prepare for the school, with the help of her experience during her training at Mary Wigman's dance school at Dresden.

[13] Boshi Sen's letters and reports give us an insight into the enthusiasm with which the process of teaching started at the USICC in the beginning of its short but significant life. His biography by Girish N. Mehra (2007) as well as his letters also portrays his disappointment later as Uday Shankar seemed to lose interest in the academy and he could see its imminent shut down.

[14] *USIC Centre News*, the fortnightly newsletters of USICC, available at the Dartington Hall Archive, UK, have been important for my research. They were edited by Rajendra Shankar and published by Vishnudas Shirali.

way one lives and in turn dances that life. Hence, a critical analysis may offend the subject of one's investigation. Transferring someone else's corporeality onto a computer screen can turn into a significantly problematic ethnographical method, with unintended misrepresentations. On the other hand, the writing could turn into a full-fledged hagiography (Fig.1.1).

Even though I recognise myself to be partial insider, I have tried to let the archive inform my writing as much as possible. Initially born from an idea of writing about Shankar's dance form, the research was pushed beyond the rhetoric generated on Shankar about being the ambassador of Indian culture in the West, how beautiful he was, and what a body he had as a dancer, and how large a number of his audience were women. In terms of his dance, it became clear that many writers have not really thought much about his dance and the dance form as an art product that finally got documented (fortunately for all of us) in his film *Kalpana*. His visions on stagecraft and designing of performance remained largely outside the mainstream artistic discourse. His pedagogy of dance and rhythms resonating and related to everyday life in a country he visually and kinaesthetically tried to make a sense of—did not seem to warrant serious academic engagement. Many of his movement explorations were seen as either too simplistic or too trivial to warrant analytical attention. Finally, the most important reason for the complete disarray of organised published material on his vast transcultural journey across continents is because there is no organised collection, except at the Dartington Hall Archives. Amateur collections of personal documentation exist but they have not been properly organised by him or anyone qualified to do so in a systematic manner or shared for academic access.

The quest in this research has been largely to follow his work and dance, as I realised that a binary has been created between Uday Shankar, the genius choreographer/oriental dancer, and Uday Shankar, a man with a troubled family life and a history of a series of intimacies. I have kept deliberately away from his personal relationships and the assessment of those as a part of who and what he was as a dancer. This involved the subjective and intimate processing of his journey across different times and spaces, seen on stage, respected, partnered, been trained by, and remembered by many people in many countries, with love, admiration, respect, and also bitterness. During the vast extent of the geographical as

Fig. 1.1 Uday Shankar dancing in Ascona, Switzerland (1926) (Photo by Alice Boner. © *Legacy Alice Boner, Rietberg Museum, Zurich*)

well as cultural distances that Shankar's dance journey covered, it is understandable that many of the writings including mine shall be a process of knowing only bits and pieces and not the whole or the extent of his visions and engagements.

Reading and Writing Shankar's Dance: Composite Identity, Changing Visions

All writings about Shankar's dance, including those by Amala Shankar, frequently talk about the great attraction of Shankar and his ability to command the attention and admiration of the audience. The discourse on the reception of his dance almost inevitably centres around how many women where there in the audience, what their reactions were, and how the audience admired this not so dark, tall, handsome man with sharp and bright features, and how he mesmerised the audience, breaking the stereotype of the subjugated figure of the native Indian subject. Shankar also seemed to have enjoyed this. Amala Shankar in her book *Sat Sagarer Pare* (1934) talks about a performance at the International Colonial Exposition, where she saw Shankar dancing. She writes that after Shankar danced as Indra, the clapping went on and there were 19 curtain calls. Seeing that the claps were not stopping, Shankar repeated his dance again, now without the music. The only music was his ankle bells. This time the audience went wild. Amala mentions another occasion when after 30 odd minutes of curtain calls and incessant clapping when Shankar appeared on stage and finally said, 'thank you', some woman sitting in the front row whispered, 'My god! He talks!' It becomes important then to understand what Shankar's dance may have meant at that juncture of life, when he was instinctively trying to produce dance works and choreographies without much proper training. Was it only the attractive body that he knew he had that drew the audience? Was it the construction of an imaginary oriental other, which was presented in an attractive package for the Western audience to be able to appreciate and enjoy? Was Shankar's dance more of a display of the oriental culture, before he actually became aware of his responsibility as an Indian dancer? Was his acceptance by the Indian critics framed by the oriental lens through which the West had framed him?

The pedagogy of the Western modern dance did not make sense to him in the exact ways they were being experimented with and taught, but his urge was to acknowledge the past and to move towards the future in the Indian context, not by rejection of one for the other but through an exploration of tradition and innovation as possibilities of moving.

In the book *New Directions in Indian Dance*, Kapila Vatsyayan writes about Shankar's dance:

> His experiments were thus of two kinds. The first may be termed as the desire for revival in which Indian mythology and legend were presented through beautiful spectacle. The second was the expression of the sensitive man's reaction to ugly mechanisation of life.... For the myth and legend he utilized long, flowing languorous movements in a slow tempo, usually executed to ektala or teentala. For numbers like 'Labour and Machinery', he used jerky movements, which were not necessarily performed to any given raga. Only percussion was used as accompaniment. (Vatsyayan 2003: 20–21)

According to Vatsyayan:

> The dancer was no longer in a position to interpret or improvise according to the poetic line or the recurrent musical melody. Another significant step was taken. The dance was no longer based on a distinctive kinetic hypothesis; there was no basic pose, which had to be repeated. Movements were chosen on their expressive quality rather than for the abstract pattern which they could evolve in a given geometric motif. (Quoted in Sarkar Munsi 2008: 88)

Shankar's processes were varied. From representations and creative experiments based on traditional performance practices already popular all over India, his works were created by selection of the narrative as just a skeletal idea that was expanded through creative processes of simultaneous explorations of music and dance. For him, dance was the tool, and music as well as theatrical techniques its essential accompaniments for facilitating the creative process. Even through his experimental pedagogy, it is this creative stimulus that Shankar wanted to train his disciples to understand and nurture, 'which would bring in elements of individuality into movements created in relation as well as reaction to contexts, emotions, or events—an aspect of dance that the students subsequently became very confident about, unlike classical dancers who are often at a loss when asked to compose a new dance' (Sarkar Munsi 2008: 97). The challenge posed by the newness of an open and free form—a form free to develop and go its own way in order to explore any theme, music, or grammar—posed a challenge to the hegemonic hold of the south Indian orthodox brahmins on the dance scene of India. This cannot be ruled out in any analysis of the politics of representation of that time.

Problematic Negotiations Around Gender

While writing this book, sitting heavy are two questions that I see problematically posited, and rather simplistically negotiated in the works of Uday Shankar and in most of the writings on him. The first one of them is the question of gender and the other is that of patriarchy. A feminist perspective has become a consistent tool, as Shankar's own life, his professional or personal negotiations with a series of decisive women partners pushes me to draw upon histories of gender and agency discourses to understand the choices that become evident throughout Shankar's life journey. I am led by the two distinct strands of transcultural histories that ran parallel to create many oriental Western women dancers and mostly male Indian counterparts like Shankar.

Shankar's dance choreographies as well as writings on his social affiliations, configure him as a member of the patriarchal upper middle-class, upper caste (brahmin) family. Shankar's charm, his work and travels, as well as his life in/with dance got him a great deal of female attention. On the one hand, he learnt to respect women, as they played very important parts in his professional life. On the other hand, his almost flippantly charming attitude and vision for success and global recognition may have been the reason he shifted from one relationship to another, often leaving hurt and bitter women on his trail. While his personal relationships are of no use to me for this book, the professional contributions of women such as Alice Boner (the Swiss sculptress who funded and managed Shankar's Hindoo Ballet Troupe at the beginning of his organised dance travels), Beatrice Straight (the daughter of Dorothy Elmhirst of Dartington Hall, who initiated and oversaw the patronage of the Hall Trust for USICC, Almora), Simkie or Simone Barbiere (his dance partner and teacher at the USICC, Almora) facilitated Shankar's negotiations of transcultural terrains that required skills and abilities beyond dancing and choreography. That these relations did not remain professional would not have been of any consequence, except for the fact that there seems to be a connection between his moving on from each of the relationships and a sense of disengagement that appears linked to the waning of the past professional interest. In letters written by Boner, Straight, and the

Elmhirsts, one sees a repeated pattern of moving on. This research is not about the personal ups and downs as I said before, but they get registered in the performance/location maps that emerge through the writing.

Discussing the issue of gender in my essay 'Emergence of the Contemporary Woman Dancer', I wrote, 'It is also necessary to acknowledge that his touring company accommodating male as well female dancers, became the face of Indian dance abroad for a long period of time between the 1930s and the 1950s, actually performing at the same spaces as the largest ballet troupes of European countries…' (Sarkar Munsi 2011: 229–30). Shankar chose to present solo and duets (with a female partner) and also in trios (presenting himself with two women dancers) before he created a dance troupe. At a time when many colonial expositions and the internal debates regarding the Nautch girl or the Devadasi system was attracting reformist attention, he set out with a troupe of male and female dancers, to represent India as a land of cultural richness, and in that effort the image was not of patriarchy but of a festive coexistence of both genders. In Amala Shankar's descriptions in her book we get descriptions of immense respect that troupe received with members appearing well groomed and disciplined. Shankar's concern regarding the respect that the troupe must receive, and the importance he attached to being skilled enough to be at par with the top ranking professional troupes headed by European dancers, made him train his dancers—both male and female in social as well as dance skills.

The readings on gendering need complicating when one looks at the representation of the temple iconography in Shankar's mythological themes and movements vis-à-vis his representation of modern themes such as the mechanisation of the society. It is important to note that women characters in Shankar's choreographies and his class instructions worked to create ordinary everyday women characters from different strata of the Indian society. Students were asked to refer to their experiences to create such representations. This is in complete contrast to the classical dances, where most women characters are either celestial or royal beings. Shankar's dancers' emotive references were often used by him to produce gender-by-culture and gender-by-context according to the need of the productions. Often falling back on heteronormative, socialised expectations, his female characters would show much more of facial reactions to show love, joy, fear, anger, disgust, sadness, and other emotions, than the male ones, when using the finer emotive/expressive principles of bhava and rasa.

Shankar's admiration of the sculpted dynamism of the bodies, of both humans as well as gods, and the desire to achieve a representation of the unfinished suggestions through those static sculptures on the temple walls also created or reconstructed the typical gendered positions of male and female bodies in connection to each other. In Shankar's dances as recorded in the clips with Simkie, or in *Kalpana*, one can find signifiers of patriarchy in a tilt of the head of the female body or a protective embrace of the male by holding the female with one hand over her shoulder, side by side with extremely empowering moments of embodied female presences. The content, characters, and storytelling often project a casual conservatism, along with patriarchal nationalism, side by side with emancipatory declarations of women's rights to public spaces, workers' and peasants' rights to machine and land, and a total rejection of religious fundamentalism will come through in the analysis in different chapters.

On the other hand, gender-switches in movements were a part of Shankar's classes as well as choreographies. His earlier portrayals of women's roles in dances in London and Paris (i.e. dressed as the Rajput bride—as photographed by Alice Boner between 1926 and 1929), adds yet another layer of complications regarding his ideas of public and private negotiation of gender and sexuality, and give us an added incentive to investigate his position vis-a-vis the developing modern dance scenario of the time. A curious dichotomy, of pushing women as well as men students to acknowledge contemporary times in his class creatively, while sticking to very traditional patriarchal tropes of gendered bodies in many of the choreographed items appeared to be a fluid but confusing process—of belonging/performing two worlds at the same time. His experiments allowed easy shifts between genders. Thus, ungendered movements as well as hyper-gendering were considered useful skills to navigate, and continued to be taught as part of the movement grammars making it difficult to read connections between Shankar's personal and choreographic gender constructs.

The Question of Authenticity, Modern Dance, and Transmission

The second troublesome question involves the dichotomy between 'authenticity' and 'modernity'. Joan Erdman, in her essay on 'Performance as Translation', writes that even though Shankar 'was convinced of his own authenticity, the difficulty in finding themes, partners, musical accompaniment, appropriate venues, and sponsors forced him to try different combinations and methods' (Erdman 1987: 73). Shankar was caught up between two different expectations around the idea of 'authentic' Indian dance all his life. In him, both the West and the East invested certain responsibilities of delivering the 'authentic' movements that they could identify as fulfilling of his duty as an Indian dancer. Clear in the expectations and disappointments of his critics is the fact that Shankar could not fulfil the demands of presenting the historical (read brahminical) identity that the Indian cultural sphere wanted him to present to the world, for India. His troupe was named Uday Shankar's Hindoo/Hindu Dancers', his signature dances were about gods and goddesses, but he was and remained a secular Indian by choice. The use of the words Hindoo or Hindu seems a decision to create a specific and exclusive geopolitical identity for his company of dancers. Equally clear in the reviews is the fact that the majority of the critics and entrepreneurs in the West were ready only to accept him as a representation or a presenter of the stereotypes that the West was by then very comfortable allocating to colonised and exotic subjects. In the middle of these expectations, Shankar wanted to have the creative freedom to explore traditional and new sensibility on his own terms. His journey was towards establishing a modern institution that would teach traditional styles of dance along with his own dance process as a sign of controlling and compromising his modernist instincts. Discussing this push and pull, Ashish Rajadhyaksha quotes Kapila Vatsyayan and writes, 'Uday Shankar discovered—soon, perhaps all too soon—that 'there was a rich storehouse of the classical styles to be explored, and there were those gurus of gigantic stature at whose feet he had to sit to know more…' (Rajadhyaksha 2009: 146).[15] Rajadhyaksha is possibly referring to the effort by Shankar to locate regional dance forms from different parts of India in 1930. Shankar started inviting master teachers to teach the distinctive regional performance forms in mid-1930s in an effort to learn a range of techniques. Some of these dances were recognised as classical dances much later.

While there is quite a consistent denial of Uday Shankar's status as a modern dancer among the dance community in India, the overall

[15] This is a significant remark on the way Shankar's modern experiments were always pulled back by his need to portray his allegiance to the classical trainings that were handed down through the traditional system of learning dance under a master–teacher's tutelage that is known as *Guru–Shishya Parampara*.

scholastic acceptance is building with writings that have placed him quite clearly within the modern spectrum of dance. At the same time, many of his disciples reproduce his dance items and choreographies time and again and stay within a restricted boundary by reproducing what he did in his classes 80 years before. This present trend of following on the 'authentic' path shown by Shankar stops today's dancers from living and dancing in the current times. The significance of his global conversation through dance between the two World Wars is not explored or meaningful to many who claim his legacy. The deification of Shankar within a small community of his admirers without exploring his idea of dance education and research lessens the significance of his contribution towards building a modern gender-equal institution. Acknowledging his 'Indian'ness and excluding his transcultural, translocational explorations, actually limits his (modern) vision.

This book aspires to be a temporary closure to a pilgrimage, into the past of a fascinating male dancer who was born in the first year of the twentieth century, whose quest for his artistic identity took off and never arrived at the desired destination. For me, it has been the culmination of a journey across the world to establish a close relationship with the available documentation on this almost forgotten Indian dancer, who fascinated the world with some intangible yet striking attractions he could create through his dance as well as choreography. It has been a long-term endeavour that will unravel in the next five chapters— through the analytical readings of the documental evidences, records, and published and unpublished writings. Between the remnants of Uday Shankar, preserved or left neglected and unnoticed in the archives and the embodied knowledge and the memories of his dance, writing this history has been a fascinating journey.

Timeline

The timeline of fifty years (approximately 1920–1970) of Shankar's relationship with dance that this book operates on is significant. The first thirty years (1920–1950) are seen as his transcultural/translocational journey that is the principle construct through which Shankar emerges as a transnational dance artist. It begins at the moment of a deliberate choice that Shankar himself made to change his own status as a student of visual art to that of a migrant oriental dancer, searching for a viable career (either as a part-time or a full-time occupation) by honing his instinctive creative skills to in dance.

The next twenty years (1950–1970) have been seen differently by me—as a more contained home/region-bound Shankar continued his experiments with dance art and worked on mixed-media choreographies. The post-*Kalpana* phase that has seen Shankar's production of the second shadow play on Buddha (1953), as well as his landmark productions *Samanya Kshati* (1961), *Prakriti Ananda* (1966) and his critically received mixed-media production, *Shankarscope* (1970). This phase saw a series of acknowledgements (though dismissed by many as insufficient by many) of his life-long work by the Ministry of Culture in India. It also saw the birth of USICC Kolkata. mainly as an effort by Amala Shankar. It also saw the disintegration of the troupe that Shankar headed till the early 1960s, and Shankar distancing himself from his family and finally creating Uday Shankar Ballet Troupe which consisted of trained dancers from the USICC Kolkata and the Academy of Dance, Drama and Music (that became absorbed within the Rabindra Bharati University established in 1961). The troupe went on many national and two international tours in 1962 and 1968. The last one was significant as Amala Shankar distanced herself from this particular one, and Shankar fell ill during this tour and had to return to India without finishing his commitments. Many of his disciples post 1960s, Shanti Bose, Sadhan Guha, Polly Guha, and others remained active and had made a space for themselves as associates of Uday Shankar, who were trained directly by him, especially in the regional and vernacular cultural space of West Bengal. Thus, the transcultural/translocational and multi-stranded modernist experimentations that Shankar was acknowledged for in his journey from 1920, is literally and discursively found to become contained into a more localised and revitalising effort post 1960s. Even though his creative journey became limited by health and social circumstances in his last years, he worked hard without much support, in hope to retrace glories of the pedagogical and creative strength that he was known for internationally at one point of time. This complex stage is negotiated in different publications and discourses on Shankar through claims and counterclaims.

One way to understand Shankar's engagement is to map his dance journey across five distinctly different phases. They are: (1) The entry into the world of performance in the early 1920s through working with Shyam Shankar Chowdhuri and Anna Pavlova; (2) His meeting with Alice Boner and his acquaintance with Indian art in the years 1926–1936; (3) The plans and establishment of an institution with help from the Dartington Hall in the years 1937–1944; (4) Making of *Kalpana* (the making of which lasted from 1945 till 1948) and efforts at mixed/multimedia experiments thereafter; and (5) Institutional acceptance (starting with SNA award 1960) and his efforts to revitalise the past glories. A related timeline—which I activate from the time Uday Shankar (8 December 1900–26 September 1977), leaves for his home for a formal training in Arts, is in no sense trying to cover all major events. Instead it is my effort to make sense of his relationship with multiple geopolitical as well as cultural locations. I propose to do so through these five divisions in his journey, to situate him in a chronological frame with some clarity.

Phase 1

1917	He joined Sir J. J. School of Art, Bombay (now known as Mumbai).
1920	He travelled to London to enrol as a student at the Royal College of Art.
1922	Shankar first appeared on stage in one of his father's stage productions. He danced at a garden party in London organised for King George the Vth in 1922. Russian prima ballerina Anna Pavlova noticed and connected to him around the same time after seeing his performance.
1923	Shankar choreographed for and performed with Anna Pavlova for her *Oriental Impressions* programme in Covent Garden and toured America for nine months.
1924	Shankar participated in the British Empire Exhibition in Paris.

Phase 2

1926	Swiss sculptor Alice Boner saw Shankar's performance at Boner had seen Uday Shankar dance for the first time while visiting an exhibition in Zurich's prestigious Kunsthaus.
1928	Boner moved to Paris, Shankar began his classes and pianist Simone Barbier (Simkie) joined the classes as a dance student.

1930	Returning to India Shankar travelled across the country with Boner to learn about India and its cultural practices. This journey began on 9 January 1930 and lasted till October of 1930.
1931	Shankar with Boner as his manager, formed a troupe and performed at the Colonial Exposition in Paris. They registered a Company together. His troupe consisted of Timirbaran, Amala(Later Shankar), his brothers Ravi, Devendra and Rajendra, his cousin Kanaklata, and Simkie, among others.
1931–1933	Shankar was contracted for a tour of the United States by Sol Hurok.
1931	Shankar and his troupe toured India and had 42 performances all over India. They saw the performance of Tagore's dance drama in Kolkata and also met Tagore. They met Margaret Barr, the modern dancer as well.
1933–1937	Shankar was introduced to the Elmhirsts of the Dartington Hall by Margaret Barr. He visited and performed at the Hall several times.

Phase 3

1937–1938	He worked on the idea of forming an institution with Beatrice Straight and founded the Uday Shankar India Culture Centre in Almora, now in the state of Uttarakhand, India.
1939–1944	The school for dance, drama, and music ran successfully for a short span of 4 + years and closed during World War II. Shankar got married to Amala Nandi in 1942. *Ramleela*, Shankar's first experimental shadow play was created and premiered.

Phase 4

1945	Shankar started his work with the feature film *Kalpana* in Madras (now Chennai), India.
1948	*Kalpana* was released.

1953 Shadow play in colour on life of Buddha.

Phase 5

1960 Shankar received the very first Sangeet Natak Akademi Award in the category of 'creative dance and choreography'.
1962 He was the receiver of the Sangeet Natak Akademi Fellowship—the highest honour given by the National Academy of dance, music, and drama for his lifetime achievement.
1963 His performing troupe is dissolved.
1965 Uday and Amala Shankar opened their dance school Uday Shankar India Culture Centre, Kolkata.
1970 Shankar staged his last major and multi-art production *Shankarscope*.
1971 Uday Shankar is a recipient of India's second highest civilian award Padma Vibhushan.
1975 Visva-Bharati University awarded Uday Shankar its highest honour Desikottam in recognition of his achievements.
1977 On 26th September Uday Shankar passed away in Kolkata after a brief illness.

Shankar's journey from the first creative attempts with Anna Pavlova as an oriental authenticator of colonising white body, till his later dance creations clearly signify a drastic change in his understanding of the art. It is this changing relationship with dance, body, and movement and his everlasting quest to know and recreate the modern body that stopped many critics from being able to dismiss him as insignificant.

References

Abrahams, Ruth K. 2007. "Uday Shankar: The Early Years, 1900–1938." *Dance Chronicle* 30 (3): 363–426.

Bharucha, Rustom. 1999. "Politics of Culturalisms in an Age of Globalisation: Discrimination, Discontent and Dialogue." *Economic and Political Weekly*, 20–26 Februray: 477–89.

Chakravarti, Uma. 1996. "Wifehood, Widowhood and Adultery: Female Sexuality, Surveillance and the State in 18th Century Maharashtra." In *Social Reform, Sexuality and the State*, edited by Patricial Uberoi, 3–22. Delhi: Sage.
Coomaraswamy, Ananda K. 1937. "Uday Shankar's Indian Dancing." *Magazine Art*, 30 October: 611–13.
Craske, Oliver. 2020. *Indian Sun: The Life and Music of Ravi Shankar.* London: Faber & Faber.
Erdman, Joan L. 1987. "Performance as Translation: Uday Shankar in the West." *The Drama Review: TDR* 31 (1) (Spring): 64–88.
Foster, Susan Leigh. 2011. *Choreographing Empathy: Kinesthesia in Performance*. New York: Routledge.
Foster, Susan Leigh. 2019. *Valuing Dance: Commodities and Gifts in Motion*. New York: Oxford University Press
Ghosh, Bishakha. 2019. *Shankarnama: Smritichitre Amala Shankar (Bengali.* Kolkata: Ananda Publishers.
Khokar, Mohan. 1983. *His Dance, His Life: A Portrait of Uday Shankar.* New Delhi: Himalayan Books.
Meduri, Avanti. 1996. "Nation, Woman, Representation: The Sutured History of the Devadasi and Her Dance." Unpublished Dissertation. New York University.
Mehra, Girish N. 2007. *Nearer Heaven Than Earth.* Delhi: Rupa & Co.
Purkayastha, Prarthana. 2014. *Indian Modern Dance, Feminism, and Nationalism.* Basingstoke, UK: Palgrave Macmillan.
Rajadhyaksha, Ashish. 2009. *Indian Cinema in the Time of Celluloid: From Bollywood to the Emergency*. Bloomington/ Indianapolis: Indiana University Press.
Robins, Kavin. 2008. "The Challenge of Transcultural Diversities." *Revista CIDOB d'Afers Internationals (Boundaries: Transience and Intercultural Dynamics)* No. 82/83: 245–52.
Sarkar Munsi, Urmimala. 2008. "Boundaries and Beyond: Problems of Nomenclature in Indian Dance." In *Dance: Transcending Borders*, edited by Urmimala Sarkar Munsi, 78–98. Delhi: Tulika Books.
Sarkar Munsi, Urmimala. 2011. "Imag(in)ing The Nation: Uday Shankar's Kalpana." In *Traversing Tradition: Celebrating Dance in India*, edited by Urmimala Sarkar Munsi and Stephanie Burridge, 124–50. Delhi: Routledge.
Sarkar, Sumit. 2015. *Modern Times: India 1880s–1950s, Environment, Economy, Culture*. Ranikhet: Permanent Black.
Segal, Zohra. 2010. *Close-Up: Memories of a Life on Stage and Screen*. New Delhi: Women Unlimited (An Associate of Kali for Women).
Segal, Zohra, and Joan Landy Erdman. 1997. *Stages: The Art and Adventures of Zohra Segal.* New Delhi: Kali for Women.

Shankar (Nandi), Amala. (1934) 2007. *Sat Sagarer Pare [Bengali]*. Kolkata: A Mukherjee & Co. PVT LTD.
Soneji, Davesh. 2012. *Unfinished Gestures—Devadasis, Memory, and Modernity in South India (South Asia Across the Disciplines)*. Chicago: University of Chicago Press.
Srinivasan, Amrit. 1985. "Reform and Revival: The Devadasi and Her Dance." *Economic and Political Weekly* 20 (44): 1869–76.
Srinivasan, Priya. 2007. "The Bodies Beneath the Smoke or What's Behind the Cigarette Poster: Unearthing Kinesthetic Connections in American Dance History." *Discourses in Dance* 4 (1): 7–47.
Vatsyayan, Kapila. 1974, 2nd Reprint 1997. *Indian Classical Dance*. Delhi: Ministry of Information and Broadcasting, Government of India.
Vatsyayan, Kapila. 1995. "The Future of Dance Scholarship in India." *Dance Chronicle* 18 (3): 485–90.
Vatsyayan, Kapila. 2003. "Modern Dance: The Contribution of Uday SHankar and His Associates." In *New Directions in Indian Dance*, edited by Sunil Kothari, 20–31. Mumbai: Marg Publications.
Weber, Carl. 1991. "AC/TC: Currents of Theatrical Exchange." In *Interculturalism & Performance*, edited by Bonnie Marranca and Gautam Dasgupta, 27–37. New York: PAJ Publications.

Archival and Online Sources

Boston Public Library, Boston, Massachusetts, USA. https://www.bpl.org/.
British Library, London, UK.
Dance Archive Box Berlin, Akademie Der Kunst. Berlin, Germany. https://www.adk.de/en/programme/index.htm?we_objectID=60174.
Dartington Hall Records. Dartington Hall Trust Archives files [Devon Heritage Centre, Great Moor House, Bittern Road, Sowton, Exeter, Devon, EX2 7NL]. https://www.dartington.org/?s=archives.
———. LKE/IN/19: Title—LKE India 19: Uday Shankar India Culture Centre, 1932–1973.
———. DWE/A/8: Title—Dance 2, Shankar and other Indian Dancers.
———. DS/UK/843: Title—India Culture Trust; 1937–.
———. DS/UK/836: Title—Admin History Uday Shankar India Culture Centre; 1938–.
———. MC/Chekhov/S4/39: Series 4.General Files: A. Uday Shankar Play bills.
———. USIC Centre Newsletters 1939–1944 (Fortnightly), Ranidhara, Almora, U.P. Editors: Rajendra Shankar and Vishnudas Shirali. (Source: Dartington Archives, Devon Cultural Centre, UK).

German Dance Archives Cologne, Germany. http://www.tanzarchive.de/en/members/german-dance-archives-cologne/.
Jacob's Pillow Archives (Western Massachusetts), Boston. USA. https://www.jacobspillow.org/archives/.
Theaterwissenschaftliche Sammlung at the University of Cologne, Germany. http://www.universitaetssammlungen.de/sammlung/291.

CHAPTER 2

Modern Dance? Placing Shankar's Transculturality in Colonial South Asia

> *... there are certain peculiarities about our modernity. It could be the case that what others think of as modern, we have found unacceptable, whereas what we have cherished as valuable elements of our modernity, others do not consider to be modern at all.* (Chatterjee 1997: 3)

The 'modern' as a concept has been understood as something constantly on the move. It is an idea that immediately refers to a process of dynamic change. Taken as a definitive word, 'modernity', in the opinion of Avijit Pathak, is 'invariably related to the spirit of freedom. This freedom is rooted in the critical consciousness that it generates. It means: "Don't take things for granted. Question it, verify it, and subject it to critical scrutiny." There is nothing beyond critical examination...' (Pathak 2006: 13–14). Another associated gain of modernity is that it opens up the world. It brings intense dynamism, arouses tremendous vertical/horizontal mobility, and gives us wide-ranging exposure. The reason is that its inherent criticality leads to diverse experimentations and life projects. In the performing arts, modernity refers to the innovative and creative fluidity that is flexible and capable of interacting creatively with any existing idea or form. Partha Chatterjee's comment about the peculiarities of Indian modernity becomes important for me to justify Uday Shankar's dance as 'modern', when he himself had never been comfortable with the label. In Indian art discourses, for something to be

U. Sarkar Munsi, *Uday Shankar and His Transcultural Experimentations*, Transnational Theatre Histories,
https://doi.org/10.1007/978-3-030-93224-4_2

considered 'modernist' it needs to engage with concepts of authenticity, antiquity, tradition, and heritage, with a sense of freedom to break or oppose the existing structures or at least challenge them. This chapter refers to a set of writings by specialists in histories of Indian modernity, art and dance to create a thread of connections through Shankar's urge of creating his own dance technique, intending to challenge power structures of hereditary dance learning, performing, and teaching, in the context of 'our modernity'.

The general understanding perpetuated has been one of modernism and antiquity having co-existed in the nation-making discourse, sweeping along the creative processes that at other less anxious times would be recognised by and for themselves as efforts and works of individual creators and thinkers. In their book *Modern South East Asia: History, Culture, Political Economy*, Sugata Bose and Ayesha Jalal point out that there is an effort to identify a well-defined 'fault-line between tradition and modernity as well as Indian and European modernity that makes it impossible to take full account of the contestations that animated the creative efforts to fashion a vibrant culture and politics of anti-colonial modernity' (Bose and Jalal 2018: 99). This particular argument strengthens my reading of Uday Shankar's work and its critique as a work of fusion of traditions of the West and the East. In this context, Bose and Jalal's continued words, 'These efforts were not just staked on claims of cultural exclusivity or difference but also on imaginative cultural borrowings and intellectual adaptations that consciously transgressed the frontier between us and them' frame Shankar's reception from his critics—especially within India in the late 1930s and the 1940s.

Geeta Kapur in her book *When was Modernism: Essays on Contemporary Cultural Practice in India* (2000) asserts that Indian modernism does not fit into the same periodisation as the West, and neither does it have a 'firm canonical position in India'. 'It has a paradoxical value involving a continual double-take. Sometimes it serves to make indigenist issues and motifs progressive; sometimes it seems to subvert if not nationalism, then that on which it rests and purports to grow, that is, tradition' (Kapur 2000: 292). Describing modernity as a process of 'relating the material and the cultural worlds in a period of unprecedented change that we call the process of modernization' (Kapur 2000: 298), Kapur writes that the praxis of modernity 'produces a cultural dynamic whereby questions of autonomy, identity and authenticity come to the fore. These are desired individually but are sought to be gained in collectivity' (Kapur 2000: 298). Observing that modernisation, has been simultaneously 'desired and abhorred throughout the nationalist period' Kapur is of the opinion that it continued to survive through these contestations during the Nehruvian period. She concludes that 'Indian modernity is often quite circumspect, mediated as it is to a point of handicap by negative evaluations of the very practice that it is evolving' (Kapur 2000: 301).

Shankar's wish to be identified as an 'authentic' Indian dancer was pegged on being recognised as an uncompromising nationalist. This wish may have started with his migrant position and a desire for a space and recognition for his art practice, but over time it is seen as a matter of pride, and legitimisation of the creative art practice in which he created a glimpse of India for the world to experience. With Geeta Kapur's words it becomes easy to place Shankar in the category of a migrant/artist-in-exile figure, just as artists with a commitment to social transformation set the terms of revolt each in his/her context of community or nation, the outriders created the necessary disjuncture: the artists who established themselves in India became cultural emblems within a progressive national state, and those who left for Paris and London became equally emblematic outsiders of modern fiction. They embodied the modernist impulse of choosing metropolitan 'exile'-the first criterion of modernity, according to Raymond Williams (Kapur 2000: 304).

The mix of the past and the present, the mythical and the real, the celestial and the mundane created a shifting trajectory for Shankar's dance language, where 'new' movement vocabulary created a space of freedom both for the audience as well as the performers in his group. Through his exposure to the West he could access the ideas that excited the Western world of modern dance. But, he was also aware that he did not have the training or the ability to belong to that world. Neither did he, in all probability, want to do so. Instead he utilised the same references of cultural antiquity to remain distinctly different from the colonial modernity that threatened to engulf anything 'new' that came out of artistic creativity from any colonised country. Instinctively choosing the innovative process in making of dance and movement, he appears too uneasy to acknowledge his process as 'Avant-Garde', but drew heavily from his exposure to Western modern art in order to communicate a concept and an aesthetic through an audio-visual experience for the audience. These choices point to a 'spirit of freedom' and a 'critical consciousness' (Pathak 2006: 13) whereby 'everything including the most sacred—has to be observed, verified and interrogated'. In Pathak's opinion, this turn explains the drastic change that began to take place in the world of ideas (Pathak 2006: 13). Taking off from this observation, the next section of this chapter tries to construct Shankar's modern identity by looking at his work from two entry points of innovation and questioning of existing ideas,—both of which are complicated by his translocational/transcultural existence.

Shankar's Modern Identity: Transcultural Challenges

It is a well-documented fact that the Western modern dance movement began around the last decade of the nineteenth century when there was a conscious move to break away from the complete hegemony of and lack of freedom within the practice of classical ballet, which some of the performers had begun to resent. Many of the dancers in the West were looking towards the East for new ideas to aid freedom of expression and for the development of a new dance vocabulary. In the meanwhile, some of the dancers from the Indian subcontinent individually had started taking cues from the West with regard to the presentation style, stage techniques, and grammatical and choreographic methods. Prominent among the list of the many dancers who travelled to the West during these times are Uday Shankar, Rukmini Devi, Ram Gopal, and Madame Maneka among others. The dancers who visited the East are quite a few as well. Starting from Pavlova, La Marie, Ruth St. Denis, Ted Shawn, and many others have acknowledged direct or indirect influence of Eastern dance and aesthetics on their dance forms.

Shankar's popularity in the West can be clearly assessed by the repeated invitations year after year from the early thirties till the beginning of World War II by a presenter as astute as Sol Hurok. Meanwhile, in India an entrepreneur as successful as Haren Ghosh among many others presented and managed the dancer's performances. Shankar enjoyed unprecedented popularity and had ingredients clearly and purposefully chosen to represent and capture the attention of the audience and thereby become a box-office success.

John Martin,[1] the well-known American dance theorist/critic continued to write reviews of Shankar. At the same time he also wrote extensively about the moment of emergence of Western modern dance and its pioneers. His writings about Shankar's dance were read popularly and are mentioned often by many of Shankar's publicity materials. While giving Shankar the visibility as an oriental artist of significant calibre, his reviews also created and maintained a strictly limited space for him. He carefully segregated his expectations of the 'oriental' dancer Uday Shankar's choreographic efforts from modern dance explorations of the Western dancers. John Martin was a major presence during the heights of Shankar's popularity in America. He wrote most of the reviews during Shankar's first tour of the Americas in 1931, and consistently for the whole period of Shankar's tours in the Americas. Shankar, through his reviews, was slotted based on his choreographic products while he was specifically put forth as a practitioner of an alien art that depended heavily on narratives. Once that was established clearly, John Martin wrote generous reviews about Shankar that brought him credibility as an artist capable of creative expressions from the East. Shankar's process of creating new movements from everyday experiences and his ability to generate movements as narratives as well as for narratives never seemed to get a priority in what his dance was understood as. Martin remained interested in Shankar's performances continuing to write somewhat uncritical review in a somewhat troubling condescending tone. On December 26, 1951, The New York Times published his report, where he wrote, 'Uday Shankar and his handsome wife, Amala, brought their little company of Hindu dancers and musicians back after an absence of two years to open a short session at the Anta Playhouse...' (Dartington Hall Records).

John Martin, in his essay 'The Modern Dance: The Fourth of a Series' (1937) and later in his publications, frames the idea of modern dance entirely in terms of Western settings, audience, dancers, and dance forms. This in itself blocked any chance for non-Western dancers to name their experiments as modern, even when they were using many of the same material from the East for their vocabulary as the dancers who had become the authority in modern dance in the West. Rather than looking at the actual process, the critics of Shankar's form continued to use John

[1] Dance scholar Andre Lepecki elaborates John Martin's construct of modernist ideology, identifying the root of his understanding of dance as a potentially autonomous art—equal to all other high forms art forms by and for itself (Lepacki 2006: 4).

Martin's frames of reference of a differentiating vocabulary, stopping any claims that Shankar could make in the future.

A number of press cuttings preserved at the Dartington Hall Archives clarifies the idea of allocation or allowance of a particular space to a dancer form the orient. The reviews are preserved without any comment at the archives and hence do not lend any insight into how they were received either by Shankar or by the Elmhirsts (who later became chief patrons for Shankar's institution in Almora). One would surely like to know the reaction of Shankar at his troupe being labelled as 'Brown Dancers' in one of the reviews in the *Time*, Chicago, Illinois, 26 January 1937. Was he happy to have been mentioned as 'a crowd puller', 'an extremely popular choreographer, who returned to impress the audience with his representation of the sinuous Shiva', and how the writer mentions the pleasure of the crowd seeing 'Shankar's French girl Simkie (only occidental in the cast)' (Folder 910. Dartington Hall Archive)? Side by side are reviews such as the ones from the *Torquay Herald*, Torquay (United Kingdom) on the 1st and the 16th of November 1937, where the reviewer says, 'The dancers bring an art of rare and strange beauty and the musicians are almost as fascinating' (Folder 910. Dartington Hall Archive). Worded to present a pleasant or glowing impression, the reviews are similar in the marked absence of any detail about Shankar's dance choreographies or any critical analysis. These reviews highlight a different way of seeing and a different set of expectations that the audience needs to have when compared to the modern dancers from Europe and America.

An article by Basanta Koomar Roy, published by Hurok as a part of his elaborate brochure for the season of 1936, is titled 'Bronze God'. It follows in the same vein:

> If one's eyes are cultured enough, and his ears are delicate enough he cannot fail to notice that there are lofty phases of sheer loveliness in the dance art of Shan-Kar when his feet dance on the very heart of music; his arms dance with the music that is hidden in the very soul of beauty; and his eyes dance with the animated rays of the mystic music of the cosmos. At such moments, yes, at such moments of dynamic intensity and ineffable beauty, music itself becomes dance; and Uday Shan-Kar becomes dance itself. (MC/Chekhov/S4/39: Series 4. General Files: A. Uday Shankar Play bills. Dartington Hall Records)

It seems clear that Shankar was deeply implicated in the oriental spectacularism from across the world. The academic writings also stop short of giving Shankar a space for a modern dancer, perhaps because it is a difficult task without critically addressing the issues of pedagogy in his 'creative' process analytically. Shankar, through the five distinct phases of his life in/with dance (see Chapter 1), cannot be pinned down to one singular identity as his journey is marked by stages of modern negotiations evolving and differing in tune with his 'presence' in particular times and spaces. The fifty years of his dance career have seen Shankar begin as a successful visual art student from a colonised country turning into a migrant artist, surviving and finally succeeding in creating a space for himself and the colony that he chose to represent in his own way. The available archival material takes us through his search to develop tools to hone skills through the years while he was trying to anticipate what would create a stable career for himself in dance.

Accepting and Embodying Oriental Identity—A Choice Choreographed by a Migrant Subjecthood and Choreopolitics

In the context of this book, the concept of choreopolitics[2] is a significant marker of choice applied by a dancer/choreographer in shaping the representation of the body, the identity, the space, the grammar, the audience, the aesthetic, the patronage, and even the publicity for one's dance experiments. As a colonial subject, foregrounding the colonised country's culture and history was a political choice for Shankar.

As for his repertoire, a heterodox complexity in movement techniques and aesthetics resulted from the push and pull between the Western expectations and the Indian aesthetic principles. Shankar's list of choreographies from 1930 till 1939 (when he opened his institution in Almora), show a generous mix of dance numbers that were representations of life and celebrations from different parts of India, or dances composed on well-known myths around gods and demons. One assumes

[2] Lepacki explains the concepts of choreography saying, '[H]istorically and disciplinarily, the concept and the practice of choreography implements, needs, produces, and reproduces what William Forsythe has called an "art of command" (in Franko 2007: 17)'. He further state that the non-policed choice and freedom to express through bodies and movements created "possibility for the political to emerge" (Lepacki 2013: 13–27).

that the expectations created by reviews of his work from the West and the East may have been crucially important as the coercive or decisive element in his choice of contents. Eventually though, it raises critical questions regarding his reading of the social, economic, cultural, and political world. The exploration of his choreopolitics is incomplete without bringing in a discussion on his awareness of the important topics of colonisation, imperialism and social marginalisation or discrimination. These were important issues in the context of colonial India of the 1930s and 1940s. Shankar's choreographies do not help us understand the level of his awareness of the political scenario of the world. He maintained an artistic distance from the political upheavals and the development of fascism in Germany, where the troupe continued to tour, even while there are documents that contain ample proof of discomfort of his troupe members. Ravi Shankar's biographer, Oliver Craske writes about Rajendra Shankar's observations about Germany of 1932 in his letter to Boner. 'The whole atmosphere is fraught with an evil odour of suspense on account of the presidential election', Rajendra wrote to Boner in March. 'If Hitler comes into power, our condition in Germany will not remain enviable. From what I see he has a very big party' (Craske 2020: 44). That Shankar's choreography for the post-First World War society in Europe and America almost never tackled any of the difficult issues on war, death, or colonial subjecthood may be seen as a political choice in itself, of fashioning his dance according to the audience expectation in the West. He did not appear to be committed to any form of overt political ideology. We also never see Shankar in an active critique of colonialism as an active agent of control either in any of his dances or in any of his available writings in the long period of twenty-five years of colonial rule he danced in. In an interview with noted theatre personality Shambhu Mitra[3] in early 1970 Shankar states that he trained his group members before the foreign tours and warned them to never get involved in discussions on politics while making small talks in a party in foreign countries.

He seemed satisfied to be the oriental dancer at the beginning of his career, convinced that he had a duty of representing his country and happy to receive favourable reviews and full houses (even if he was racially identified as a 'brown' dancer). In some of his later works such

[3] See https://www.youtube.com/watch?v=JHq-uBio5vE, accessed on 25 January 2018.

as the *Rhythm of Life*, his overall critical view about the nature of governance in India becomes evident. His politics and modern views get clarity in his film *Kalpana*. The starving, toiling, labouring, protesting, and suffering bodies in his film create a somewhat sketchy but distinct picture of the political formulation and statement he was making as a citizen of India. However, this politics remains inadequately articulated through the embodied sufferings of toiling bodies, almost never openly complicated as a strong ideological statement in his work. This leads me to understand him through Homi Bhabha's thoughts on 'The space of the people' where he sees a tension between 'the pedagogic and performative' ways people are identified as a part of a nation state, as culturally shaped as well as a political being that for him turns into a problem of knowledge that haunts the symbolic formation of modern social authority. He says:

> The people are neither the beginning nor the end of the national narrative; they represent the cutting edge between the totalizing powers of the 'social' as homogeneous, consensual community, and the forces that signify the more specific address to contentious, unequal interests and identities within the population. (Bhabha 1994: 209)

The colonised, migrant male dancer is a marginalised being: (1) as a dancer, (2) from a colonised country, who is (3) a male, and (4) a migrant. Shankar fitted into the representation of the 'cutting edge' Bhabha mentions, in more ways than one. He was a figure who may be seen as apparently comfortable being the representative oriental subject who was happy to have received Western education. In his dependence on the colonial power as the indirect patron, and later the continued support from people and institutions worldwide, he remained grateful for being able to have access to patronage from the West (see Chapters 3 and 4).

The onus and rights of creativity as a subjective choreopolitical choice is something that all Western modern dancers took for granted as a mark of their sensibilities around the freedom of body and mind. By making public the quest for freedom from the aggressive control of the dance technique over their bodies, these dancers could become authorities for seeking and proclaiming a body that made a new space for themselves in the history of Western dance. For this transition many of them used the signs, motifs, images, and aesthetics of the East as colonisers' privilege, often without acknowledging or properly understanding their meanings. It is important to note that all this while for Shankar it was essential to supply proof of authenticity for the use of those same set of signs, motifs, images, and aesthetics within his own culture, specifically to prove his understanding and respect of his native land's cultural practices.

Shankar chose to come back to his own country after remaining in the West for the first part of his dance journey. This may have been a way of making a choreopolitical statement. It definitely was this locational shift that gave a different shape to the way Shankar placed himself and his art in a transcultural setting from then onwards. He made himself vulnerable through his self-assigned role of representing his own culture, over and above being irrevocably identified as an oriental subject in the West. His acceptance as a dancer/choreographer who assimilated the tradition and transitions of the changing times is found in the acknowledgements of Rabindranath Tagore[4] and Abanindranath Tagore.[5] Rajendra Shankar, Uday Shankar's brother, noted that Uday Shankar was acknowledged in 1930 after his concert performance in Kolkata by Abanindranath Tagore, the nephew of Rabindranath Tagore, and widely acknowledged as one of the modern artists of that era. Rajendra quoted Abanindranath in his essay.

> When I heard that a dancer, male, coming after years in the West was going to dance, I came prepared to suffer some kind of khichri performance. But what I saw created a strange effect. It is nothing like what we see or know of and yet its soul seems Indian and very stirring. (Rajendra Shankar 1983: 8)

Shankar was shaped through the experience of being an Other in the United Kingdom. A colonial subject, a migrant, who was trying to survive the basic daily struggles of making a living and an untrained male trying to establish himself as a dancer, he had a lot of prejudices to push back and fight. To look at the figure of this uncertain migrant, I refer to Homi Bhabha's writing on DissimiNation. Bhabha says:

[4] Rabindranath Tagore and his acknowledgement of Uday Shankar is well documented in his encouraging letters to Shankar. His interest in the establishment of the institution by Shankar also is understood in the interest expressed by his son and himself in inviting Shankar to be a part of Tagore's own institution Visva-Bharati (see Chapter 4).

[5] Abanindranath Tagore was trained initially in Western painting and then was introduced to Indian art by his teacher E. B. Havell. His knowledge of Indian art was encouraged in the similar manner as Shankar, who in turn had been encouraged by Sir William Rothenstein to study the art from his own country at the British Museum.

> DissiMination—owes something to the wit and wisdom of Jacques Derrida, but something more to my own experience of migration. I have lived that moment of the scattering of the people that in other times and other places, in the nations of others, becomes a time of gathering. Gatherings of exiles and émigrés and refugees; gathering on the edge of 'foreign' cultures; gathering at the frontiers; gatherings in the ghettos or cafes of city centres; gathering in the half-life, half-light of foreign tongues, or in the uncanny fluency of another's language; gathering the signs of approval and acceptance, degrees, discourses, disciplines; gathering the memories of underdevelopment, of other worlds lived retroactively; gathering the past in a ritual of revival; gathering the present. (Bhabha 1994: 199)

Bhabha's thoughts on the margins of the migrant's world, never really surfaced in any writing of Shankar or in any of his performances for that matter. Though it is reflected in what we know about his search for the audience and patrons that would give him some space as well as some time to prove himself through the art practice he instinctively knew how to handle. Shankar was candid enough to try and find ways of using his migrant subjecthood and identity. He used his body by turning it into a subject of oriental display. That his body was oriental enough to attract the Western gaze but not unpalatable in shape, or presence, he had understood from his interactions in London. He studied and understood his subjective vulnerability well. He made use of it sparingly, but enhanced its public appeal by optimising on the performative subjectivity that made him stand out in time as well as space as an oriental male dancer embodying sensuality and sexuality with grace and confident stage presence born out of practice. The presence he cultivated was performative of an attractive man of amicable behaviour with visible signs of an unfamiliar masculinity. Analysis of Shankar's position as a migrant get further clarified in Bhabha's writing:

> The scraps, patches and rags of daily life must be repeatedly turned into the signs of a coherent national culture, while the very act of the narrative performance interpellates a growing circle of national subjects. In the production of the nation as narration there is a split between the continuist, accumulative temporality of the pedagogical, and the repetitious, recursive strategy of the performative. It is through this process of splitting that the conceptual ambivalence of modern society becomes the site of writing the nation. (Bhabha 1994: 209)

It is easier to place Shankar in the above-mentioned structure of the 'recursive strategy of the performative', of repeated self-assertion as well as a performative signification of national culture that may be seen as an assertive choreopolitical choice as a whole. It is also the beginning of a pioneering move in terms of presentations from South Asia, whereby, many artists (from folk, classical, and contemporary dance backgrounds) now understand the requirements of the Western proscenium space and presentational aesthetics. It also has shaped the aesthetics and expectations within India to a large extent, and brought in modern sensibilities to replace the timeless continuity that rituals or even social occasions required of performances. One must also understand that Shankar was performing for colonial expositions even before he began to be contracted for his performances for tours organised by Sol Hurok. The first Colonial Exposition[6] he danced at was at the British Empire exhibition near London in 1924. In the 1930s, Hurok's tours also put him in the same league of invitees for Hurok's 'seasons' that were advertised widely in the United States and Europe with front ranking and internationally recognized modern dancers such as Mary Wigman, Ruth St. Denis, Ted Shawn, Pavlova, and many more well-known artists. The nine-month long '*Exposition Coloniale Internationale*', Paris, 1931, put him up as a part of the window display from India, out there for the whole of the Western world to see or at least hear about. The other lesser talked about presenter was the famous impresario, Aaron Richmond from Boston, Massachusetts, who invited Shankar to be a part of The Celebrity Series of Boston as part of his Celebrity Series established in 1938. Shankar and his Hindu Ballet was one of the very few troupes from South Asia invited by Aaron Richmond.

In all these above-mentioned cases of transcultural conversations, Shanker had to assume a different entity for each of the different audiences. It is not only his translational skill[7] but his translocational

[6] The colonial exhibitions/expositions were large world fairs for display of museumised life from the colonised countries. Ranging from display of ways of life of different communities from the colonies, by putting on public-view human subjects, such spectacular events forced the colonial subjects to literally live their lives authentically while on display.

[7] See Joan Erdman's 1987 article 'Performance as Translation: Uday Shankar in the West' for details.

understanding and negotiation that made him a survivor and a presence, eventually allowing a space for his own creativity to surface and present itself as his very own contribution to the modern language of dance in/from India.

Creative Dance as a Category

Shankar used the term 'creative dance' for the innovative and improvisational practice that had become well known as his process of training. His reference to 'creating' dance as a process can be linked to Randy Martin's words where he talked about the process of creating dance in the Western context. Martin wrote 'dance movement, like the capitalisation of society itself, develops unevenly, we can only expect those technical influences associated with certain historical formations to persist as residues within culture as a whole, as well as the body in particular' (Martin 1998: 173).

In absence of any detailed writing on creative dance as a genre in Indian writings, the same by Western authors help us formulate the process that Shankar created as his creative dance technique. One such writing by Janet Anderson begins with a quote from Agnes de Mille. It reads, 'Girl or boy, gifted or clumsy, learn then, if you can, to dance. You will stand up straighter and walk prouder the rest of your life. And you will be kinder and more polite in all physical matters, and less afraid' (Anderson 1952: 85). Even though there was vagueness about the actual definition of 'creative' dance, Shankar's emphasis (also often repeated by his late wife in our classes) was similar to the way creative dance promises many other life skills such as confidence, grace, attentiveness, the spirit of sharing, respect for each other, and kindness besides making a person a dancer. Amala Shankar's assertions regarding Shankar's creative pedagogy in her interview[8] relates to Anderson's observation that 'There is nothing neat and tidy about studying modern dance' (Anderson 1952: 85).

There remains a need to discuss the term creativity in the Indian context. The term, by virtue of its ability to distance itself from existing structures within traditional dance grammars and teaching processes, was a way to seek freedom of expressions without necessarily critiquing any existing modes of ongoing practice or teaching. In fact, though the constant pressure of acknowledging the past remained as a shackle on

[8] Personal interview of Smt. Amala Shankar by the author on dance classes and teaching techniques at USICC, Almora and Kolkata, July 2003.

Shankar, he was creating his own terms of reference with modern dance and body trainings. Bose and Jalal's observation that 'Colonised intellectuals were clearly seeking alternative routes of escape from the oppressive present, not all of which lay through creating illusions about our past and denouncing their modernity' (Bose and Jalal 2018: 100) actually gives us an idea about understanding Shankar's 'routes of escape'. His negotiations most definitely were that of a colonised individual. While, he may be seen as trying to walk a strategic and narrow path between 'us' and 'them', he definitely saw his endeavours as creating a bridge between the past, present, and future, as well as trying to take tradition as a space for accommodation of transition.

As an assessment of Shankar's contribution to dance in India in the modern times, Ruth Abrahams writes, 'Shankar offered three major contributions to the history of modern Indian dance: a performance structure conducive to modern theatrical demands, a newly defined relationship between Indian dance and musical accompaniment, and innovation in the choreographic process for Indian dance' (Abrahams 2007: 365). As a term of description, the word 'creative' invited many questions regarding the dance form itself. The term 'creative' dance was introduced in Shankar's classes. Though nobody has specifically mentioned the details about such an important pedagogical decision, it seems to have stayed on in Shankar's pedagogical references, in the written material as well as the newsletters for Almora. Putting the emphasis on the process of creating as a result of thinking and ideating seems to have been seen as the core idea on which movement-generation was grounded. The technique was to facilitate transference of ideas or images into movement impulses by individuals. Those 'new' movement sequences were then solidified through repeated practice and reflexive adjustments and tested out in group presentations. This training was required to increase the stamina, skill, and expertise of the dancer to be able to challenge himself or herself with the embodiment of his or her own ideas. Embodying a variety of dance techniques/forms was also to increase the range of movement possibilities for the dancer. The final outcome was the result of the multiple layers of laboratory-like process each of these created movements that Shankar helped his students and troupe members develop and experiment with.

Shankar's popular dance 'products' that were touring frequently at the beginning of the 1930s remained somewhat unreflective of the process of making them. It is later that he talked about discipline and freedom of expressions as the basis of the introductory understanding of his 'creative' technique. He also referred to the importance of understanding one's own body and the way it moves for creating one's own repertoire of movements with the help of imagination and innovation. One of his often repeated assertions was the reference to an aesthetic frame, structured by an identification of the traditionally influenced movement references and constructed by specific exposures to life and art from a specific geo-cultural identity. In any case, in the porous world of modern dance intellectual borrowing/sharing of ideas of embodiment, both from own as well other cultures, is something common in this period of transcultural conversations between the East and the West.

At the time when communicative language for Indian classical dances were structured with the help of a range of Sanskrit texts such as *Natyashastra* and *Abhinaya Darpan* that fixed the range of meanings for gestures and expressions, Shankar was also creating his pedagogic tools of dance and linking them to the specific expressive structures of *rasa* and *bhava*. Those tools made use of the same range of abilities that built the communicative systems within the classical dance grammars but were also available in their flexible and experimental ranges for creative experiments. Shankar's gestures were seen as, and most probably were, initially borrowed tools of creating a language of the dancing body within the Indian tradition as he understood the importance of a strong show of 'belonging' as an authentic Indian (Figs. 2.1 and 2.2).

Gestures would always play an important part in Shankar's technique, but they would not be the only way to narrate a story in his later works. Shankar's conscious understanding of the need to develop a dance language that did not limit the dance's communicative power to a certain culture or geography pushed him towards a more universal process of cognitive transfer, which was largely independent of spoken words, songs, or hand gestures. The facial expressions—an embodied characterisation of the content—however, resembled much of the developments in the vocabulary of both modern dance and dance theatre across the globe.

It could be because of the lack of specific training in his earlier years as a dancer that he was not interested in the set patterns dictated by dramaturgy or by classical texts such as *Natyashastra*. He appeared to have given in to the pressure of having to prove his 'Indian'ness later while he was establishing his institution in India. His hand gestures changed visibly as has been recorded in the films before and after. His own training in Kathakali can also be traced to the second half of the 1930s. Hence, it is

Fig. 2.1 Hand gestures specifically photographed as a part of choreographic compositions—from Shankar's publicity material from his tour with Sol Hurok (1937–1938) (© Folder: Brown M-63. Anonymous May 22, 1936, © Boston Public Library)

evident that Shankar's idea of 'creativity' evolved over time. It seems that at some point Shankar became conscious of the divide between the audience in India into those who admired his work and those who belonged

Fig. 2.2 Right: Shankar's photograph titled '*Hands: In infinite configuration*' in the brochure (© Folder: Brown M-63. Anonymous May 22, 1936, © Boston Public Library)

to the elite often brahmin group of *Rasikas* (the learned audience), most of whom were severely critical of his art.

Although from a brahminical background of privilege himself, Shankar seems to clearly display a strong tug-of-war between his brahminic upper class upbringing and his experience of professional showmanship and his understanding of the presentation of dance as an experimental and communicative art. Echoing Randy Martin, I would like to propose that both the classical grammar and the innovative technique of movement-generation resided comfortably within Shankar's body and his idea of the framework of movement-making in the forms of what Martin calls 'contending principles'. Randy Martin very aptly calls this 'process of self-governance, a technique for regulating techniques', by which 'the dancer must generate her own authority' (Martin 1998: 175). Shankar's changing relationship with his dance and especially the body image he presented through his dances travelled a significant distance with his earlier postures and movements (glimpses of which are available from small film clips and photographs) and his later mediations (as recorded in his film *Kalpana*), which indicate a significant distance travelled in the course of about fifteen years (from 1923/24 till 1948).

Chronologically placed, Shankar's recognition can be assigned to the successive negotiations he managed to have with significant personalities in the West, such as with Anna Pavlova, Alice Boner, Simkie, John Martin, Sol Hurok, the Elmhirsts, and many other important entities. His critics often appear to doubt his sincerity as a dance-maker because of his obvious need for the acknowledgement of Western receptions. The archive, however, uncovers two closely parallel urges in his presentations at the beginning of his success story as a choreographer—on the one hand striving to survive as an artist, and on the other hand the risk taken to provide a concrete shape to frame himself as an oriental male subject on the proscenium presenting the culture of his country of origin. His modernity was an inevitable way of processing his passion for creatively expressing himself through dance.

Shankar created his own 'peculiar' modernity. Due to the confidence he gained in being able to talk back to the West he was able to create dance presentations that worked because of his strategies to deal with the stereotypes of Western expectations. Sometimes those strategies involved the content that appealed to Western audiences by recreating the unknown romantic world of myth. In other words he was making available glimpses of another culture that was difficult to understand, through presentational tactics for short modular consumption. He mentioned other strategies such as the length of the choreographies. He was known to hold the opinion that a choreographer must know where to stop, that he/she must never produce a piece that becomes too long, and that the audience must leave the auditorium feeling a bit dissatisfied and a little hungry and wanting to see more.

Ensemble as a 'Modern' Way of Moving

Uday Shankar began his dancing career as a partner to Anna Pavlova, and had seen her work with her company of dancers. Over the years, Shankar's journey changed from an individual one to a highly intricate and developed ensemble mode of choreography as well as movement-generation over the years of his dancing career. His success as a solo dancer remained a story that influenced many others, including male dancers such as Ram Gopal[9] whose dance documentation shows the remarkable influence of Shankar's successful path. However, Shankar's career shows a remarkable shift from solos and duets to group/ensemble performances. It was in the course of teaching larger number of students in organised classes—first at the Dartington Hall and then at Almora—that one notes the mention of group work as the most important way to build a dance repertory as an ensemble.

By ensemble practice here I mean not a dance presentation in imitation of 'folk' traditions of organic ways of moving together but a new experimental form whereby it is a technique of training in theatrical communication as well as a coordinated and collaborative dance creation. This is not the same as belonging to the community through dance but instead building the skill of coordination in dancers by training them to nurture responses to each other. In Shankar's practice, ensemble (group) work refers to developing a mindset of being in the creative process together, to own and have agency in the process of choreography. It also means lending oneself in a manner that s/he becomes a part of a whole, to generate a strong sense of creating, performing, reflecting, and critiquing together rather than being concerned only about one's own dance world that creates and relies on an isolative and competitive excellence even within a group of people dancing together. The emphasis here

[9] Ram Gopal was a dancer who followed Uday Shankar's path to a certain extent to take Indian dance to the West. His dance presentations and costumes often show great similarity to Shankar's presentation of his own dances. Ram Gopal, unlike Shankar, had training in classical dances. He was hailed as a trained dancer displaying 'authentic' technique in Kathakali, Bharatanatyam, and Kathak.

is strictly on generating a particular level of awareness as well as ability to be one of a group rather than an individual dancer who even while in a crowd on stage manages to create an invisible wall of indifference towards how other dancers are moving.[10]

Shankar's choreographic works point towards a significant effort towards creating a kaleidoscopic relationship between the participants in an ensemble, as well as generating an affective relationship between the core and the margin in a choreography. The consistent nurturing of a sense of comfort within the group of dancers, between the dancers and musicians, and between the choreographer(s) and the dancers seen in these works, is easier said than done. The ideal form is utopic but even the workable one that can contribute significantly to the choreographic process can certainly not be attained by only giving instructions and expecting people to follow. This process in itself was and still remains different from the training techniques used in the classical dances where one survives the rigorous training if only s/he is an individual who is consistently competitive, perhaps even before becoming a dancer of some calibre.

The word ensemble signifies learning, creating, rehearsing, performing, creating costumes and props, working backstage, travelling, and staying together during tours. Sharing much more than the dance technique, training, or the performance space together, the ensemble becomes a community brought and bound together by 'the multiple forces of mobilization' (Martin 1998: 14). In the case of Shankar's work and troupe activities, the ensemble identity seems to be the way the creative tool is successfully used in dance and the extended corporeal mobilisation.

Building on the Idea of 'ensemble' that is easily attached to community life, ritual practices, and community performances in India, within proscenium dance it has assumed a simplistic understanding. One thinks of ensemble as large groups performing in practised unison and uniformity. In many dance choreographies, the aim is to be able to create a perfect ensemble output or product and to achieve that by ensuring a rigorous practice process. Whereas, in theatre, especially the genre of group theatre, ensemble refers to a specific technique or process which has been

[10] In classical forms of dances in India the training starts with focus on individual skill, with a sense of competition for the dancer to emerge as the best one in the class. Even group choreographies for classical Indian dances are a number of skilled bodies put together on stage.

developed and fine-tuned as a way of moving away from character-based individually oriented theatre acting. For Shankar, the essential qualities seemed to have been: self and interpersonal reflexivity; experiments in proxemic communication; building or enhancing unpredictability that is possible with multiple participants working with the common consciousness for achieving a communicative and alert togetherness; being and claiming the agency for creative processes of dance-making together; and finally, developing on the idea of corporeal interdependence and techniques to generate togetherness as a kinaesthetic idea to take it beyond only imitative and clone-like movements.

The power of improvised-assimilative dance-making can be seen amplying in Shankar's later works. This process drew its strength from assimilating stimulations and triggers to move in coordination, consciously encouraging participant dancers as well as musicians to use the stimulations and triggers to act as reference points for expressing one's subjectivity while working in a group. Much like theatre exercises and stimulations, this process encouraged participants to retreat into their own body archive while also getting constant impetus from other co-participants doing the same thing at the same time in the same space. Thus, one's own 'new' movement idea is always materialised through the whole ensemble observing. This is at once humbling like all collaborative movement works in such spaces. It is shared and therefore is everyone's work but at the same time it also acquires strength of conviction as one sees many different bodies performing the same movements perhaps with slight modifications making it possible for the 'original' creator to now become a collaborator for the same movement structure that s/he has created and to assimilate changes on the way to get a reviewed output without much ado.

Uday Shankar's principle of creating a dance in an ensemble, thus, followed a different ownership logic. There are ample reasons to dislike and discard this logic if one actually does not really believe or is not invested in the idea of the ensemble. As I said earlier, dancers trained for expertise and excellence in particular techniques may be discomforted by such a shared concept of contribution and communication. But ensemble technique remains a different space altogether, inhabited more by theatre artists than dancers. For Shankar, this remained the way to imagine as well as source movements beyond one's own bodily possibilities while seeing the movement being refereed and reviewed through the proper review process possible in an equitable manner only in an ensemble space.

Methods and Material in Choreography: Ways of Communicating Through Dance

Shankar's inspirations came from several sources such as the architectural remains in India, the everyday presence of dance in community life that he saw and documented, his instinctive sense of and responses to music, the gradual opening up of his horizon through his experience as a professional showman and a performer, and very often accidental meetings that turned into useful and path-breaking new turns in patronage as well as the realisation of his experimental ideas. It is important to relate to the conceptual relationship between materials and methods in his work in order to identify the idea of the modern in his dance.

Sculptures and Their Interpretations

Indian temple sculptures have been an inspiration to classical dance forms such as Bharatanatyam and Odissi very directly. Referring to the sculptural bodies of celestial dancers and their postures, the classicists have justified and validated through historical and mythical references the grammatic structures introduced into dance vocabularies in different parts of the Indian subcontinent. Iconography of these spectacular material remains has been useful to study dance as a part of art history as well as an important documentation of dance in the past. Shankar's introduction to sculptures were in two stages—first through William Rothenstein, his teacher at the Royal College of Art, and while looking at the actual remnants in India, through the eyes of his sculptress friend /patron Alice Boner (see Chapter 3 for details). The sculptures became the stories, the movement inspirations, and the aesthetic infrastructure of Shankar's dance vocabulary, and his material building blocks for designing the static and dynamic possibilities for the moving bodies.

Everyday Life Through an Ethnographic Viewing and Documentation of India

Uday Shankar's childhood reference to dance is recognised through repeated reference by Shankar, his brothers, and later writers about Shankar, to a man named Matadin. Matadin's name, however, never comes up without the mention of his caste identity of shoe-makers (*Chamar*). In the need to communicate how inclusive and rooted

Shankar's practice was in his childhood memories, this story has been perpetuated by people who continue to repeat this memory in print. Many of the articles also mention the later meeting of Shankar with Matadin when Shankar sought out Matadin on one of his return trips to India in the 1930s to acknowledge him in public. The caste of this natural dancer may or may not have mattered to Shankar. His dance was a source of inspiration and motivation for Shankar's upper caste sensibility. He mentioned Matadin time and again in his talks, interviews, and writings—seemingly in awe of the natural, untrained bodies in rural, caste-segregated societies. Rajendra Shankar writes: 'During Holi he would watch the dances of the "Chamars" and specially their leader, Matadin, who created a strange fascination for young Uday with his curious movements, sometimes comic and vulgar, and sometimes very soft and serious' (Rajendra Shankar 1983: 4). For the elite upbringing of many Hindu upper caste individuals like Shankar in India such distances and lack of knowledge about each other are normalised through the segregated ways of life. Shankar tried to fill in the gaps by spending a whole year of 1930 roaming about different parts of India, seeing and sometimes even filming life, dance, and festivities (see Chapter 3 for more details). The ethnographic experience of the moving of individual bodies, crowd behaviour, agricultural seasons, and community events, fed into Shankar's sense of choreographing a presence and representations for proscenium experiences. The material collected over the years added to the material for his 'construction' of new choreographies.

Musical Instruments and Musical Accompaniment

The third support and incentive came in the form of innovative ideas of musical accompaniment. Shankar's work, right from the first half of the twentieth century when he started his independent concert presentations, remained dependent on the specific bodies that he had available for his creative process. It also remained, as we shall see through the other chapters as well, controlled by the musical accompaniment that was a constant necessity as a conversation between the moving bodies and the rhythm, mood, and culture specific ambiance. Shankar's well-crafted design of creating a performance piece required the support of the famous musicians he had with him. Hence, even for his solo performances in the beginning of his public career as a dancer he was not a solo performer. The musicians like Timirbaran Bhattacharya, Vishnudas

Shirali, Ustad Alauddin Khan, and Ravi Shankar performed with and for him, sometimes leading the dance movements, and at other times being led by them. The music established the mythical, cultural, social, and gendered references that created a bridge between the dancers and the audience all around the world.

Amala Shankar often talked about the creation of particular musical pieces, rather accidentally, with the idea being born on the dining table where a *sawaal jawaab* (a conversation in rhythms)—'Dhi-nak-na-tin'—'Ti-nak-na-tin' with cutleries led to the birth of a musical piece for *Kalpana*. Hence, choreography was a creativity-based conversation between the music and the movements where the music was not composed beforehand as a structure governing the dance.

For Shankar musical accompaniment was an important requirement. It needed to carry a strong reference to the East, sometimes including musical instruments such as gongs and gamelans for beyond the borders of South Asia. It is only that, unlike the concert dances in the West, within the Indian context it was difficult to distinguish between music, dance, and theatre as different genres as all three continued to be woven together in most of the participatory class exercises as well as presentational forms on stage. Shankar's choreographic structures were connected closely to the musical structure that in most cases was also created through a process of interaction with the idea of the choreography.

Dance at and The Dartington Hall and Visva-Bharati University

For Shankar, one of the most important inspirations to push his creativity came from the Elmhirsts of Dartington Hall in the United Kingdom who partially funded and backed Visva-Bharati of Rabindranath Tagore, Kalakshetra of Rukmini Devi, and the American Dance Festival (USA). The Hall also funded the Elmgrant Trust for Uday Shankar's dance academy in Almora. The Hall's modern art education model and Tagore's view of holistic education for teaching visual and performing arts in a place close to nature provided different alternatives and Shankar was helped by the Elmhirsts to choose the institutional structure that was most suitable for a multi-disciplinary teaching of a theory–practice interface around dance and other related arts (see Chapter 4 for more details).

Mary Wigman School and the Heterogeneity of Available Technique Through Zohra Segal

The second inspiration came in the form of the trained dancer Zohra Segal, trained under Mary Wigman (Segal 2010: 45–46) in Germany in Modern Dance, who was put in charge of the syllabus-building process at USICC, Almora. The school aspired to become an ideal performing art academy with a vision of overall development in performative skills and knowledge. The materials came together with Shankar's thoughts on developing a strong pedagogy. It strengthened Shankar's creative process linked to but not restricted by the material he identified as his artistic inspiration. The important point to note is the 'heterogeneity of technique' that Randy Martin and Susan L. Foster (Randy Martin 1998: 176) have talked about while referring to intertextuality in dance techniques. Explaining this manner of reference to intertextuality and heterogeneity of movements Randy Martin writes, 'Susan Foster has indicated that this heterogeneity of technique marks a certain moment in the history of dance technique when, particularly among professionals, commodification itself usurps a given technical affiliation' (Martin 1998: 176). Intertextuality in Shankar's movement repertoire developed over time, not along a specifically designed and planned path but experimentally. In that journey new knowledge about the varied structures within the dance from different regions of India unravelled themselves as Shankar got reintroduced to his own country and its cultural repertoire as a subject looking at it from far, almost as if through an outsider's (Western) eyes. This translocationality configured Shankar and his dance, enriched his process of both 'being' and constantly 'becoming' the figure that eventually came to be referred to popularly as the Ambassador of Indian culture.

Expectations: Managing the Push and Pull of Tradition and Modernity

Shankar was too traditional for the West to be able to allow him to inhabit the same kinaesthetic sphere with Western modern dancers. The West could at best allow him the label of a representative of the East. He was at the same time too innovative and taking too much liberty for the East to digest. For the same reason his audience differed vastly depending on the space of performance. The range of spaces varied from open-air grounds and make shift stages in different parts of India to the largest and most well-equipped auditoria, City Halls, and Opera Houses all over the world. He consistently strived to keep up with the techniques of communication that also needed to be completely re-adjusted to these different settings. His audience became familiar to his choreographies and came with a specific expectation, especially during his yearly tours of Europe and America. This was ensured by careful advertising by Hurok through the release of publicity material, much like for all the other performers he presented. Such publicity materials are often what help us to understand the audience that was expected for Shankar's shows. This audience was served with a specific image to build their aesthetic expectation and the advertisements often painted a very different picture for Shankar's performances than they would for modern dancers of the West. This expectation eventually may have been the inevitable path that Shankar saw as his only option, at least till he was still negotiating hard to reach a level of stability in terms of his reception. A cyclic inevitability, that pushed him to dance to what was popular and liked, led to being loved for what he danced. This popularity caught him in a bind, keeping him from breaking this cycle for quite a long time. This whirlpool seems to have been broken by him, for the first time, when he started his institution in Almora. Pedagogy became his escape route from the stronghold of expectations, both in the East and the West.

Shankar's career touched its peak in terms of popularity, visibility, and creativity for the first time in 1931 with his partnership and eventual business contract (signed in 1931) with Alice Boner. India was sixteen years away from freedom and the world was struggling to normalise itself between the two world wars. The colonial powers were struggling to keep their colonies under control with increasing oppression and violence. The Indian elite were getting Western education. Links between the colony and the British had grown in terms of cultural awareness about each other. The idea of the 'other' was one that both the colonisers as well as the colonised recognised as a significant category. Dance was a definite domain of traditional, hereditary knowledge within the nationalistic project in India. The way it was taught, learnt, imbibed, and transmitted curtailed and severely restricted any way of going beyond the *Guru–Shishya Parampara*. These restrictions effectively discouraged modes of communication with the modern knowledge systems successfully by bestowing the responsibility of being the gate-keeper to the heritage. Hence, there was a great distance created between the imagined antiquity of the classical dances and anything that is 'modern' and therefore 'foreign' and 'new'. For colonial India, modern knowledge needed to be adapted to the Indian value systems, otherwise it was resisted passionately as a colonial vice trying to influence minds to embrace Western values and norms and to reject antiquity and traditional knowledge. Chatterjee notes that:

> By the second half of the 19th century, we see the emergence of 'national' societies for the pursuit of the modern knowledges. The learned societies of the earlier era had both European and Indian members. The new institutions were exclusively for Indian members and devoted to the cultivation and spread of the modern sciences and arts among Indians, if possible in the Indian languages. They were, in other words, institutions for the 'nationalisation' of the modern knowledges, located in a space somewhat set apart from the field of universal discourse, a space where discourse would be modern, and yet 'national'. (Chatterjee 1997: 16)

Shankar seems to fit this picture perfectly. Between the push and pull of tradition and transition, Shankar had managed to arrive at a space of negotiation where his dance would have both the traditional and the modern element. I see his decision clearly as one where he would dance the 'national' but be the 'modern' choreographer.

Alongside Chatterjee's views to separately classify 'our' modernity as an independent and specific socio-cultural negotiation, the concept of multiple modernities actually strengthens our understanding of Shankar's encounter of the 'modern'. Not as a new structured movement system but as a process allowing creativity beyond the established grammar of the hegemonic dance genres. He was taking on the West as well as the East in his contestation and also pushing us to look at Eisenstadt's theorisation (as elaborated by Gerhard Preyer and Michael Sussman) of multiple modernities, whereby the modernisation process may be seen neither as one single homogenised pattern of societal change nor a road towards an universal goal for the whole humanity and where multiple modernities signify a shifting process of modification of existing patterns of existence, of norms, beliefs, communication, and interaction. 'There are many modernities and no one single version of modernisation' (Preyer and Sussman 2016: 10–11).

Pallabi Chakravorty argues that the 'new dimensions of modernity as experienced in India' dependent on the changing nature of the public culture in turn was linked to the changing nature of patronage and formation of independent India (Chakravorty 2006: 59). Her observations that 'modernity today is no longer a prerogative of the west' (2006: ibid.), is important here in the context of the continuing my argument on the specific encounters between Indian dance and modernity. I suggest that first Tagore and then Shankar were driven by the ongoing reforms movement in the cultural ecology of India in the early twentieth century to identify two principle ideas regarding what they must ensure about reception of their work with dance. Shankar may have been following Tagore's advise when he—much like Tagore, wanted to see dance as an acceptable and respectable performance practice in India. He also seems to have followed Tagore's ideas of searching for the new within the older existing practices.

The Changing Scenario

While elaborating 'the story of nationalist emancipation' Partha Chatterjee says, 'The story of nationalist emancipation is necessarily a story of betrayal. Because it could confer freedom only by imposing a whole set of new controls, it could define a cultural identity for a nation only by excluding many from its fold...' (Chatterjee 1997: 154). Chatterjee's words explain the hierarchisation of the citizenry, in the process of nation building to create differential rights and claims to cultural capital and antiquity. It also helps us understand the logic behind classicisation in dance, whereby traditional practitioners were marginalised, and all modern endeavours were devalued by being identified as being against the national culture and tradition. Rustom Bharucha put forth this history in an apt manner within performance history:

> In the more institutionalized sectors of cultural practice as well, there was a vacuous retrieval of the past through an 'invention of tradition', whereby a 'back to the roots' anti-modern/anti-realist/anti-western policy was crudely, yet tenaciously propagated by the state and its accomplices. These proponents of an authentic 'Indianness' were, for the most part, neither native visionaries nor ideologues, but cultural bureaucrats who exemplified the 'intellectual laziness' that marks the defunct state of the national bourgeoisie... (Bharucha 1993: 33)

Writing about the reforms, Pallabi Chakravorty alerts us regarding the changes that anticipated power shift in the dance scenario. She writes that male master teachers of Kathak dance, had already been settling in Delhi since the 1930s, and in the post-independence drive to reform the cultural practices they were officially recognised as the bearers of the traditional knowledge (Chakravorty 2006: 118). This trajectory of the creation of the 'pure' form was applied in Bharatanatyam, Kuchipudi, Odissi, and other neoclassical forms where sanitisation process was followed by handing over the rights to carry on with teaching the now-cleansed form to the next generations to the men and women of the higher castes. Any dance in order for it to be accepted and be included in historical documentation as 'Indian' had to have an added characterisation such as 'pure' and/or 'traditional'. The purification process would inevitably include vigorous rewriting of its performance history involving hereditary women dancers, delinking it from its lower caste associations, and the process of trying to link it to ancient Sanskritic sources in order to establish its pure and/or sacred origin. In the process, marginalising the lives and dances of hereditary women performers to 'rescue' them while appropriating their dance was legitimised. Simultaneously some dancers such as Shankar, were identified as 'imitators' and therefore 'infiltrators' into the 'pure' traditional practices. This was done as a seemingly well-meaning preventive measure by the gate-keepers of Indian 'culture' and 'tradition' for providing a secure space and patronage to a particular form of brahminic indigeneity, which needed to curate its affiliates through caste hierarchy as well as inherited practices of citizenry. The reformers came from different caste hierarchies. In *Unfinished Gestures*, Davesh Soneji quotes the reformer Muthulakshmi Reddy from her archival files, 'I appeal to you who are mothers to make the future of your children bright, happy, and glorious and make them respectable and useful citizens—Muthulakshmi Reddy (1932, 614)' (Soneji 2012: 19). Soneji also observes, 'Devadasi reform was necessarily an altruistic act, and in the discourse of "rescue," devadasis could only be marked as "victims"' (Soneji 2012: 19).

The elite planners of Independent India, many of whom were products of Western higher education, were complex in their ideas of modernity, in the ways they reacted to the idea of the concept of 'western dance and music' and saw imitation of the West in many endeavours of creativity. This complexity was reflected in the frequent references to tradition in cultural policies. While the regional dance practices were used to project the colourful lifestyles and community identities that would showcase India's 'unity in diversity', the classical dances came into existence through an elaborate process of revival and restructuring of certain regional forms of dance and simultaneous of reconstruction of its history. The history records many erasures of spaces occupied by hereditary dance practitioners, along with systematic restructuring of the dance and its presentational principles. 'In this process the link with the *Natyashastra* was deliberately sought and established, and, in most cases, even the name of the forms were newly invented' (Sarkar Munsi 2008: 78).

Towards Modern Dance: Tagore as an Influence

According to Geeta Kapur the works of India's transitional modernity are 'ranged across three decades' from the 1930s to the 1950s (Kapur 2000: 287). Shankar's dance temporally fits this frame. His trip to India with Alice Boner and their visit to Tagore's University in 1930 is well documented in Boner's photographic collection. It becomes important to link the works of these two important personalities, whose endeavours enriched India's dance ecology significantly.

Tagore's school was established in 1901 in Santiniketan, West Bengal. Here, despite the negativity about dance in particular and performing arts in general among middle-class Indians, he included classes on music, drama, and visual arts. He could not include dance because of the severe aversion that many parents had towards dance. Hence the institution began without any specialized dance teacher. According to Santidev Ghosh, Tagore's well-known disciple, the dance practice faced a lot of opposition and therefore was slotted as evening games practice in the routine.[11] To help students acquire a large movement vocabulary and expertise he continued to invite specialist dancers from many parts of India and foreign countries. He encouraged creativity using his own poetry and participated in the plays as well as trained his students and participated in dance-dramas created out of his own texts. 'Tagore's principal motivation in using bodily movements as part of his understanding of education seems to have been the experience and expression of

[11] Ghosh, in his writings, mentioned that the monthly newsletter of the institution published the news of the new dance class taught by two experts from Tripura strategically by mentioning them as 'rhythmic physical exercises ... to the rhythm of the Manipuri drum—Mridangam' (quoted in Ghosh 1983: 9–10).

freedom, the sense of joy in bringing the body and mind together in the process of undertaking explorations through music, poetry, dance, and drama' (Sarkar Munsi 2008: 82–83). Tagore's modern outlook regarding holistic education and acknowledgement of dance as a communicative tool is understood from his following writing:

> In all parts of the world, dance as a communicative tool gets respect as part of the arts practices. We have started relating it to the fallen in our society because the elite have stopped dancing. But dance continues to exist in many forms among different communities. Yet the urban elite has a problem in thinking of those dances as their own—even if they are beautiful—as a result of class consciousness. (Quoted in Ghosh 1983: 4)

L.K. Elmhirst of the Dartington Hall began working as a volunteer for Tagore's village welfare work in 1921. The Elmhirsts were enamoured by Tagore's work and vision in his institution in Santiniketan and designed much of the Dartington Hall experiment in the same pattern.[12] Their association was consolidated over years through various exchanges and visits including a visit to the Hall by Tagore and his daughter-in-law, Pratima Devi (in-charge of dance-related activities at Santiniketan). Tagore created a teaching method called '*Bhavanritya*' or expressive dance. I have argued 'Tagore admired and followed the development of modern dance techniques in the West acknowledging them as an outcome of the creative urge in dancers. He also understood the dynamics of the Eastern body and, thus, looked towards the multiple dance forms of Asian countries like Indonesia, Thailand, and Ceylon for their movement genres, dresses, and presentation techniques for use in Indian dance' (Sarkar Munsi 2008: 85).

The comparison between the plans and execution of the process of inclusion of dance, first in Tagore's institution at Santiniketan and then at Shankar's institution in Almora, clearly highlights many similarities in the form of the instinctive cultural contributions that Tagore and Shankar wanted their institutions to make towards modern India. Tagore's plans were much more holistic. He had a definite vision of a particular form of holistic education that would maintain a rootedness for all students in the everyday realities of India, while creating a world-class university

[12] Later, Elmhirsts also funded the USICC, and their association with Shankar ushered in a significant era of change in dance in India.

that would create future opportunities at par with all such universities. Within that Tagore created a specific space for art education that would put similar emphasis on visual arts, crafts, and all forms of performing arts such as dance, music, and theatre. Shankar had his vision very focused on dance, but for his institution he envisioned an inclusive space for artistic training where learning from expert gurus or master teachers would go hand in hand with experiencing choreography, scenography, performance management, as well as documentation, and research. During his visit to Santiniketan in 1930 and after, Shankar must have seen the structure of the teaching programmes, as he had also witnessed at The Dartington Hall from 1934 onwards.

I have previously argued that Tagore had already been recognised for his endeavours in creating a pedagogy for art education first at a school level and then in Visva-Bharati University. Shankar was fascinated by this idea of a possibility that could give a secure space for dance education that could be safely placed alongside a larger field of art education in the plans that he had for creating an institution. While Shankar was influenced by Tagore, his own maturity shaped Tagore's opinion of his work over time, becoming reflected in Tagore's acknowledgement of him as a mature creative artist. From the 1930s till 1940,[13] they were continuing to engage with the idea of cultural consciousness, identity-specific nurturing of thoughts and art, nationalism, and creativity in their own ways. Regarding the creative consciousness embodied in these contributions to the history of dance in India, I have argued:

> Tagore has been criticised for having ventured into a territory that he knew nothing about. He worked with different forms of dance, both from India and abroad, in an attempt to create a more communicative dance language. This, however, according to the critics remained a collection of forms to work with and did not really coalesce into a single idiom or grammar. Shankar, on the other hand, was disapproved of for simply taking

[13] Tagore started his experiment with teaching using his idea of an inclusive education in 1910 and he got his Nobel prize in 1913. Shankar's first performances with Anna Pavlova were in 1923/1924. I take the time of 1930–1940, as the time when they were aware of each other and also were in touch. It is the period which also shows a great deal of similarities in the ways in which their use of dance forms from different regions in India helped them energise their method of using dance as a communicative art.

> elements from different dance forms and using these to create his own dance idiom, and for appropriating various techniques without undergoing proper training in any particular style. (Sarkar Munsi 2008: 79)

Tagore as a Predecessor of Shankar in Dance Education

Tagore also appears to have been influenced by the idea of cleansing and reforms. As will be discussed in detail in Chapter 4, in a letter to Uday Shankar, Rabindranath Tagore referred to dance as that which 'caters for a diseased mind' and is represented by the 'professional dancing girls' (see Chapter 4: 160 for details). A wave of change was encompassing the dance-related discourse in the East around the 1920s. Many dancers kept on experimenting on an individual basis with different forms, both Western and Eastern, such as Rukmini Devi (later Arundale), Srimati Hutheesingh (later Tagore), Zohra Mumtaz (later Segal), and Uday Shankar to mention just a few. Rukmini Devi went abroad to learn ballet and came in contact with Pavlova; Uday Shankar went to learn art but became a dancer with Pavlova; Zohra Segal and Srimati Tagore both went to the Mary Wigman School from two different parts of India. Though none of these above-mentioned dancers pursued what they learnt directly, they came back to go their own ways in contributing significantly to dance in India. Rukmini Devi established the traditional dance school named Kalakshetra and was actively responsible in the classicisation process for Bharatanatyam. Zohra joined Shankar's troupe initially and then moved on to theatre/films. Srimati Tagore became a student of Santiniketan and was well known for her dance and choreography.

One has to place Shankar's dance institution in Almora in a particular historically significant time in India around the first half of the twentieth century that may be identified as the phase of rapid growth in art institutions. Recognising this Ashish Rajadhyaksha writes:

> In the context of the Numerous institutions were geared to the invention of a modern aesthetics in the early twentieth century, the foremost being Santiniketan (Kala Bhavan, 1919; Visva-Bharati University, 1921), Kerala Kalamandalam (1930), Kalakshetra (1935), Uday Shankar India Culture Centre (1938), Gandharva Mahavidyalaya (1901) and Bhatkhande Vidyapeeth (1926). (Rajadhyaksha 2009: 144)

As a continuation of pre-independence developments, the nation's policy makers decided to establish the Sangeet Natak Akademi (Academy of Music and Theatre) in 1953, along with the Lalit Kala Akademi (Academy of Fine Arts), and the Sahitya Akademi (Academy of Letters) in 1954 for the promotion, recovery, restructuring, and patronage of the lost and neglected forms of visual and performing arts. The Sangeet Natak Akademi's report of 1953–1959 states that its intention is to encourage 'the new awakening and cultural resurgence' to be encouraged 'under a system of patronage hitherto unknown to the Indian Arts'.

The pre-independence institutions mentioned by Rajadhyaksha were structured by the principal vision of the person(s) who set it up in the first place, but these institutions got recognized later keeping the original structure of the institution as unchanged as possible. The post-independence institutions were part of a holistic plan of cultural growth and incentive with the state acting as its planner, chief patron, as well as the upholder of sovereignty. Pre-independence institutions such as Visva-Bharati and USICC are significant as they put in place modern pedagogies culled out of experiences in transcultural, and translocational circumstances. A review of Tagore's ideas of incorporation of dance in education helps us locate Shankar's hope and desire for a specialised dance institution in the institutional history of India. The timing and patronage for Tagore's institution to consolidate its dance-related curriculum coincides largely with Shankar's effort in an almost similar area. Though the structure and particular history of USICC, Almora, is discussed in detail in Chapter 4, the current discussion is necessary to place Shankar's tryst with modernity into one single scape.

Was Creative Dance Modern Enough:

Shankar was never a part of elite society even though he was a brahmin. His struggle to become accepted as a dancer and his success at catching the attention of famous critics as well as dance connoisseurs definitely means we need to investigate his identity negotiations through those struggling moments of his 'writing of the nation'. He never seized to be a part-outsider in the world of dance.

The reading of his performance strategies as his politics, of individualistic and somewhat self-centred survival as a dancer and an authentic citizen of India needs to be complicated. His presentation of the Orient as an exaggerated hyper-exoticised land on the one hand, and as a society of diverse living traditions formed around survival, labour, celebrations, and modern innovations on the other hand makes the transcultural and translocational negotiations worthy of detailed discussion. As a migrant artist, an admired choreographer, and a frequent presenter of Oriental spectacles using eastern dance aesthetics—touring, mostly successfully, across Europe and the Americas, Shankar demands a more nuanced reading. His negotiations continued to be shaped by the reception and the anticipated kinaesthetic expectations which by and for themselves made him a dancer with a modern understanding of performance reception.

This assorted mobilisation of translocationality raises important questions. How was Shankar's work of attempting to bring the East and the West together different from any of the later East–West encounters? Did the problem lie in the tension that existed between the processes of 'Sanskritisation' and 'Westernisation' in Indian dance at that point in history? While, on the one hand, Shankar's 'form-less', 'technique-less'(!) dance was the primary focus of the critique, on the other hand his acknowledgement of the existing forms of classical dance also came under censure, for it was believed that he was trying to appropriate movements from different dance traditions. In the process, his emphasis on greater freedom for the development of an explorative dance vocabulary, at times for its specific use in the choreography of a narrative, and also for the sheer joy of creating new movements was dismissed as appropriation and, therefore, was not even analysed academically. The responsibility for this kind of misunderstanding and misinterpretation of Shankar's experiments, in my opinion, lies more with the successors of Shankar, much like the successors of Tagore, who took only his form as the binding principle and not his philosophy.

The works of Tagore and Shankar, in opening up dance to a process of experimentation and to the coming together of multiple forms have generally been seen as a way to self-discovery and self-definition. Both of them worked on the principle of building a respectful attitude towards other cultural practices, creating the opportunity to learn more about them, as well as assimilating their movements in dance. Uday Shankar perhaps had the vision to do what many dancers are wanting to do now. Not shackled by any one form of dance training, he was a free man, free to explore and take motifs and movements, and his method became known as creative method, whereby, he also, like many Western dancers was responding to his urge to express and communicate through his body. He worked hard to make his form different from the Western techniques and he based creation on movement principles from regional dances of India, a choice made by many performers of later years while creating something of their own.

As already discussed in many writings about Shankar, his modernity is understood as the urge to create not only new dance but a system for creating new movements of dance. This also leads to discussions by Abrahams (2007), Khullar (2018), and Purkayastha (2014) regarding whether he was modern enough. As a way to understand his ways to live and breathe through his art, it may be interesting to look at Shankar's encounters with the modern moment. I see it as a constantly evolving one. Born necessarily as a product of multiple geopolitical pulls—it needs to be seen as his ongoing quest through his embodied negotiations with the world around him. I would also like to suggest at this point that once he was accepted as a successful representative of Indian dance, there was a tremendous amount of support extended to him and his work by the intellectuals and nationalist leaders within India. His support came in the form of encouragement from Rabindranath Tagore, Jawaharlal Nehru, Netaji Subhash Chandra Bose, Pearl Buch, Sardar Patel, Mahatma Gandhi, the Dartington Hall Trust, and many others. His creations often seem to be striving to anticipate a postcolonial time, when the nation would have its own independence.

References

Abrahams, Ruth K. 2007. "Uday Shankar: The Early Years, 1900–1938." *Dance Chronicle* 30 (3): 363–426.

Anderson, Janet. 1952. *Modern Dance*. 2nd edition. New York: Chelsea House.

Bhabha, Homi. 1994. *The Location of Culture*. London and New York: Routledge.

Bharucha, Rustom. 1993. *Theatre and the World: Performance and the Politics of Culture*. London and New York: Routledge.

Bose, Sugata, and Ayesha Jalal. 2018. *Modern South Asia: History, Culture, Political Economy*. New Delhi: Routledge.

Chakravorty, Pallabi. 2006. "Dancing into Modernity: Multiple Narratives of India's Kathak Dance." *Dance Research Journal* 38 (1&2): 115–37.

Chatterjee, Partha. (1997) 1999. *The Nation and Its Fragments: Colonial and Postcolonial Histories (Reprint)*. New Delhi: Oxford University Press.

Craske, Oliver. 2020. *Indian Sun: The Life and Music of Ravi Shankar*. London: Faber & Faber.

Erdman, Joan L. 1987. "Performance as Translation: Uday Shankar in the West." *The Drama Review: TDR* 31 (1 (Spring)): 64–88.

Franko, Mark. 2007. "Dance and the Political: States of Exception." In *Dance Discourses: Keywords in Dance Research*, eds. Susanne Franco and Marina Nordera, 11–28. London: Routledge.

Ghosh, Santidev. 1983. *Adhunik Bharatiyo Nritya (in Bengali)*. Kolkata: Ananda Publishers.

Kapur, Geeta. 2000. *When Was Modern: Essay on Contemporary Cultural Practice in India*. Delhi: Tulika Books.

Khullar, Sonal. 2018. "Almora Dreams: Art and Life at the Uday Shankar India Cultural Centre, 1939–44." *Marg* 69 (4): 14–31.

Lepacki, André. 2013. "Choreopolice and Choreopolitics: Or, the Task of the Dancer." *TDR* 57 (4): 13–27.

Lepecki, Andre. 2006. *Exhausting Dance: Performance and Politics of Movement*. New York and London: Routledge.

Martin, John. 1937. "The Dance: Hindu Center; Shan-Kar to Preserve Indian Arts." *The New York Times*, February 14, p. 8.

Martin, John. 1951. "Shankar Dancers in Program Here; Uday, Amala and Company of Hindu Musicians Return After Two-Year Absence." *The New York Times*, December 26, p. 18.

Martin, Randy. 1998. *Critical Moves: Dance Studies in Theory and Politics*. Durham and London: Duke University Press.

Pathak, Avijit. 2006. *Modernity, Globalization and Identity: Towards a Reflexive Quest*. Delhi: Aakar Books.

Preyer, G., and M. Sussman, eds. 2016. "Introduction on Shmuel N. Eisenstadt's Sociology: The Path to Multiple Modernities." In *Varieties of Multiple Modernities*, 1–29. Leiden: Brill.

Purkayastha, Prarthana. 2014. *Indian Modern Dance, Feminism, and Nationalism*. Basingstoke, UK: Palgrave Macmillan.

Rajadhyaksha, Ashish. 2009. *Indian Cinema in the Time of Celluloid: From Bollywood to the Emergency*. New Delhi; Bloomingdon: Tulika Books/Indiana University Press.

Roy, Basanta Koomar. 1936. Brochure published by Sol Hurok. *MC/Chekhov/S4/39: Series 4. General Files: A. Uday Shankar Play Bills*. Devon: Dartington Hall Records.

Segal, Zohra. 2010. *Close-Up: Memories of a Life on Stage and Screen*. New Delhi: Women Unlimited (An Associate of Kali for Women).

Shankar, Rajendra. 1983. "Personal Reminiscences of Uday SHankar." In *Uday SHankar*, ed. Sunil Kothari and Mohan Khokar, 4–10. New Delhi: RIMPA and the Uday Shankar Festival '83 Committee.

Sarkar Munsi, Urmimala. 2008. "Boundaries and Beyond: Problems of Nomenclature in Indian Dance." In *Dance: Transcending Borders*, ed. Urmimala Sarkar Munsi, 78–98. Delhi: Tulika Books.

Soneji, Davesh. 2012. *Unfinished Gestures—Devadasis, Memory, and Modernity in South India (South Asia Across the Disciplines)*. Chicago: University of Chicago Press.

Archival/Online Sources

Interview of Uday Shankar by Shambhu Mitra. https://www.youtube.com/watch?v=JHq-uBio5vE, accessed on 25 January 2018.

Legacy Alice Boner, Reitberg Museum Collection at https://emp-web-101.zetcom.ch/eMP/eMuseumPlus?service=RedirectService&sp=Scollection&sp=SfieldValue&sp=0&sp=0&sp=3&sp=SdetailList&sp=0&sp=Sdetail&sp=0&sp=F

Segal, Zohra. Interview by Kapila Vatsyayan. "Zinda Itihas Zohra Sehgal", EP #01, Doordarshan National. https://www.youtube.com/watch?v=PxUD37ze-Ho. Accessed on 13 June 2019.

USIC Centre Newsletters 1939–1944 (Fortnightly), Ranidhara, Almora, U.P. Editors: Rajendra Shankar and Vishnudas Shirali (Source: Dartington Archives, Devon Cultural Centre, UK).

CHAPTER 3

Dancing 'Oriental' Masculinity: Uday Shankar and His Experiments in Modern Dance

The story of otherness and of marginality has recently become so central to theoretical discussion that it is difficult both to respond satisfactorily to the demand and to take on the dubious role of the Real Other to speak the 'truth' on otherness... (Trinh T. Minh Ha 1991: 185)

Reading Shankar's own writings, the writings of people who knew his work and were his contemporaries, along with the later biographical as well as published research by scholars makes one realise that Shankar is seen through a lens of orientalism. Hence, the nuanced details of his growth over the years are completely or significantly overlooked in the summing up of his place in Indian dance history. He is sometimes called the 'other' and sometimes dismissed as 'untrained' and mostly given no right to be remembered among the many celebrated and well-known dancers of India. All this is legitimised because he is seen as an intruder in the world of performance, where his entry is seen as an undeserved but a lucky one at a time when the West was hungry for the oriental other to entertain them. In this chapter my aim is to make an attempt at placing Shankar's dance/d life in an order of temporal progression and changing choreopolitical negotiations.

U. Sarkar Munsi, *Uday Shankar and His Transcultural Experimentations*, Transnational Theatre Histories,
https://doi.org/10.1007/978-3-030-93224-4_3

India as Reference

According to Edward Said, the Orient was Orientalised not only because it was discovered to be 'Oriental' in all those ways considered commonplace by an average nineteenth-century European but also because it could be, that is it submitted to being made Oriental (Said 2003: 13–14). As the chapter delves into Uday Shankar's early negotiations and the management of his own identity, we start with the proposition that his artistic journey started with submitting to 'being made Oriental'. Many critics say that Shankar did not know anything much about India when he started his dance journey but had identified exactly what in him attracted the audience in which part of the universe. He knew why his oriental body was a saleable product to top level impresarios all over the world. His dance items say that he sold the exotic orient to the places and people who wanted to retain the colonial mystical understanding and nostalgia. A large section of his choreographies were around his self-projection of an attractive male body, while a few others produced a cross dressed-queer identity. Some of the choreographies had completely contemporary content, while others used content from the epics such as Mahabharata or Ramayana that were common in the regional mythological performances.

This chapter aspires to see his work as a journey, from the untrained, oriental entertainer catering to the imaginations of the 'west' to a person who recognised and chose specific processes of changing his relationship with dance with a lot of care and deliberate work. In this understanding of Shankar's creative process, I also want to refer to the way this pedagogy, however fragile and unsubstantiated by theorising and grammatical structuring, got incorporated into his later works. Late Narendra Sharma mentioned this journey in his personal interview. He said:

> Shankar probably would never have wanted to be remembered through restaging of his dance choreographies. It may also be difficult and uninteresting to restage Shankar's dance without them appearing to be out of date or at least aging. However, what remains alive and fully up to date is his technique of imagining movements—new ones—from new realities around us, new ideas, different rhythms, and sound experiences, imaginations, emotions, and moods. All these new inspirations can be the roots for endless responses in the form of movements. (Sharma, Personal Interview 2004)

In the reading of this journey of self-education, experimentation, and pedagogical explorations, his negotiations with Orientalism and the idea of masculinity in dance are important to investigate, and animated through the mobilisations of his translocational/transcultural identity. These lenses structure Uday Shankar as a changing entity with his locations adding layers of necessary and nuanced processes to his dance and choreography.

Almost all the writings about Shankar begin with tracing his love for movements and rhythms from childhood. As discussed earlier, Rajendra Shankar's reminiscences in the book *Uday Shankar* (1983) mention that Uday Shankar lived in three locations in Rajasthan, Uttar Pradesh, and Bengal during his childhood, also mentioning Shankar's fascination with Matadin's dance (see Chapter 2) in the same essay (Rajendra Shankar, Rajendra 1983: 4). This 'fascination' remains located at the 'festivals' of the above-mentioned three states, that Rajendra identifies as roots of Shankar's love for dance and aesthetic understanding. Rajendra's writing further helps us to identify the next location in a 'modern stage in London' where their father Shyam Shankar presented a performance of a fantasy named *The Great Mughal's Chamber of Dreams*, written and directed by Shyam Shankar himself. The performance was staged in the aid of the bereaved families of the Indian soldiers killed in the First World War. Uday Shankar is known to have assisted his father with stage designs, magic effects, music, and musical accompaniment. This chapter shall highlight the stages of Shankar's journey in what emerges as a superimposition of locations, pushing me to see Shankar's body as the tool as well the space where the map materialises through the temporal frame. Starting with Anna Pavlova's dance company to the few prestigious shows his father's contacts brought him which were spaces of full-blown Orientalism practised in British society, but were ready to offer a certain space to him as an artist on the fringe. He was definitely moving towards making a 'space' for himself by accepting the patronage and appreciation that, however, came with a heavy responsibility to perform what through this chapter gets clarity through the discourse of 'Oriental masculinity' (Barber 2015: 440–45).

Once he chose to dance, Shankar tried hard to negotiate between his wish and right to project his national culture and his aspiration to be recognised as dancer of international standard. He chose to foreground a seemingly confident culturally empowered status of a migrant artist.

As a colonial male subject his intention seems to have been to participate creatively in the colonising country's diverse and complex cultural life. I would argue that Shankar's contribution to dance needs to be read as a process rather than a summation of the outcomes of tours, institutional affiliations, and a list of choreographies. Similarly, his experiments with movement-making principles that have continued to escape understanding need to be addressed through an understanding of the different phases of Shankar's life. These processes were shared and developed by him in collaboration with a number of persons who have played very distinct parts in the way the 'work' of developing the processes grew over the years. It then got shared with the few batches of students at the Uday Shankar India Culture centre (USICC) in Almora (1939–1944). When the Centre became functional again in Kolkata (1965–2015), Amala Shankar recreated, to the best of her abilities, the teaching processes of USICC, Almora.

The flattening of the dancing body into a written page and a number of photographs is many a time the only way to access something as dynamic and ephemeral as dance. Hence, scholarship on Shankar lays excessive importance on the film *Kalpana*, where Shankar with his ideas and his dance has been captured lock, stock, and barrel. The dance community is still re-creating his dance 'items' by seeing and imitating his movements in the film. But this imitative reproduction belittles the process of training the dancing body that he emphasised so greatly through his life's work. My effort in this chapter will be to understand his work as a whole. I shall consider the added complexity of the omnipresent and powerful patron(s) to understand the visible as well as invisible structures of regulatory/emancipatory constructions that made his products what they were while highlighting his processes as his escape from those regulations.

It is widely acknowledged that Shankar's almost accidental introduction to the world of dance and subsequent concert tours throughout Europe and the United States of America in the 1920s familiarised him with the artistic practices as well as the taste of the audiences of that time in those countries. So widespread was his influence and his audience base that several mentions of his influence on musical and performance experiments are acknowledged by his contemporaries in both the East and the West. Ruth Abrahams writes about the American dancer/choreographer Agnes de Mille's account of Shankar's influence in 1933 on Antony Tudor's ballet style saying that though he later rejected the notion that Shankar had influenced him, Tudor at one point was greatly impressed.

Abrahams quoted Mille where she says 'the sense that the arms and hands are an extra voice and not merely appendages to the spine remained a hallmark of his style'. Abrahams further continues that:

> Leonard Bernstein also admitted to a direct influence of Shankar on his early musical development. After he attended one of Shankar's Boston concerts in 1938, when he was a Harvard undergraduate, he incorporated approximations of tonalities and rhythmic patterns from the Indian music he heard produced by Shankar and his music director, Vishnudass Shirali, into several passages of his own works of the period, including his original score for a Harvard Theatre production of Aristophanes' The Birds. (Abrahams 2007: 364)

Shankar was admired and publicly acknowledged by critics and artists who appeared impressed with the professional showmanship and acumen that he acquired as his experience grew with time. Thus, the observations that were once indulgent and tolerant of the 'orientalist display' soon changed into admiration of his presentational/choreographic skills. As his visits to the West became regular occurrences, he also acquired a fairly large group of women admirers among the western audience (Robinson 1994; Abrahams 2007; Erdman 1997) to begin with, but he also acquired a dedicated audience that looked forward to his visits to their countries. Shankar seemed to have been the major attraction as he appeared in numerous solos and duets as were his large group of musicians, post the 1930s when the orchestra was a live ensemble of a range of wind, string, and percussion instruments along with vocal singers all of whom sat on the stage. Renowned art historian and philosopher Ananda Coomaraswamy acknowledged Shankar's success in presenting stories and myths from India in and through his dance. He also admired the way in which Shankar used a variety of instrumental music from India to explore the roots of the eastern performance traditions (Coomaraswamy 1937: 611–13). In the writings of Coomaraswamy there is an acknowledgement of the clearly identifiable Indian aesthetic in the expressive/communicative power in Shankar's dance and his use of music for a fluid conceptualisation of cultural knowledge for audiences from different geographies.

There appears to have been a significant number of people openly critical of Shankar's creative experiments and his daring move of trying to dance without any formal training. They continued to look at him as an imposter who took advantage of opportunities that presented themselves to him due to his presence in Europe at an opportune time. But Shankar's performances were extremely popular and attracted a large audience made up of common people from all walks of life in India. In his own scant writing endeavours Shankar identified himself as a dreamer, someone who dreamt of the ideal dance technique, the ideal art institution, the ideal creative language of the body and mind. His urge to explore the 'limitless field' of creativity in dance, as Tagore had suggested in a letter, came largely through his dedicated pursuit of a movement language that would carry all characters identifiable as 'Indian' but would at the same time be something that he could call his own. Quoting Rabindranath Tagore, Shankar had written that:

> I would like to quote here a few lines from Rabindranath Tagore's letter to me written to me sometime in the 1930s. 'I know you feel it deep within your heart that the path of realisation of your dreams stretches long before you, where new inspirations wait for you and where you must create in a limitless field, new forms of living beauty. We hope your creations will not be a mere imitation of the past nor burdened with narrow provincialism'. (Shankar 2001: 11)

Bondage of the Oriental Subjecthood

The concept of 'orientalism' explained through the works of Edward Said becomes one of the appropriate conceptual formulations that define the principle rubric through which one can see Shankar's aesthetics, dance, as well as his reception in the West. While acknowledging the discourse and critique around his conceptualisation of 'orientalism', I need to place the much discussed frame of reference of Shankar and his image as the acknowledged 'male dancer from the East' in relation to the references of the orient created by Said's writings. Said wrote that:

> orientalism was ultimately a political vision of reality whose structure promoted the difference between the familiar (Europe, the West, 'us') and the strange (the Orient, the East, 'them'). This vision in a sense created and then served the two worlds thus conceived. Orientals lived in their world, 'we' lived in ours. The vision and material reality propped each other up, kept each other going. A certain freedom of intercourse was always the Westerner's privilege; because his was the stronger culture, he

could penetrate, he could wrestle with, he could give shape and meaning to the great Asiatic mystery, as Disraeli once called it. (Said 2003: 43–44)

Shankar did not write much about his journey. In one of the essays (re-published after his death) about his love of dance he wrote about his experience at the Royal College of Arts, London University with his teacher, the then Principal, Sir William Rothenstein who asked Shankar to meet him in his office after seeing Shankar's painting in class. Shankar writes that:

> I met him accordingly, and he said, 'I was in India for a long time and have seen wonders in arts and crafts. I can see in your art that you are very much interested in our European way of modern painting. Why take this disease to India? Why not keep in your Indian style and improve on it?' He handed me a letter saying, 'Give this to the Curator of the British Museum, he will help you, and you don't need to come for a month to join your classes.'
> So I met the curator. He took me to a lonely room and showed me a large table with hundreds of voluminous books on Indian art and craft.... So, I spent one month looking through those books—one month was not enough. For the first time I realized what a great heritage in art and culture we had in our country, and for that I am most grateful to Sir William Rothenstein. (Shankar 2001: 7)[1]

The focused artistic knowledge and aesthetic engagement regarding India, for Shankar, seems to have begun under the guidance of Indian art and sculpted iconography with the help of Rothenstein at the Royal Academy of Art. Rothenstein was not at all supportive at first about Shankar's father pushing Shankar into performance. He wrote to Shankar's father insisting that Shankar had a great future as a visual artist. He conceded in his memoirs later, reminiscing of going to one of Shankar's first performances, he wrote that 'I went to one of them [performances]. I saw at once I had been wrong; Uday Shankar's dancing, his poise, and gestures, had the grace and gravity I saw in the players and

[1] 'My Love for Dance' is one of the very few published materials available that has been written by Uday Shankar himself on his own life. This was reproduced from *Uday Shankar: A Photo—Biography*, ed. Sunil Kothari and Mohan Khokar, 1983 in *Nartaki: A Quarterly Journal in Indian Dance, A Special Issue on Uday Shankar* 1 No. 4, 2001.

dancers in India. There was a religious atmosphere throughout Uday's entertainment' (Rothenstein 1931: 177–78).

Rothenstein's idea that Shankar could benefit from knowing the art and craft of his own country and 'improve' on them instead, points to the consciousness of a distinction between Eastern and Western modernity, and a positioning of Western modernity against an Eastern traditionalism. He advised Shankar to ground himself in a particular form of art that would create a different aesthetic of the modern times for him, keeping the 'pure' and exotic in him safely distinguished as the 'other'. This distinction of the Indian as 'traditional' was of course informed by the colonial orientalist tropes. Fortunately for Shankar, his exposure to his own country filtered through both his Western guidance and his capacity to absorb everyday practices of human life gradually emerged as one of a kind and that is clear in the following words, published much after his death. He wrote, 'My country brought new impulses to me. I found that the older conception of our Indian dances has lost essential truths and its interpretation has become mechanical. It must not only express a dramatic action or an emotion but each movement of the dancer must be penetrated by the living idea' (Shankar 2001: 10). He also clarifies that, 'I always seek in my dances, simplicity, power and beauty, and I think that is why my dances have succeeded in having a universal appeal—still remaining purely Indian without any influence of the West' (Shankar 2001: 11).

Shankar's status as neither the 'Western' and nor the 'Eastern' dancer also got complicated by his being neither the 'classical' nor the 'modern' dancer. In fact, his not being a trained dancer or a practising visual artist set him away from most forms of classification, with the help of the politics of exclusion through non-categorisation rather than inclusion of any kind.

Finding the Representative Male Body: Anna Pavlova's Collaboration with Shankar

Shankar's dance journey is traced back to his experience of making two choreographies for Anna Pavlova. The requirements that Pavlova seemed to have placed before him as an untrained artist was not to create a full-fledged dance routine, but to create two choreographies/tableaus that would showcase particular cultural symbols, movements, gestures, and everyday life from the exotic land that Pavlova wanted to frame herself in—to expand her repertoire. Pavlova's portrayal neither had to be authentic nor representative of Indian women, it had to bring her appreciation. Shankar complied and the rest is history.

Shankar acknowledged Anna Pavlova in his essay[2] saying that:

> I came back to India, after staying 11 years at a stretch in Europe, to organize a troupe with a real Indian orchestra to take back to Europe. I travelled all over India for one year continuously and saw the wonders of my country. I saw the dances, temples, mosques, architectures, cave paintings, etc., and studied as much as I could. I was overwhelmed with joy seeing these and fully realised what Sir William Rothenstein and Anna Pavlova had said about India. (Shankar 2001: 10)

Pavlova is one of the earliest translocational influences on Shankar. His work with her remains the first documented proof of Shankar's readiness to perform as the oriental 'male' and as the dance partner of the Russian Ballet dancer. The learnt/imitated oriental hyper-femininity, constructed through her experience and perfected through the imaginations of Shankar, gave Pavlova the characters she wanted to dance. This collaboration and Shankar's presence provided the authentic Oriental male presence to validate the role of the oriental female dancer that Pavlova wanted to portray. Pavlova's idea of representation of life in dance gets expressed in her article 'An Answer to Critics of the Ballet' published in the American Magazine, *The Dance* (1926). It is referred to by Oleg Kerensky in her biography, *Anna Pavlova* (1973), where he quotes her on her idea of the function of dance. He quotes:

> Pavlova's article is worth quoting fairly extensively. 'The purpose of dancing is not to show men as they look when they go about their work, a little grubby, a little sordid, a little pathetic. Contrarily, the function of dancing is to give man a sight of an unreal world, beautiful, dazzling as his dreams. For dancing is pure romance and it is by the grace of romance that man sees himself, not as he is, but as he should like to be... beautiful, free, healthy, happy, carefree... (Kerensky 1973: 101)

Oleg Kerensky further writes that:

> Pavlova's interest in art and dance was deep and genuine and *Ajanta Frescoes* was only one of three Indian Ballets which had premieres during her brief Covent Garden season in 1923. *Ajanta Frescoes* derived from

[2] Ibid.

> her emotion when she saw the Ajanta temples and the caves, and the second India ballet, *Hindu Wedding*, was suggested to her when she saw a wedding ceremony in London. (Kerensky 1973: 94)

A detailed discussion in Kerensky's book tells us that once introduced to the female musician of Indian origin, Comolata Bannerjee, at her Indian music recital in Ivy House, London, Pavlova became interested in Indian music and dance and asked Bannerjee to write the scores for *Hindu Wedding*. It is around this time that Bannerjee introduced Pavlova to Uday Shankar. It is very important here to note what Kerensky writes at the beginning of the choreographic collaboration between Pavlova and Shankar, whereby two ballets *Hindu Wedding* and a Radha and Krishna duet, were created as a part of the Ballet *Oriental Impressions* and premiered on 13 September 1923. He wrote that:

> Shankar worked for three months with Pavlova and her company, teaching them Indian-style movements. He himself danced Krishna to Pavlova's Radha. In this Pax de Deux, for which Miss Bannerjee also wrote the music, Pavlova was all gentle submissiveness to Shankar's handsome lover-god. The costumes were made of genuine Indian fabrics and the dance was obviously more authentic than in *Ajanta Frescoes*..... Pavlova toured with Shankar as her partner for nine months in Canada, Mexico and all over the United States. (Kerensky 1973: 94–95)

Kerensky noted that 'she became the oriental dancer' during the performance (Kerensky 1973: 95), even though the Ballet was not a success except among the Indian audience.

In her interviews she is known often to have said of Shankar that he was endowed with one of the finest and most perfect bodies. Neither was Shankar in the decision-making position, nor was he equipped with adequate knowledge about the East that he was to represent in the plans for the choreographies. Shankar eagerly jumped into the new, though, temporary position. Pavlova had already made up her mind about getting Shankar to choreograph the two ballets with 'Hindu' themes and conflation of the national and the religious identity through the use of the word 'Hindu / Hindoo' appeared and stayed attached to Shankar's dance for years to come.

Pavlova's motive was clear though. She was persuasive because she wanted Shankar to work for her for those two choreographies without any long-term intention or promise of engaging him as a creative director or any such thing. For her he was the supplier of an out of bounds form of embodied knowledge, along with the presentably brown but not too brown body of an exotic male dancer from a colonised country.

Both Shankar and Pavlova seem to have gained something beyond the choreographic output that made history. Though neither of them knew then, it set the beginning of Shankar's path to international fame. Pavlova utilised these performances to display her ability to do a variety of roles and movements. Shankar also was impressed by the way dancers in Pavlova's troupe kept on their struggle for achieving the best in and through their dance. For him the troupe's organisation, discipline, and showmanship remained an example that he always stated as his motivation to train himself and others from his country. He saw this as essential not only to dance but an addition to becoming capable of choreographing, conducting, and presenting a performance. After touring with the two Oriental dance presentations as a part of her repertoire for nearly nine months, Pavlova persuaded Shankar to go back to his own country and get to know his own culture more intimately. He moved away to concentrate on becoming a dancer, as well as building his relationship with Indian dance traditions. Though Shankar was replaced by Pavlova's long-time associate Algeranoff, in her performance, Pavlova continued to recommend Shankar as an able choreographer to Hurok and many others in later years.

A new phase of translocational identity formation can be noted as he left Pavlova's troupe. In 1924 Shankar danced at the British Empire Exhibition at the Wembley Stadium, and soon after left for Paris to relocate there for the next five years. This was a phase filled with vulnerability as Shankar soon became an impoverished artist nobody knew or cared for. In Rajendra Shankar's word, 'He struggled, starved, worked and sweated but never gave up. He got hold of many dance partners, French, German, Italian, English, and even Arab, to build up dance items and present them in cabarets' (Shankar, Rajendra 2001: 19). Rajendra also writes that Uday Shankar used to go to the Louvre and read archival materials to know more about his own country's history. During this phase, Coomaraswamy's book, *Mirror of Gestures* (1917) inspired Shankar to create *Indra Dance*, which became one of his most famous solos in the later times (Shankar, Rajendra 2001: 19). At this stage in 1925, Shankar was also developing himself as an Oriental dancer/entertainer wanting to fashion himself in ways that his livelihood would be best ensured. An anecdote on his presence and reception at that time is recorded by Rajendra Shankar. He writes that in those cabaret performances Shankar had to appear every evening and perform and also drink with the customers. He 'was taught to swallow an ounce of olive oil before so that he could later throw out the drinks.... A Maharaja watching him one night felt nauseated at the protruding ribs and asked him to be taken off. Incidentally, he stayed as a state guest of the same Maharaja when he returned with fame to India' (Shankar, Rajendra 2001: 19). Shankar's students from Almora, the doting audience that he had in the later years of his established career as a dancer, and people like us who have only seen him in the late sixties have a difficult time imagining this particular image, of a half fed, skeletal figure, dancing at cabarets to earn barely enough to make a living.

Locating the Birth of Agency in the Transcultural Negotiations

The next section of the chapter shall highlight the important developments in Shankar's dance career between 1926 and 1944. Alice Boner (Shankar's admirer/mentor/friend/business partner from 1929 to 1939 and the manager of his first properly organised troupe), Simkie, the French pianist (his dance partner and an important part of his dance company as well as in his institution in Almora), Sol Hurok (the famous impresario), Zohra Segal (who became a part of Shankar's troupe after her two year training at Mary Wigman's school in Dresden and was an important member of the USICC faculty), and Beatrice Straight and Mr. and Mrs. Elmhirst (of the Dartington Hall, England) who facilitated the funding that funded USICC) shall be discussed as significant translocational facilitators. These are all people without whom his creative endeavours would not have matured into a pedagogical stage through the concretisation of the idea of the USICC in Almora. A historiographic revisiting of the archives generates a need to acknowledge multiple co-collaborators who have left their marks on Shankar's achievements.

Alice Boner and the Idea of the Sculpted Male Body

Ignored by many authors, the collaboration between Alice Boner and Uday Shankar yielded the most significant and prolonged experimentation as well as articulation of translocational exchange and conversation, whereby multiple locations connected in Shankar's trajectory through the expertise available to Boner (Sarkar Munsi 2021: 26–35). Shankar as a trained visual artist benefitted immensely by turning his instinctive understanding into available material for dance creativity through Boner's artistic and managerial sensitivities. Boner in turn, continued to influence Shankar's activities till the mid-1930s, though Shankar's shifting locations and growing circle of acquaintance seemed to reset his priorities again and again (Fig. 3.1).

While visiting an exhibition in Zurich's prestigious Kunsthaus, Alice Boner met Uday Shankar during one of his performances in the city in 1926. This meeting was to be a turning point in both Boner's as well Shankar's life. In hindsight, it may be said that this meeting was also an extremely significant moment in the history of Indian modern dance. About this meeting, marking the beginning of a long period of collaboration between Boner and Shankar, Ruth Abrahams (2007) wrote that:

> The meeting proved mutually significant, as Shankar agreed to pose for Boner, a well-to-do leader in Parisian literary and art circles, so that 'she could make of him figurines in clay which were cast in bronze'. For Shankar, the encounter served as yet another turning point in his career, for by 1926, Boner (1889–1981) was an established artist, her work in sculpture and painting acclaimed by both the public and other artists. (Abrahams 2007: 394)

Some of Shankar's solo, duet, and group choreographies developed over the period 1926–1931—evolving with his increasing practice and understanding of dance specifically from India as well as from other parts of the world. As he shifted from London to Paris in 1928, Shankar started his studio classes. The shaping of the next phase of Shankar's career can be seen as being the handiwork of Alice Boner and himself together. his quest to understand and know more about the aesthetics and presentational aspects of dance intensified. Boner shifted to Paris in 1928 as

Fig. 3.1 Alice Boner's Sculpture of Uday Shankar (© Alice Boner Institute)

well, after becoming familiar with Shankar's effort to create a dance repertoire for himself. She also encouraged his goal to create a dance troupe that would represent India through a range of performances. Boner's involvement and her viewing, photographing, sketching, and sculpting of Shankar's body and his movements seem to have mutually benefitted the two artists who made their own art works out of the same material, i.e., Shankar's dancing body. His work as an oriental entertainer slowly was replaced by his wish to dance and create choreographies. He was a trained visual artist, and he was trained to understand artistic creations. His aesthetic visions saw fruition with strong support from Boner. From 1926 till 1929, the influence of Alice Boner's representation of his body and dance[3] in her drawings, sculpture, and photographs remains as the remnant of this whole period of Shankar's extended practice in visual and dance art. Boner's artistic sketches of Shankar's movements and musculature hint at a transformative period where the trained visual artist in Shankar allowed his own body to become the model for another artist. This seems to have been an unique way of fine tuning his dance art.

Many European artists and dancers visited India during the early part of the twentieth century. A growing interest in the cultures of the colonised countries along with a fascination for artistic practices such as dance and music as well as the crafts and arts of little known cultures of Asia drew many artists to Asia. Shankar is known to have taken a tour of India and Southeast Asia with Boner in 1930. Boner's fascination with India matched Shankar's artistic instincts and ability to encourage a collaboration that proved fruitful in the next few years. It is therefore extremely important to place alongside Uday Shankar's interpretation of 'Indian culture', Alice Boner's contribution in framing that particular version of Indian culture for him. With Boner's encouragement and patronage, Shankar was also able to buy a range of musical instruments he came across during the tour and started collecting them.

Shankar's performance in Paris was prepared with support from Boner in more ways than one. She became the advisor, artistic manager, the benefactor, and the overall support of Shankar's endeavours and creative journey. During this phase, Boner's ideas and influence shaped Shankar's career and also created the artistic space for him to explore the possibilities of creativity without being troubled by administrative work. Boner's handling of tours, in and outside Europe, her handling of publicity, her help in creating the costumes, and her overall aesthetic and artistic sensibilities provided the much required encouragement for Shankar to explore and expand his artistic capabilities. At this time, Boner arranged

[3] See online collection Alice Boner and Uday Shankar in Reitberg Museum, Zurich. https://emp-web-101.zetcom.ch/eMP/eMuseumPlus?service=RedirectService&sp=Scollection&sp=SfieldValue&sp=0&sp=0&sp=3&sp=SdetailList&sp=0&sp=Sdetail&sp=0&sp=F. Accessed on 15 August 2021.

and accompanied Shankar on his trip to India, extending over nearly a year. The sizeable film footage/recordings from this tour are proof of the range of cultural practices experienced by both of them. Uday Shankar became fascinated by the local forms of art practice on the one hand, while being enamoured by the temples and sculptures they saw on the other. The photos and documentation of the tours undertaken by the both of them, visiting historical sites as well as experiencing the ways of life and culture of South Asia and Southeast Asia, present ample proof of the way in which this phase shaped the way Shankar viewed dance and dance cultures for the rest of his life. Shankar's fascination with the sculpturesque quality of dance movements, which became a permanent and important part of his dance repertoire, seems to have germinated from his viewing the sculptures in the temples of India with Boner. Boner's contribution to Shankar's life, beside the intellectual stimulations and the aesthetic orientation, were posters and photographs (taken on an Exakta camera) and other publicity materials for Shankar's Dance Company that Boner made for Shankar's performance in Paris and delicate watercolour paintings of scenes from a Kathakali routine, the dance drama style she regarded as the highest form of theatre.

Travelling across India, Boner and Shankar experienced the presence of community solidarities across the land, forms of coexistence, sharing of the eco-system, labour, social, and ritual practices. The harmonious ways of life in a space shared by humans and non-humans reaffirmed ideas of cohabitation in a shared space, faith, and support systems. The tour was meant to be for the specific purpose of observation and documentation of life and dance in the rural corners of India's less travelled geographies. It also helped Shankar understand and experience the remnants of India's past as documented on the ancient architectural ruins.

The film documentation that exists from this trip needs specific discussion. The trip undertaken by Shankar and Boner left its imprint on all the dances that Shankar visualised and finally documented in *Kalpana*. Fortunately a short eleven minute long film footage of their 1930 journey within India, covering Udaipur, Varanasi, Puri, and other unnamed spaces, had been compiled as a part of a recent touring exhibition of the Alice Boner Archive Project. The collected clips are compiled under the title 'A Film by Uday Shankar and Alice Boner' for documentation purpose (Legacy Alice Boner, Museum Rietberg, Zurich).

The above-mentioned film footage may have provided Shankar with creative ideas regarding embodied aesthetics from different dances in

India that were as much for his knowledge of bodily possibilities already present in Indian dance, as for him to utilise in his dance compositions. The film footage is an eye opener. It had an extraordinarily steady but silent footage of celebrations and a procession in Varanasi in its first section. In that section one can see a spectacular event with a large number of people in traditional gear and with people dancing in groups amongst a busy avenue filled with the stalls of the market. In the second section a celebration is captured in Udaipur, where groups of women in long skirts and with their faces and heads covered in a traditional manner have been filmed. It bears a striking resemblance to similar choreographies and costumes for Rajasthani women dancers that Shankar recreated in *Kalpana* after almost sixteen years. The third section is a short footage of the Puri temple Ratha Yatra event, a spectacle in its own right. And the short last section is on a group of Santhal Adivasi dancers who are seen dancing together in a semi-circular formation seen often even in current times. After their tour of India, Boner became Shankar's business manager and artistic adviser.

Boner's presence had been etched on the way Shankar interpreted many of his visions of Indian culture. Imagining lines within iconographic movements in temple sculptures was a specialised technique that Alice Boner brought to his viewing and sketching exercises, as is known through all her documentations from that tour and also her research. Her photographs of sculptures and subsequent ones of Shankar in the same posture makes it possible for the observer to understand a live process of transference of embodied knowledge from the live body to a two dimensional photograph or a three dimensional representation of the same moving body. This processual understanding seems to have become evident in Shankar's pedagogical venture in USICC later (Fig. 3.2).

The trip was also a chance for Boner (as a collector and a visual artist) and Shankar (as a dancer-choreographer) to locate possible 'authentic material' in the form of local dance costumes, ornaments, textiles, musical instruments, and props that could be used for their choreographic endeavours after going back to Paris. By this time Shankar, as well as Boner with her collector's eye and ability, had become aware of the need for an authentication of an all Indian troupe of performers that would take them a long way to becoming a true representation of Indian culture. This quest for knowledge took Boner and Shankar to faraway places in the North Eastern parts of India. The other extreme they travelled to was to the state of Kerala which is the home of Kathakali and many other

Fig. 3.2 From the series of movement captures of Uday Shankar dancing as a woman in 1929 (Photo: Alice Boner © Legacy Alice Boner. © Museum of Rietberg, Zurich)

specialised forms of art. The impressions of dances from Manipur and Kerala and the culture specific practices of these places influenced Shankar deeply and had a clearly visible influence in his later pedagogical and creative ventures. This was also a period during which Shankar's confidence in creating art was encouraged by his immersive and keen contact with forms such as Kathakali and other community ritual and performance practices from the different regions of India. Boner collected and documented sculptures and created a knowledge bank for Shankar to use in his performances.

An artistic partnership/business venture resulted out of this extraordinary exchange. The Deed for 'A French Limited Liability Company' was registered under the name 'Compagnie Uday Shankar: Danses & Musique Hindus' in France on 23 December 1931. The deed spelled out a capital of 25,000 francs put into equal amounts of 12,500 francs each by Boner and Shankar at the time of the formation of the company. The Deed of

Partnership made on 23 December 1931 of the agreement between Alice Boner and Uday Shankar, now available at the Dartington Hall Archives, states that:

> *PART I – OBJECT – DENOMINATION – DURATION – HEAD OFFICE*
> *Art. 2 – The Company's object is - creation, acquisition, sale and exploitations of all establishments and undertakings, organisation of performances, concerts exhibitions, auditions and lectures with view of acquainting the public with Hindu music and choreographic art and, generally, all business and undertakings, for the account of the company or third parties, in France and everywhere abroad, in connection with the above objects, in the most extensive and wide acceptance, the preceding enumeration being of an enunciative and not of limitative character*. (Dartington Hall Records, LKE—India. 19, 1932–1938)

Art entrepreneurships, common in Europe and America, were not as common in the colonised worlds. Alice Boner took on herself the responsibility of managing Shankar's newly formed dance company. The first show of the company, arranged by Boner on March 1931 in Paris, saw his dance and musical presentations being critically acclaimed. Shankar had arrived! He had made a leap from being an oriental dancer to a choreographer, being presented by internationally reputed presenters and entrepreneurs. Boner needs to be acknowledged for having astutely planned and arranged a long tour of France and Switzerland. During this prolonged tour, Shankar's company was invited to participate in the Paris Exposition in 1931. A significant stage of transition for Shankar was the colonial Exposition in Paris. The reception of the bodies from faraway lands was already exoticised and had found an audience in the colonial expositions since the early 1900s. A range of exhibits, from a zoo-like display of the exotic and the untamed subjects from Asia and Africa to an elevated position of representative performances from distance colonised cultures were part of these expositions already. Shankar had performed in such displays before, but the 1931 exposition saw him better equipped and organised as a choreographer.

Shankar's own performance and the glimpses of his showmanship caught the attention of Sol Hurok, a famous European producer of concert theatre presentations in the United States, who invited him for a tour of America in 1931. It was also the first time, at the Paris Exposition, that Shankar met Amala Nandi (then only eleven years old) who was at the Exposition with her father. She later became his wife and dance partner.

Alice Boner and Shankar signed a contract with Hurok's company for three years of touring. With this exposure, Shankar became a known name in the world of dance. Uday Shankar and his company of dancers and musicians toured Europe and America extensively. Through these years, Boner supported 'Shankar's troupe of Hindu Dancers and Musicians'—the name the troupe had become famous by. She helped the company with her artistic, aesthetic, and administrative expertise. Hurok continued to arrange several shows in Europe and America for Shankar, presenting him alongside the already famous German modern dancer Mary Wigman, oriental dancer/choreographer Ruth St. Denis, and others. Shankar's circle of admirers, acquaintances, and well-wishers grew in number. Subsequent years saw Shankar's recognition worldwide as a dancer with an extraordinary understanding of showmanship and stage presence. In 1933 Shankar got to know Mr. and Mrs. Elmhirst of Dartington Hall and that resulted in the beginning of the support and patronage from the Hall.

Over the years, Shankar's fame increased. He also did not require Boner to manage his company. Boner's quiet withdrawal from Shankar's life as a celebrity and his performance activities is well documented in the archives of Dartington Hall. She continued to be associated with Shankar's troupe till 1938, though she had already disentangled herself from most of the day-to-day activities of the troupe. In the planning stage and finalisation of the name for the Almora Centre that Shankar finally began in 1939, Boner seemed to have assumed an advisory role. Their company was dissolved in 1939.

Alice Boner's influence remained imprinted on the configuration of the body in Shankar's work where Shankar pushed the limits of body balance in his dance compositions such as *Kartikeya* (created in 1933) and many other dances. One of the best examples is a posture that Shankar holds through eight beats, standing on his right leg, slightly bent at the knee. His upper body is in a reclining position on the left, while his left foot is up across his body to point to his right with the big toe held away at a ninety degree angle to his pointed foot. The hands are both in front, spread in an imagination of holding a sword parallel to the ground with both hands. The diagonal line created by the angular position of the stable right foot on the ground continues through his body from the hip up and finally to the head.

In one of his last correspondences dated 12 March 1939, archived at the Dartington Hall Records, Shankar wrote to Boner about the Centre being named 'Uday Shankar India Culture Centre'. He wrote, 'We have purposely used the name 'Culture Centre' because as time progresses, we hope not only to have Dance and Art represented here but also Music, Painting, Sculpture, Drama, and even general education' (Dartington Hall Records).

Simkie: A Westerner Who Danced 'as an Indian'

In her writings, Erdman highlighted the fact that 'Shankar taught his French partner, Simkie, to dance as an Indian' (Erdman 1987: 66). She further continued:

> Simkie was not promoted as a westerner who had learned Indian dance. She was so convincingly Indian that spectators usually thought she was an Indian. Only if they came backstage to meet her did they learn her nationality. She was also warmly and approvingly received in India, according to interviews with troupe members and others who recalled her appearances there. (Erdman 1987: 68)

Simkie's contribution goes largely unacknowledged in the post-Almora years of Shankar's life. Shankar's wonderous stage presence as well as magical charisma managed to render most of his women partners powerless in terms of presence in more ways than one. As it became clear from several conversations with Amala Shankar and Narendra Sharma and the video clips available on the internet, Simkie's dance movements looked different from the later techniques and movement idioms that became Shankar's signature repertoire in later times. But she was the only dancer who began dancing with Shankar in the second half of the 1920s and continued her journey with him to USICC in Almora. From 1925, she was his dance partner in tours throughout the world. She taught some of the technique classes in Almora and also got married to one of the troupe members later. They remained in Almora till the institution started showing signs of disintegration. Shankar's photographs from 1928 to 1935 mostly show Simkie as his dance partner, while she also was part of many group dances that were a part of the troupe's regular reper (Fig. 3.3).

Rajendra Shankar wrote that:

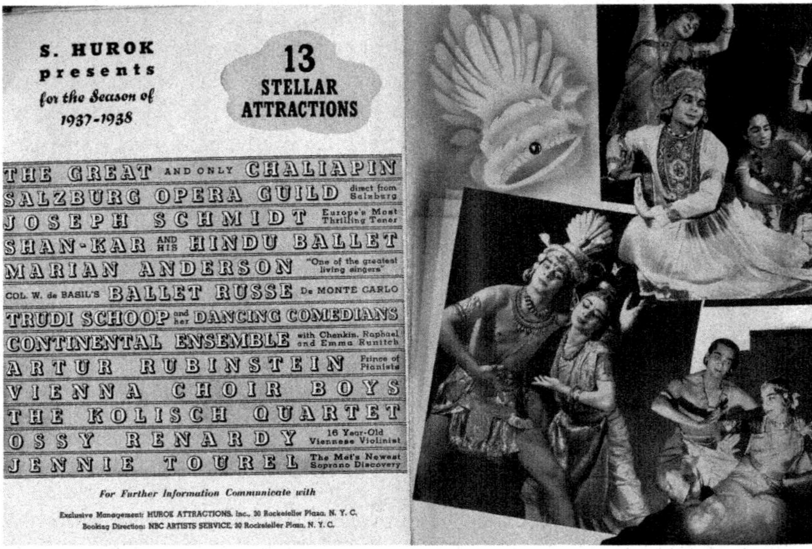

Fig. 3.3 Hurok's publicity brochure showing the 'Steller Attractions' of the season with a collage of photos of Shankar, Simkie, Zohra, and Madhavan (1937–1938) (© Boston Public Library)

> Simkie joined as a student. Resident of Paris, and a pianist she showed great aptitude and helped him in the orchestration of his music and finally became his partner. Things were looking up and he got a chance to perform at the Paris Exposition Internationale of 1925… he and Simkie formed the troupe, they packed their costumes in a box and had copies of notated music which would be handed over to the local orchestra for a few rehearsals and then the final show. (Shankar, Rajendra 2001: 19–20)

Shankar's experiments with his artistic inspirations connected different locations and histories through his collaborations with individuals and their creative urges. One such formulation and representation of his homeland, through the scores of the 'Indian' dances he composed with the assistance from Simkie, may be marked as a beginning for the later elaborate musical accompaniments that Shankar managed to get together as live accompaniment to his choreographic presentations. In her discussion about Shankar's dancing partner for the larger part of the late 1920s and 1930s, Ruth Abrahams writes that Simkie joined Shankar's studio classes in Paris formally in 1928. This was in preparation of Shankar's efforts to create a troupe of dancers and musicians. Abrahams writes:

> Shankar reappeared in Paris, according to a review on January 3, 1929. The brief concert elicited the critics' praise and their enthusiastic approval of his new partner, Simkie. Parisian by birth, Simkie, *n'ee* Simone Barbiere... she soon became an exponent of his dance style. By 1929, Simkie had learned Shankar's repertoire with such proficiency, understanding, and grace that she became his professional partner. (Abrahams 2007: 395)

It is well known that Simkie and Shankar were very popular as an oriental dancing pair. This period is also documented in the form of advertisements and promotional materials that are commonly preserved all over the world in different libraries and archives. It becomes clear that the popularity of Shankar's performances grew as his recognition as a choreographer and a dancer assimilated the presence of a troupe of talented co-performers, who were never acknowledged as independent individuals but seen as enhancing Shankar's image and presence. Abrahams writes about this:

> Simkie was independently recognized for her unique and sensitive interpretations of Shankar's choreography. Shankar himself noted that Simkie was 'the only woman who embodied the qualities needed to convey the god-like choreography better than any Indian woman I could find'. (Abrahams 2007: 395)

Simkie was an important member of the troupe. Whatever their personal relationships may have been, the duo was represented as dance partners and one may find evidence of this from a huge number of photographs from the 1930s. Simkie and Shankar are also photographed in a sequence of postures as Parvati and Shiva by Alice Boner (Sarkar Munsi 2021: 60–62),[4] in postures that portray her as a demure, petite, beautiful presence to his posture of a lover/partner, with Shankar appearing very male and overtly protective in most of the photos. I would like to contemplate if and to what extent Simkie's presence structured the image of the male partner/dancer for Shankar. Or was he simply giving structure and shape to his already firm ideas of embodying/representing

[4] Ibid.

the male identity? From the available film clips and photographs it seems that Simkie was partnering Shankar to help frame him with her hyper-feminine submissive presence. Zohra and Amala of course were never as hyper-feminine as Simkie and one can find in many photos that the both of them emanated more actively an agentive body language. Simkie seems to have structured the dancer Shankar's image of those particularly important formative years. With her instinctive understanding of gestural femininity within gender coded displays, Simkie's presence enhanced Shankar's oriental masculinity for the audience.[5]

Zohra Segal: The Trained Pedagogue

My search through the untitled photos preserved at the Cologne Dance Archive in Germany helped me find an unidentified photo of a laughing young woman with long hair in a leotard. In the leaflet from 1936 she was mentioned as an ex-student who now worked with the Uday Shankar Centre. Another copy of the same photo, accidentally discovered after a longer search, surfaced in the same archive on which Mary Wigman had written the name 'Zorah Muntaz' in pencil. One can read the details of this extraordinary experience in Zohra Segal's writings. Regarding her training at the Wigman School, she wrote:

> The Wigman School stint was hard work, but I felt I was at an advantageous position as teachers looked on me almost with leniency; almost awed by my nationality. They were surprised at my having come to Germany to learn dancing.... Mary Wigman, who was the kindest of teachers as far as I was concerned (other girls were terrified of her), told me explicitly never to imitate the German girls in my work, but to try and evoke an inner flow, fused with my inherent rhythm. (Segal 2010: 45)

Zohra believed that this training, in building upon one's own inner flow of movements, helped her to take up dancing in India with ease. Simultaneously she also acknowledged Wigman's rigorous training with fourteen hour long schedules of practice, as well as a controlled regimen of relaxation helped her think of dance pedagogy in the later years at the USICC, Almora. This pedagogy created the base for her to design a body training/dance programme that incorporated improvisation, technique, disciplined movement structures, as well as free explorations with

[5] https://roughinhere.wordpress.com/2010/11/07/rare-uday-shankar-dance-footage-playing-on-ravis-tv-set/. Accessed on 21 August 2019.

everyday movements for USICC. This we shall examine in detail in Chapter 4.

Zohra Mumtazullah Khan (a name Zohra herself shortened by the time she was at the Mary Wigman's school in Dresden, Germany), a well-known stage and screen presence in the later part of her life, also needs to be situated within the scopes of the translocational connections that cross-fertilised many of Shankar's transcultural conversations in the time between the two world wars. Zohra has left two autobiographies and has also been documented in numerous interviews. In her autobiography, *Close-up*, she included a letter to her uncle (who she called Memphis) that she wrote on 9 August 1932 from Dresden. She wrote, 'In the meanwhile I tried to do something else—fly to Paris with a brother and sister to meet Uday Shankar, the Indian dancer. He was not in Paris just then and I never got a reply to my letter' (Segal 2010: 41).

In her letter dated 29 August 1932, Zohra Segal mentioned Mary Wigman as the kindest teacher as far as she was concerned, while others were terrified of her. She also said that the training process at Mary Wigman's School entailed very hard work. Zohra mentioned that much like Shankar's teachers and mentors from the West, Wigman advised her never to imitate the girls from Germany but to try to follow her inner instincts and flows and go according to her inner rhythms (Segal 2010: 44–45).

Zohra's training with Mary Wigman concluded in a Diploma in Dance from the Academy after little more than two years of having worked very hard at Wigman's School in Dresden. As mentioned by her in her autobiography, in a letter to her uncle written on 25 June 1933, she says she came second in her class. She often expressed her marvel at the result, in spite of not knowing German and having no previous dance training. She also expressed her surprise at having become a very hard-working student and doing well in her class even though she had seen dance performances only twice in her life (Segal 2010: 47–48). Zohra joined Shankar's troupe along with her sister Uzra in 1935. The connections had been initially made while Shankar was visiting Wigman's Academy in Dresden in 1933, during his troupes' visit to Mary Wigman's School in Dresden.

Zohra mentions in her autobiography that she started working at the Queen Mary School in Lahore after her return to India in 1933 (Segal 2010: 60). Her classes were called Music Drill as there could not be any dance class in a Muslim school where most girls were in purdah. She taught English to the junior classes, was the swimming instructor, and also helped with administrative works. This trained her well for the overall administrative work as well as the teaching that she took up at Shankar's Academy in 1939.

In her autobiography Zohra Segal assigned Chapter 4 to *1935–1938: The Uday Shankar Ballet Company* and Chapter 5 to *1938–1943: The second return* to started her association as a troupe member after she was taught the dance movements hurriedly by Simkie, who she remembered as a patient and kind teacher. She also mentions Alice Boner as the then manager of the troupe who was horrified at the stiffness of Zohra's movements. Her hurried inclusion into Shankar's troupe was before the commencement of the tour of Japan that was to begin on 11 August 1935 (Segal 2010: 63–66). Zohra wrote about her 'very first dance tour' itinerary that included Burma, Singapore, and the Malay Peninsula, during which they performed at 'Rangoon, Moulmen, Kuala Lumpur, and visited Mandalay and Penang' (Segal 2010: 67).

It is from her writing that one gets to understand how the dancers were trained and empowered to be in charge of their own costume and make-up, unlike the already established role of the dresser that was a part of the artists' performance world in the West. The idea of the self-sufficient performer that was very much part of the learning process at the Uday Shankar India Culture Centre in Almora in the later years and in its second version at Kolkata, saw its germination here as a part of an artistic understanding of the experiences gathered from the different worlds of performers from both the East and the West. In this context Zohra wrote, 'I learnt the art of applying make-up to an Indian face in order to highlight those facial expressions which form an integral part of our dancing, to be responsible for my own costumes and jewellery (packing and unpacking being the job of artists and not dressers)' (Segal 2010: 67).

She also talked about learning several other intrinsic values and norms as Shankar's contribution to the artistic training and pedagogic dimensions within Indian dance, and acknowledged Shankar's training, showmanship, and professionalism which he imbibed into all his troupe members in her interview to Kapila Vatsyayan[6] and in her own writings. She mentioned that she learnt a lot of things besides dance during the first tour. These included stage discipline along with the requirement of self-discipline, of punctuality, and 'almost religious atmosphere during

[6] Kapila Vatsysyan interviewed Zohra Segal for the archives of Indira Gandhi National Centre for the Arts (IGNCA), Delhi.

a performance' (Segal 2010: 67). She also mentioned that the troupe members had to learn to be prepared and ready to catch a train or a boat at any time of the day or night as well as be able to rest and catch up with sleep and rest anywhere and everywhere. They had to learn to prioritise performances and related requirements over everything else, to arrive at the venue of the performance with enough time (at least one hour in hand) so that they may prepare to be in the performance in all ways possible. Zohra's writings talk about the importance of exercising before the shows, without actually mentioning the word 'warm up' by saying that the members were supposed to shed all other involvements by,

> first practicing the daily exercises and later going over the difficult movements of the dances, enabling you to step onto the stage with complete confidence and ease. Surely travelling with a troupe is one of the most enjoyable way of living! All your worries of eating and sleeping are taken care of, you have enough to spend on little luxuries, sight seeings and buying presents for the family, and in the evenings you are occupied with a task to which you are dedicated. (Segal 2010: 67)

The tour in Zohra's opinion was a success artistically but not financially. The next tour mentioned by Zohra started on January 1936 and continued through Aden, Palestine, Syria, Iraq, Egypt, Greece, the Balkan states, Czechoslovakia, Italy, Switzerland, and Paris. Zohra also wrote about the continued association, during which she toured the world, and also visited Dartington Hall along with the rest of the members of Shankar's troupe and finally went to Almora to join the USICC in 1939.

1935–1938 was the period that was emphasised as extremely important in the planning and preparation for the institution Shankar wanted to establish. Zohra's writings tell us about the addition of trained dancers and musicians into the troupe. In her opinion the troupe started growing more professionally equipped, holding their own in terms of having their own musicians to conduct the live music for all shows. She mentioned that Vishnudas Shirali (music composer), Ustad Alauddin Khan (the already well known Sitar maestro), Shankar's brothers—Rajendra and Debendra, and also Ravi (who was training under Ustad Alauddin Khan as a budding sitarist) joined the troupe. A trained Kathakali dancer, Madhavan Nair, and Zohra's sister Uzra also were welcomed as new members.

One of the incidents after a performance in 1936 is described by Zohra. She mentions that after a performance in London, Lord Linlithgow, the then Viceroy of India—visiting London at that time—came backstage to meet Zohra and Uzra because of connections with their uncle. He asked the family connections of Simkie unknowingly—unaware of her French origin. So much of the 'Parvati incarnate' Simkie was, that according to Zohra, this man had no way of knowing that she was not Indian. Zohra continued to say that Sir Feroze Khan Noon, accompanying the Viceroy, saved the situation by claiming Simkie as his niece (Segal 2010: 73). Zohra's casual mentioning of such incidents[7] is supposed to be taken in a lighter vein. But these incidents help to consolidate our understanding of the role all parties concerned played in the construction of the image of the 'oriental other'. From Zohra's description, it also became clear that it was important to claim royal or high birth for the female dancers, which ensured a certain amount of 'oriental' prestige to the colonised subjects by playing to the imagination of the West, helping themselves to escape the inevitable position of an entertainer.

An important contribution from Zohra's chapter '1938–1943: *The Second Return*' in her biography *Close-up* is the acknowledgement of the exposure of Shankar and Zohra to Balinese cultural practices during a trip to Bali on which Shankar took Zohra along. She described their stay in Bali to experience life and social and cultural practices that comprised of their experiences of rituals, rites of passage, and festivities. This description also helped the readers understand the continued influence of the dance costumes and ornaments that Shankar acquired from Bali and also improvised from. The specific influence of the aesthetic of the East (made up of a great deal of dress material, as well as ornaments and musical instruments from the southern part of India and Indonesia) are documented in the photos of Shankar right from 1930 onwards. The metal head-dresses, armlets, wristlets, and necklaces, and the later improvised versions of the same in flexible materials such as golden-embossed Rexine,[8] became part of the common ornaments that ensured easier and lighter ways of carrying them on long-distance journeys. These specific sets of designs became signature styles for Shankar and later for his wife Amala Shankar's costume

[7] Similar incidents are mentioned by Zohra in her autobiography *Close-Up* (2010) in pages 73–75.

[8] A strong coated cloth with leather-like finish and texture and used especially for bookbinding, was commonly used for making belts and ornaments.

collections. Important in Zohra's description is also a rare glimpse of the continued explorations of 'other' relatively lesser-known cultures into which Shankar wanted to conduct his own personal search for dance aesthetics. His interest in further enriching transcultural grammatic and performative principles made him eager to search for the possible expansion and consolidation of the dance vocabulary of the East (Segal 2010: 76–83).

Zohra's contribution in the pedagogical structure of Shankar's teaching plans and curriculum in Almora and Shankar having concretised the plans for Zohra to have the responsibility of formalising the curriculum led to the continued association between Zohra and Shankar himself. She remained with the USICC till Kameshwar Segal, her husband (a student of the Centre) was asked to leave the USICC due to disciplinary measures taken for some student unrest. Zohra's moving away may have been the death blow to the disciplinary and pedagogical structure. Zohra continued to be an ardent admirer of the efforts of Shankar and acknowledge his efforts as modern, futuristic, and innovative in her autobiography and numerous interviews on television. Subtly different and mature in personality and expectations, Zohra was a figure of significance, and never just an additional member of the troupe to enhance Shankar's presence on stage.

Amala Nandi: Dancer—Documenter Extraordinaire

To begin to understand an extraordinary association that started in 1931 in Paris, one has to refer to Uday Shankar's wife and partner Amala Shankar's self-documentation and memoir of the Paris Exposition and a tour of Europe with Shankar and his group. Amala was in Paris for the Paris Colonial Exposition in 1931 with her father Akshay Nandi and so was Shankar with his mother and two brothers, Devendra and Rajendra, Simkie, Shankar's uncle, and his cousin Kanaklata, and Alice Boner. Alice Boner had rented a large house for Shankar's family and the troupe and the regular rehearsals were held in a large hall in that house. Shankar was performing at the exposition. Amala was there with her father at the Hindoostan Pavilion, where her father's jewellery shop 'Economic Jewellery Works' had been selected to put up a stall (Fig. 3.4).

The experience of her tour of Europe from November 1931 to October 1933, with Shankar and his troupe had been recorded by Amala after her return to India, once she went back to a regular education and

Fig. 3.4 Uday and Amala Shankar on the cover of a publicity folder, 1950 (© Personal archive of the author)

her life back at home. This little known book, *Sat Sagarer Pare* ([1934] 2007), a Bengali documentation of the troupe's travels through Europe between the two world wars is one of the key sources of description of the first long European tour, that Shankar was contracted for in 1931. Amala Shankar may never have understood the extent of her contribution towards the documentation of Shankar's work in those years, but this remains one of the best and useful contributions towards piecing together Shankar's legacy.

One of the chapters in the book is about the chance meeting of Uday Shankar and Amala's father Akshay Nandi, which led to the father and the daughter being invited to Shankar's house for a dinner with his family. Conversations there and Amala's ability to learn and follow dance movements led to Shankar asking Amala's father for his permission to include her as one of the members for the upcoming Europe tour after the colonial exposition ended. Amala had already been chosen to represent India in certain dance programmes at the Exposition's evening programmes, by the dancer Nyota Inyoka (a Vaudeville dancer born of a

French mother and an Indian father in Pondicherry and settled in Paris) who was impressed by Amala's looks and ability to learn dance gestures. Eleven year old Amala in her book does not seem to be over-awed or enamoured by Shankar at this point. She mentions one dance named, *Kaliya Daman*, in which she played the role of the snake with eight heads while Shankar played the role of god Krishna. She was just one year older to Uday Shankar's youngest brother Rabindra Shankar (Robu), who later became famous the world over as Sitar Maestro known by the name Ravi Shankar. Uday Shankar's mother took special care of this young girl, who had been permitted by her family to tour Europe for almost two years as a member of Shankar's troupe.

Amala, in her memoir has divided the dance tour of Europe into three chapters in her book, Chapters 13, 14, and 15, which are especially important in *Sat Sagarer Paare* as they deal with the details of each and every performance, the journeys, and the audience and the reception. Amala named her thirteenth chapter '*Amader Nrityaabhijan*' (literally meaning Our Dance Tour), followed by the second and third part of the tour in the fourteenth and fifteenth chapter. The tour was almost two years long. The first part of the tour started on 29 December 1931, with sixteen troupe members. The troupe included five women—Shankar's mother, the Swiss Sculptress Alice Boner (who Amala mentions as the 'Mohila Oddhokkho' or the woman director), Miss Simone (Simkie), Shankar's cousin Kanaklata (who was addressed as Meena), and Amala herself (with Aparajita as her stage name). The other members of the troupe were the two brothers of Shankar, Mr. Bogner (the French manager), Shankar's uncle (who was also Meena's father), music director Timir Baran, and other musicians (not specified by Amala in her book), and of course Shankar himself. Unlike other writings such as Ruth K. Abrahams' detailed history of Shankar's early days, this narrative by Amala, a teenager, is able to reconstruct the first long international tour of Europe in detail. The trip started with eighty odd musical instruments as well as trunks full of costumes, props, and accessories for the performances that had been planned. Amala was thrilled to join Uday Shankar and his troupe after they finished their contract to perform at the International Colonial Exposition in Paris. She herself had acquired some experience of dancing under Nyota Inyoka's guidance at the Hindoostan Pavilion as well.

According to the dates mentioned in *Sat Sagarer Pare* by Amala, the first of the shows was in the city of Liz on 30 December 1931. This started a long journey across Europe with performances at the best of concerts and performance proscenium spaces available in the post-World War I cities across Europe. Between the 15 and 19 of January 1932, Shankar's troupe visited Mary Wigman's school in Dresden where Amala Shankar met Zohra, who she mentions as 'a princess from Kashmir' without writing her name. In the month of February 1932, Shankar's troupe presented thirty-six performances in Germany itself. All of them were extremely well attended and well received according to her (Amala Shankar [1934] 2007: 120).

These descriptions are important to understand the level of professionalism that Shankar and Boner achieved in terms of presentational acumen and organisation. This structure of professionalism learnt and admired by Shankar from his exposure to Anna Pavlova's troupe management and presentational strategies became a standard maintained religiously in after years as well by Uday and Amala Shankar. In Amala Shankar's travelogue, dates of shows and descriptions of the venues and audiences are accompanied by specific memorable anecdotes that establish different levels of communication between these Indian members of the troupe and the people they met as audience, patrons, organisers, and journalists.

Amala mentioned their visit to Munich (Germany) and the performance, saying that they were to perform in Munich and as usual the biggest auditorium had been booked for the performance. In the middle of the performance the President of the Munich city council came up on the stage to present a bouquet of flowers to Uday Shankar, Amala Shankar, Simkie, and Kanaklata. Simultaneously, people from the audience also started showering the dancers with garlands and flowers that they had brought with them. The three women picked up all the flowers on the stage as they did not want the audience to feel bad about not being acknowledged for their blessings. Next day the newspapers were full of descriptions of how the act of picking up the flowers also appeared dance-like to the audience (Amala Shankar [1934] 2007: 114). In another section, on performances in Budapest, she wrote that in Budapest the troupe's performance was organised at the Opera House which was the venue for the best of performances. According to the newspapers that Amala and the members read, the only other performance that had become so popular after the First World War was by Anna Pavlova's troupe (Amala Shankar [1934] 2007: 124).

Some of these writings are worth mentioning for understanding the expanse of Shankar's influence and the reception that his troupe received. Her descriptions of the performances are accompanied by details of travel across the unfamiliar terrains of Europe, across signs of death and destructions of the First World War in the Western Front and breathtakingly beautiful geographies. While Shankar's interviews remained silent about the details of this trip, Amala's writings documented Shankar's journey to success, as his troupe became internationally known as the Hindoo Ballet Troupe that soon caught the attention of the internationally renowned presenter, Sol Hurok. While looking at Shankar's legacy, for me Amala Shankar's book stands witness to her journey with Uday Shankar, in real time with him across Europe in 1931–1932, and also in terms of the conceptual span of translocational and transcultural expanse that it covered and manipulated in terms of the cultural expressions according to the expectations of orientalism, nationalism, and modernism. While Amala continued her journey (discussed in detail in Chapter 6) with Shankar in different roles in the next stages of his journey, this phase remained a significant entry point for her into the proscenium space under the guidance of an extraordinary personality.

With Sol Hurok: (Re)Discovery of Self—Skill and Presentation of the Collective Body in Performance

Walking into the Boston Public Library the first day in continuation of some investigative search online and going up to the counter to request the attendant to find a particular folder named 'Uday Shan-Kar' was part of my archival work that had become a routine activity in the summer of 2017. I was soon looking at a red cloth covered folder, given to the library by 'anonymous'. It was a collection of publicity materials from the years 1936–1937, published by the Nicolas Publishing Company, Inc. for the company 'Hurok Attractions' in New York. The file also contained the photos sent by Shankar in preparation for the tour of America that Sol Hurok organised for Shankar at the beginning of their long association, and some reviews by famous critics who wrote regularly for American newspapers. Shankar was presented alongside other very prominent dancers and performing troupes, already well-recognised in the international circuit for dance in the post-World War I era.

The numerous reviews were revelations as well. Trying to read them critically to discern differences of attitude towards choreographies and to assess the qualitative aspects of the dance and the performance, I was looking for a reading of the exotic other, commonly the way to write about efforts by the 'other' less familiar cultures from all over the world. Such Orientalist othering irks us dance scholars from non-western cultures as the difference is not seen as an aesthetic or intellectual one but instead as a work of entertaining exotic quality, worth seeing for its representation of an inferior culture and as a result an inferior practice and ability. One of the reviews, which had also been used as a part of the publicity material by Hurok, written by Rene Daumal for the January 1936 *Hound and Horn*, reads:

> The beauty of these musicians and dancers, of their instruments, of their very attitude of sustained attention, of continual reality, as well as of their accurate and yet most real harmony of their costumes, the truth of all that, the complete absence of scenery, that marching, sonorous splendour, that dance that moves, and that moving music that exactly fills the duration signifying eternal immobility, all that marvel, I still believe, sometimes, to have dreamed it only, as one dreams of an ancient country of wiser and more beautiful people, as one dream of golden age. (From Anonymous folder, dated May 22, 1936, Boston Public Library)[9]

In the first autobiographical book written by Hurok and Ruth Good, he talks about a full evening's performance in 'Indian style', as 'lazy Hindu dramas running for hours beautifully and sumptuously produced, but played with great leisure' (Hurok and Good 1947: 160). This line may be read as a mildly worded but clearly critical opinion coming from a definite gap in understanding the aesthetic appeal or the content. But this was definitely written by him in retrospect after having already spent the first fifteen years of presenting Shankar's performances all over the Western world. According to Ruth Abrahams, Hurok did not much like either the new genre of modern dance of Mary Wigman or the 'ethnic' dance that Shankar was presenting, as he was a staunch admirer of Russian Ballet. Mary Wigman's last tour of America was with Hurok in 1932–1933, and Shankar's tour was from December 1931–1933, along with Vicente Escudero's from Spain (The Last Impresario 1994: 151). Shankar and Escudero had both been recommended to Hurok by Pavlova. Being a skilled curator already, he recognised the artistic prowess and commercial potential of both these artists and thereby finalised both their contracts.

[9] Anonymous folder from Boston Public Library.

This started a long business relationship between Shankar and Hurok. Sol Hurok, already established as a leading presenter and co-curator, travelled to the Paris Exposition and viewed Shankar's choreography. It was on 26 December 1932 that 'Uday Shankar and his company of Hindu Dancers and Musicians' presented their first show during the International Dance Festival organised by Hurok, at the New Yorker Theatre in New York city. Shankar mentioned this as a landmark in his life and so did Rajendra Shankar in their writings respectively (in Nartanam 2001). On the international success of Shankar's presentations and Hurok's continued pushing of his troupe towards intercontinental journeys for tours across Europe and America certainly meant that economically as well as reception-wise Hurok was sure of a profit. Of this, Ruth Abrahams wrote:

> Hurok himself admitted that he was unprepared for Shankar's overwhelming triumph in the United States. The positive public reaction was so staggering that six major New York arts critics printed rave reviews in their respective newspapers. (Abrahams 2007: 407–8)

According to Abrahams, the audience seemed to be really impressed by the spectacle. They were being introduced to a new East that was not represented by the figures of the poor, repressed, colonised, unfed bodies or only by mythical representations of royalty, brought to be on display as colonial bounty. These were performers representing and presenting an unfamiliar spectacle of dance, music, drama, and festivities.

Shankar was the centre of this attraction. He was definitely the principle draw for the audience. The troupe performed to full houses over and over again. As an impresario who prided himself for having the greatest ability to see the future of any performer, the reception of 'Shan-Kar' (as spelled in Hurok's publicity material) impressed him. Samuel S. Madell wrote in The New York City American, on 27 December 1932, 'There is something of godly impressiveness in the appearance Shan-Kar, and in his dancing'. He was probably echoing the fascination of the crowd at the body of the dancer that is male but not muscular, oriental but not dark and sweaty, masculine but with a promise of curves that the dancer was not afraid to use in his artistic endeavour. The fascination seemed to be centred around the grace and not the strength of the male dancer, a quality that was usually expected of female ballerinas and modern dancers of the time. While the West was stereotyping dance and dance bodies through their colonisers' lenses, it seems that the Eastern bodies were accorded a much softer masculinity in comparison to the raw energies and untamed presence of the African continent. On the other hand, the soft flowing demureness of the East often imitated by female dancers such as Ruth St. Denis and Maud Allen seem to be as much products of stereotypes as the colonised submissive body of the Oriental male dancer. Uday Shankar was an interesting presence in that context. He was more male than the small male dancers of the South East Asian countries, but was adorable enough in his presence for the fantasies of the Eastern sensibilities to be kept alive. Huge admirations of Shankar's hands, long neck, serpent-like 'boneless' movements, sinuous grace, were mentioned by critiques over and over again, and have become usual terms of references for his dance. Shankar's famous wave-like arm movements of flowing muscles, that he continued to use in some of his choreographies and two very significant sequences in his film *Kalpana* much later, added to his attraction. The audience was mesmerised to see the magical ripple of muscles in a carefully controlled flow of movements from shoulder to finger tips and back. Most publicity materials by Hurok carefully utilised these references repeatedly. In this context, Abrahams wrote:

> As in Europe Shankar's 1933 tour of the United States reaped many plaudits for his unique offering and special talent. One reason for the continued strong press coverage and increased sponsorship from the American intellectual community was the addition of Ren´e Daumal to handle the press for the American tour. Daumal was a respected author and humanist-philosopher whose first work, published when he was eighteen, had become a classic. An admirer of Tagore and the Theosophist Annie Besant, he was drawn to the humanism he found in the religions and philosophies of Asia, and particularly those of India. Joining Shankar in the latter part of November 1932, he remained with him until early March, 1933, when Shankar returned to England. (Abrahams 2007: 408)

Robinson, Hurok's biographer, has described the inter-dependence that made both Hurok and Shankar depend on each other for their careers. They both understood and took full advantage of this mutually beneficial situation. Such transcultural transactions led to increasing awareness of each other's world as well as ability and a greater awareness of the power that each brought to the other's world, both professionally and commercially. It was actually about putting a negotiated price or value to art and art-reception creating a transactional relationship between an artistic effort and a number of distant markets. Shankar's art was described by critics as well as Hurok himself in terms that clearly pronounced him as a big attraction, as well as a box-office hit. Shankar's stage presence as a sexually attractive male dancer made him especially appealing to female members of the audience. This was read by Hurok as a charisma that was enhanced by the quality of interaction between the female co-dancers and Shankar himself in the choreographies, where many times he would be the only male on the stage. John Martin had joined New York Times in 1927 first as a dance writer and then as a staff dance critic. Hurok mentioned him as 'the first American dance critic' (Robinson 1994: 147) and cultivated him carefully. Martin wrote about Hurok's dance presentations extensively and also played a very significant part in presenting dance as something more than just an entertainment and an exotic activity.

Robinson wrote:

> By the time he [Shankar] made his solo debut in New York, then, in late December 1932, Shan-Kar was well known among dance enthusiasts, including John Martin, who had written a long advance piece for the New York Times calling his appearance 'one of the most provocative and delightful events of the dance season'. For his part Hurok was optimistic about how well Shan-Kar would do, but 'I never anticipated his being a smash hit'. What drew the predominantly female sold-out houses, Hurok believed, was Shan-Kar's sex appeal, enhanced by the adoring female dancers who surrounded and worshipped him like some Hindu god. He was received as a matinee idol .... With this string of commercial and artistic successes, Hurok by the end of 1932 firmly established himself as New York's—and America's—leading presenter of dance events. (Robinson 1994: 152)

This particular take on Shankar's work has been used by critics from India as well as from the West. While Indian critics repeatedly dismissed Shankar's efforts as deeply influenced by the West, the West continued to welcome his 'oriental' dance presented to the accompaniment of 'deliciously weird Eastern music' (Illustration 8). The translocational/transcultural reception therefore points to the interesting emergence of a masculinity that was something in-between and was an independent artistic choice rather than a plain representation of something that is either completely Eastern or Western. But imposing a binary was essential for both the East and the West, as that made the power relations easier to understand and carry out by the artist himself as well as the worlds he or she is traversing delicately (Fig. 3.5).

This observation is strengthened by Trinh T. Minh–ha's thoughts, she writes:

> The margins, our sites of survival, become our fighting grounds and their site for pilgrimage. Thus, while we turn around and reclaim them as our exclusive territory, they happily approve, for the divisions between margin and center should be preserved, and as clearly demarcated as possible, if the two positions are to remain intact in their power relations… (Minh–ha 1991: 17)

Fig. 3.5 Hurok's publicity material (© Anonymous file No. M 463, Boston Public Library)

Shankar remained apparently happily classified therefore. In fact, he perpetuated the image and became comfortable claiming the Indian-ness that the Indians critics often had trouble seeing. The expanse of translocational advantages and the influences in terms of time as well as space seem to have made it easier for Shankar to locate his art more and more deeply within the Indian cultural context, even before he started his institution in Almora in 1939. His artistic relationship with the country of his birth, in fact, was facilitated by Sol Hurok further. The Impresario's choice of the exotic Indian dancer may have begun with his wanting to honour Pavlova's recommendation and to introduce an Oriental performance as a variety within his usual list of performers, but he soon understood Shankar's ability to draw the audience consistently. The ethnocentric[10] choices that Shankar continued to make and Hurok continued to patronise over the years that they worked with each other brought both these men fame and recognition consistently. Shankar's troupe claimed a deliberately ethnocentric space as the 'Hindoo (Hindu) dancers', and Hurok had no problem with this convenient identification. Thus, a relationship of convenience or adjustment may be read between the 'margin' and the 'center' that Trinh T. Minh–ha mentions by writing:

> They accept the margins; so do we. For without the margin, there is no center, no heart .... By displacing, it never allows this classifying world to exert its classificatory power without returning it to its own ethnocentric classifications. All the while, it points to an elsewhere-within-here whose boundaries would continue to compel frenzied attempts at 'baptizing' through logocentric naming and objectivizing to reflect on themselves as they face their own constricting apparatus of refined grids and partitioning walls. (Minh-ha 1991: 17)

It was during the early 1930s (Abrahams 2007) with Hurok that Shankar met the Elmhirsts of Dartington Hall, which actually brought about the consolidation of Shankar's pedagogical activities through the establishment of an institution for the promotion of the arts in India. It was also during the early 1930s that Shankar visited Mary Wigman's School in Dresden. Scant documentation exists about

[10] Ethnocentrism may be defined as a yardstick for judging all cultural practices and norms of other communities other than one's own—created by communities themselves. The term ethnocentrism refers then to the common process of human groups identifying themselves culturally superior when compared to all others.

Fig. 3.6 Shankar in Hurok's publicity Prochure (© Anonymous file No. 463, Boston Public Library)

Shankar's exchanges with Mary Wigman, Ruth St. Denis, Kurt Jooss, Rudolf Laban, and others. All these dancers made their historical mark on the world dance map and Shankar existed and shared many of the same cultural spaces, but never actually belonged in them. His form was separated and often marginalised by the critics and dance presenters as well as the audience and more importantly by Shankar himself. So while trying to be a part of the same dance scene, he was also probably conscious of the fact that he never wanted to separate his embodied practices from their cultural context and representation. Hence, his transcultural location may have helped him choose and fashion his tools for building, bit by tiny bit, with important components based on his own experiences as a male performer who never was fully able to move away from the identification that he acquired as a colonised, immigrant, male dancer. In later years we also find him settling down with the identity that he managed to build and the justification he fashioned around it.

Though Shankar and his troupe were presented by Sol Hurok for a number of seasons, his association with Hurok went through several ups and downs. As Shankar became an established and world renowned dancer through Hurok's presentation of his company, Hurok also established himself as a specialised dance impresario in America (Fig. 3.6).

Performing Masculinity: Engaging in a Transnational Cultural Circuit and the Obsession with Shiva

The British system of creating a structure of knowledge for colonised cultures had an undeniable influence on the way knowledge became available to a certain class of people who had a way of being part of the knowledge system/circuit through mobility as well as education. Ananda Coomaraswamy's writing on Shiva, in his collection of essays *The Dance of Siva: Fourteen Indian Essays*, were widely read. He wrote about Siva (Nataraja):

> The essential significance of Siva's dance is threefold: First: It is the image of his rhythmic play as the source of all movements within the cosmos. Secondly: The purpose of his dance is to release the countless souls of men from the snare of illusion. Thirdly: The place of dance, Chidambaram, the centre of Universe, is within the heart'... It is not strange that the figure of Nataraja has commanded the adorations of so many generations past. (Coomaraswamy 1918: 65–66)

For Shankar, Shiva as a male god was a fascination. And he was not alone. Shiva became the ideal character for many male dancers of that time. Shankar worked on several choreographies—solos, duets, as well as group performances that had at their centre the representation of

Shiva/Nataraja, as the lord of dance. This becomes relevant as the first notable mention of Shankar's performance *Dance of Shiva* in 1924, while he was still struggling after his disconnect with Pavlova. Shankar's big break was in 1924 when after a long time of hardship, he got invited to perform at the British Empire Exhibition at Wembley, very near London. Mohan Khokar quoted Shankar in this context:

> I danced the dance of Shiva. Music I myself gave to be composed and some good musicians were there who played the orchestra. As they played I danced. Without knowing anything about Shiva's dance, I just jumped around, most probably. What I did, god knows, but it proved a big success and they bravoed me. I could not realise why they liked it so much. (Khokar 1983: 42)

It is clear from Shankar's admissions that he hardly had any idea of what or how to perform the dance of Shiva when he was starting to imagine that as a performance. Khokar mentions in this context that while he was touring the Americas with Pavlova, Shankar had been gifted a copy of *The Mirror of Gestures*, a translation of the *Abhinaya Darpana* of Nandikesvara by Ananda K. Coomaraswamy and Gopala Krishnayya Duggirala that had been published in 1917, by Coomaraswamy himself. After having left the book unread for a year and a half, Shankar started reading it one night in Paris. He was struck by the picture of *Nataraja* he found in the book. Khokar wrote about Shankar's experience at this point:

> Then I discovered that this is not merely a pose but the centre of hundreds of movements that moved from one to another and finished with that pose. I invented the movements which I thought emanated from the Nataraja pose. Of course, at that time I did not know at all who Nataraja was or what he represented. Later, this idea of movements radiating from a source and merging back into it I used in a number of my compositions. (Khokar 1983: 42)

Similar inspirations to dance in the role of Shiva seem to have struck other male dancers of the time. The proof lies in Ted Shawn's choreography of Shiva's dance almost around the same time. His ideas showed some similarities to the imaginations of the East that were generated and in hindsight seem to be part of the same cultural circuit (created out of information, ideas, and pedagogy) that Shankar was part of. The fascination with the *Tandava*[11] vs the *Lasya*[12] as male and female energies, the conceptual embodiment of physical and conceptual masculinity, and the visual reference to Shiva and his actions as portrayed in iconographic representations were some of the ideas that seem to have been common for dances created by Uday Shankar 1924 and by Ted Shawn in 1925. Ted Shawn created his choreography '*Cosmic Dance of Shiva*' during his far Eastern tour in 1925. In an audio recording archived at the Jacob's Pillow Archive in Massachusetts, Ted Shawn's talk on the '*Cosmic Dance of Shiva*' mentions that the dance and the set were composed and designed by Shawn during his India tour. He mentions that he had the 'Ring of Fire' constructed as per the eleventh-century depictions of Shiva. He also mentions acquiring pieces of jewellery that he thought would represent Shiva in the closest manner. Describing his process of trying to understand the role of Nataraja he was about to take on, Shawn says on the tape that:

> The Last thing I have to say is that a Friend of mine, Boshi Sen,[13] a devout Hindu, who had had a fine western education but remained a devout Hindu, travelled with me to many parts of India, to Banaras a holy city and Allahabad another holy city, and took me to holy men, and interpreted and got them to talk to me about Shiva, and eventually after 5 or 6 months I said to him that Boshi you have been very patient with me. I now realise your motive was for me to find out that this was too enormous a theme for me to package into one neat little dance, How can I dance the creation and destruction in a single dance. He laughed and said no that wasn't my motive, because you don't have to do it. All you have to do, make the form of the dance and present the form and the body and say 'Lord Shiva here am I and Dance through me' and Shiva will dance. And

[11] According to the Natyashastra chapter 4, *Tandava* refers to a specific rigorous form of dance that is believed to have been created by Taṇḍu after receiving instructions from Shiva.

[12] Lāsya is the form of dance associated with women. It is believed to have been danced by Siva's consort Parvati, and then taught by her to Usha, the daughter of a sage.

[13] Boshi Sen is mentioned as a friend who was important as an advisor, expert for Ted Shawn and Ruth St. Denis during their tour of India. He and his wife Gertrude were close friends and associates of the Elmhirsts and Rabindranath Tagore. Boshi Sen also remained very important first as a mediator for the patronage extended by the Elmhirsts towards support extended to Uday Shankar and his art, by the Elmhirsts. Finally, he remained associated with Shankar and his work as one of important advisors/administrators for the USICC, right from its planning stage till its closure.

> that is what I have done in all these years that I have danced this dance, I have said, 'Lord Shiva , dance through me', and he has... (Transcription of Ted Shawn's talk, Jacob's Pillow Archives)

Shiva continued to influence other male dancers such as Ram Gopal in later years as well. But with regards to Shankar's Orientalist representation of himself, it is clear that he considered himself a representative of Indian culture and the iconographical world. Shawn was an outsider but with significant interest in accessing Indian culture to draw inspirations from it in terms of movements and spirituality. Shankar's writings have not really expressed any spiritual connection, but instead seem to be motivated by the possibilities of movements embedded within the idea of Shiva. Both these men wanted to imagine the movements of Shiva within a year of each other. I imagine Shankar's words when he says, 'I invented the movements' as an honest confession. But I also see them as a record of the flow of movements and postures of the figure of *Nataraja* through body memory and not through the stories that Shankar confesses to have not known before he danced the dance of Shiva. These words also signify the base of Shankar's journey in terms of his imagination and the embodiment of the cultural constructs of the geography he wanted to represent.

Shankar first choreographed *Tandava Nrittya*, also known as *Shiva Tandava* in the late 1920s and started performing it regularly in the 1930s. This was a solo dance, a representation of Shiva that was extremely popular and remained one of the biggest favourites of the audience at home and abroad throughout his performative years. In the 1930s he also choreographed a duet named *Shiva Parvati Nrittya Dwandva*, which was a duet based on the story of a quarrel between Shiva and his wife Parvati, where they compete with each other to establish who the better dancer amongst them is.

Shankar's Shiva has stood apart and possibly above many other versions of the same theme that have been recorded as a part of the huge repertoire coming out of the representational dances composed on Indian life, culture, and performances all over the world since the 1920s and 30s. Time and again, Shankar has been called '*Nataraja*' (Lord of Dance) incarnate. Ravi Shankar has gone as far as to say that he was Shiva on and off stage, in his dance, his way of thinking, and in the way he lived his life admired and followed by numerous women, smitten totally by his persona as well as appearance. However, according to Ravi Shankar's biography (2020) Uday Shankar also 'cultivated the idea of himself as a Krishna figure', in Raslila—a dance of Krishna with multiple women admirers (Craske 2020: 47).

Dance on the Theme of Labour: Similar yet Dissimilar Choreographies

A later example of another one of Shankar's dance choreographies, this one essentially an ensemble one, is important in discussing a comparative context alongside a choreographed piece by Ted Shawn on the same theme. Both Ted Shawn and Shankar choreographed around the theme of labouring bodies. While Shawn's piece was called '*The Labour Symphony*' (1934), Shankar's choreography was named '*Labour and Machinery*' (late 1940s).

Shawn's important work in 1934 was something that created an 'intersection between labour and dance received its fullest exploration a year later with *Labor Symphony* (1934)' (Scolieri, https://danceinteractive.jacobspillow.org/themes-essays/men-in-dance/ted-shawn-defense-male-dancer/). Shawn's performance (filmed and preserved at the Jacob's Pillow Archives) brought out reactions of admiration in 1934–1935. A review by *The Boston Globe* on May 4 1935, quoted by Christena Schlundt, read:

> The new Labor Symphony was boldly pantomimic and breath-taking to many. The Boston Globe wrote that "In the dance of the field workers, Shawn's genius as a choreographer is most apparent. Here ... a living Parthenon frieze moved in swift beautiful patterns, a thing of exquisite composition, yet purely beautiful. (Schlundt 1967: 23)

Shawn's programme notes on *Labor Symphony* read, 'The four movements of this dance, as in true symphonic structure, are danced without pause. The theme of each movement being stated in solo by Mr. Shawn and immediately developed by the entire ensemble.' The note names the principle sections (movements) as: (1) Labor of the Fields; (2) Labor of the Forests; (3) Labor of the Seas; and (4) Mechanised Labor. Paul A. Scolieri writes in his article 'Ted Shawn and his male dancers, 1933–1940–Jacob's Pillow Dance Interactive' that:

> The final section is a stunning 'machine dance' wherein the dancers perform elaborate sequences patterned after automated pistons, cogs, and gears. In one section, the dancers form a living telegraph: their lower bodies create the machine's pulsing rhythm with stringent sideways strides as their sleeve-covered arms slide across their bare chests, giving the appearance of spewing dots and dashes of a ticker tape. (Scolieri, https://danceinteractive.jacobspillow.org/themes-essays/men-in-dance/ted-shawn-defense-male-dancer/)

Shankar's, *Labour and Machinery*, shortened to suit the new medium became an important part of his film *Kalpana* that is often compared to *Metropolis*, a 1927 silent German expressionist film directed by Fritz Lang. In the first section in *Kalpana*, *Labour and Machinery*, a choreography that was much later restaged (with some alterations) by Amala Shankar in the late 1970s at USICC, was already a stage production of Shankar's in the beginning of the 1940s. The USIC Centre News, the newsletter of the Centre, dated 28 April 1940 mentions 'Dada's (Uday Shankar's) new ballet dealing with labour and machinery is progressing steadily, in which five girls are taking part' (USIC Centre News, 28 April 1940: 4 © Dartington Hall Records, Devon). This presentation with a larger cast eventually became the piece that showcased Shankar's idea of labouring bodies, their pains and exploitations, the overall mechanisation process of human bodies and labour for maximisation of profit, and a systematic erosion of agricultural land in favour of growing urban presence.

Labour and Machinery was described in Shankar's programme notes (Khokar 1983: 178) as a story of a peaceful community living in a small and tranquil village, where the residents worked hard on the lands under the guidance of the village elder, until some outsiders lured them to leave their age-old practice and join a new factory. The story unfolded to show extreme and often violent exploitation of the workers and the complete mechanisation of their lives. One young man (played by Shankar) emerged as the leader of the community and was the most enthusiastic participant in this life-changing endeavour. The grinding labour, the loss of independence, and the exploitation by the factory owners mechanised the community that began resembling assorted pieces of machinery. The travails and turbulences of a rebellion finally brought the realisation among the members of the community and the young man sought the Village elder's advise. The hour long performance ended with the dawn of a new era, where the community finds a middle path that would help them use science to their benefit. A simple message highlighting the utility of the modern knowledge, while continuing with traditional harmonious ways of life was put forth with a festive event as the finale.

This story, like many of Shankar's production contents, was based on an utopian idea of a good/bad binary and somewhat simplistic rendition of the inevitability of the cyclic disorders related to postcolonial growth and the advance of capitalism. It created an 'either/or' world through the choreography. But what kept the audience spellbound through the elaborate representations of individual labouring bodies covered in sweat and soot, and the ensemble representation of mechanised labour was the developing of a series of unusual but dedicated movements such as use of abrupt mechanical and rhythmic shifts to create sharp angles using joints like the knee, the elbow, the wrist, the neck, and the hip. Shankar's *Labour and Machinery* also had an elaborate section on replacement of human labour with mechanical labour to produce an efficient assembly-like affect. Side by side, there were movements such as shaving, combing of hair, eating, sitting, running, that were turned into repeated mechanised and stylised representations of human activities, to represent the human bodies as tools in the life inside the factory.

In a section known as 'head-less' dance,[14] the sequence portraying mobilizing of the mechanised bodies builds up by adding movement segments part-by-part. This is started by first pulling an invisible string from one side of a line of four bodies by the overseer, who initiates simultaneous right to left movements of the neck for all the four bodies. This is followed by the overseer moving to each body and activating their hips by pushing imaginary buttons from both sides of the hips. As the overseer pulls another imaginary rope from one side all the hips start moving right and left to combine with the neck movements. Slow build- up of additional movements for all bodies and the indication of complete control being in the hands of the controller and not the bodies themselves project the regulated human bodies as coordinated and programmed parts of a whole, to be seen as a large machine.

[14] The same sequence was restructured to be included in Kalpana (p. 252).

Working Through Patterns of Orientalised Gendering: Between Masculinity and Colonial Effiminisation

It would be useful to understand Shankar's choice of presence and representation that he chose for himself and his dance and choreographies to respond to the scope of a stereotyped understanding of one's own culture. Reading his life and dance through the tools of intersectionality[15] will help us configure the multiple labels that fit his complex identification of self within various cultural and social matrixes. Consistently through the chapter the apparently apolitical and artistic choices that Shankar is seen making, may be read as negotiations for existing and surviving within 'the overlapping and conflicting dynamics of race, gender, class, sexuality, nation, and other inequalities' (Cho et al. 2013: 788).

The urge within him to traverse between two or more geographies was to make a successful career in and around dance. In the process, aesthetic/gender/race/caste-class stereotypes were consistently negotiated by him by allowing a constant interplay between the multiple stereotypes that he became framed by, in terms of intersecting positions of privilege and vulnerability. Intersectionality thus becomes an 'analytic disposition, a way of thinking about and conducting analyses' (Cho et al. 2013: 795), throughout this chapter, where 'the adaptation of an intersectional way of thinking about the problem of sameness and difference and its relation to power' (ibid.) has been the thread for the analytical process. Shankar's years as a male oriental dancer—occupying the same stage as the well-known modern dancers of the West, but never considered or given the same status as them makes him always seemingly basking in the glory of success and yet always hovering at the precipice between hope and despair.

The idea of intersectionality also lends itself 'as an analytical tool[16] to capture and engage contextual dynamics of power' (Cho et al. 2013: 788)

[15] Intersectionality here is used as an is an analytical tool to locate the multiple identities shaping and structuring Shankar's life and art, as a migrant of colour facing multiple subordinations.

[16] Kimberle Williams Crenshaw's initial idea of 'Intersectionality' (1989) reached Indian academic arena formally in 2015 through Nivedita Menon's work on 'Is Feminism About Women: A Critical View on Intersectionality from India', though there has been extensive scholarship on multiple identities and co-construction of marginalities within the political and socio-economic writings in India.

providing the possibilities to look at Shankar's earlier photographs where the ambiguity of the gender representation in his work comes out clearly.

Shankar's photos through his career show us a variety of negotiations with gender identities, auto-exoticism, performative masculinity, sexualities, and expressions of sensuality. These readings are based on all the photos that had been shared widely through the media by him as publicity material, as well as those printed in different books, besides those which are available in archives across the world. On the one hand are his photographs dressed as a nautch girl where he appears to be dancing as a female dancer/impersonator. On the other hand, one wonders about the role that he was performing, looking at him holding a sword with his teeth in a daringly provocative stance that could be read as distinctly beyond gender binaries. In his first solo performance in Paris on 11 January 1926, at the Théâtre Comédie des Champs-Elysées, Shankar presented a solo 'Danse Nuptial' (literally meaning 'The wedding Dance') dressed in a saree with ornaments and make-up and hair styled for a woman. He was clearly still trying to work on ideas of representation of the Indian bride and marriage that worked well for his choreographies for Pavlova. It was common for men to cross-dress in traditional Indian performances, therefore, as an authentic Oriental subject his presentation was tolerated, in spite, of some severe criticism, if one has to go by the few reviews that survive. But the reviews also show a certain amount of indulgence for the strange charms of the East. One of the reviews reads:

> Uday Shankar dances in a feminine costume, a Wedding Dance that is unique, in which the travesty has nothing of the suggestive or unpleasantness that it usually has. In these dances, sensuality is spiritualized, idealized to the point of losing all its qualities of embarrassment. Beauty, harmony, and the perfection of movement, and poise leave us completely absorbed and subjugated. (Review excerpt, La Tribune de Genève, 18 October 1929 quoted in Abrahams 1986, 72)[17]

The review is important in more ways than one. It shows an effort in the West, towards a normalisation of the effeminacy and female impersonations (see Chapter 1) by Shankar towards the beginning of his dance

[17] This is part of a performance review published in *La Tribune de Genève*, 18 October 1929, from Ruth Abrahams' unpublished Ph.D. thesis, 'The Life and Art of Uday Shankar', 1986.

journey in the West. Secondly, it reaffirms the readiness to accept the East as a space where there are different visual experiences of seeing the sexual and the sensual as spiritual. Thirdly, it appeals to the Western audiences to see the East, not in a position of subjugation but as a different cultural context. This and other such experiments in turn also tell us that Shankar himself was informed by the Western ideas that defined the Orient as an effeminate, un-understandable, emotional, and exotic space that needed explication. But soon he also wanted the control of that performative explication within his embodied aesthetic.

In the context of Shankar's ease with his masculinity, however, there has to be a separate set of arguments. Can there be a working definition of masculinity in the specific context of dance? And then again is there a specific masculinity that can be assigned to the specific context of 'dance in/from the east' that entered the international aesthetic register and market place as the 'oriental' cultural expression specifically coming from the colonised south Asian country, India? Jennifer Fisher and Anthony Shey in the *Introduction* to their edited book *When Men Dance: Choreographing Masculinities Across Borders* write:

> the term is so often associated with biologically defined males, and that it tends to be accompanied by notions of its presumed opposite, 'femininity'. Beyond that, the debates correctly begin, given what masculinity can mean in different contexts, and given the slippage that can occur between conceptions of 'sexuality' and 'gender'. (Fisher and Shey 2009: 3)

The notion of masculinity, often intersectional, is consistent with socialised structures of thinking and behaving as per the norms, expectations, and requirements of being a male. In case of body idioms and movement patterns in dance, masculine and feminine imprint is clearly visible in grammars and choreographies in more ways than one. Here the obvious connection between patriarchy and masculinity becomes important in the dance idiom and choices made in any choreographic work.

The idea of performing 'Oriental' masculinities (Barber 2015) opens up possibilities of looking beyond transcultural and translocational readings of Shankar in multiple manners. Barber's essay on the contemporary Vietnamese population in London and the ethnic profiling and stereotyping that they regularly face in the so-called cosmopolitan city lent several terminologies for trying to sharpen the analysis of Shankar's apparent acceptance of the stereotyping that he faced from the East as well as the West. A number of popular photos often used in the publicity material by Sol Hurok (for USA and Europe), and Haren Ghosh (for India) portray inevitably Shankar as the quintessential male partner to a submissive demure female partner, be it Simkie or Amala Shankar. I would like to read in these archival materials, Shankar's choice of using the colonial 'logics of biological size and sexual preferences' that are often used to 'effeminise' (Barber 2015: 451) the colonised Oriental body of the male, as tools to utilise these stereotypes to his advantage at different points in his life. Once he established his troupe, and had a somewhat acceptable presence among the Western audience, the choreographic narratives around gods such as Shiva and Krishna with a clear male godly presence highlighted by a markedly subordinate female partner helped Shankar negotiate the gendering encountered in his performance in the 1930s. Shankar does not seem to have been a 'passive recipient' (Barber 2015: 446) of any of the orientalising processes, by the time he started going on regular tours with his troupe. A range of strategies that Barber identifies in her writing, such as (a) 'risk-taking or risky performances of masculinity'; (b) 'practices of self-orientalism[18]'; and, 'auto-exoticising[19]' (Barber 2015: 446–48) may be identified as important strategies used often by Shankar as well.

'His audience loved him' is what we hear time and again. Similarly to Barber's observation, Shankar could use and turn the whole oriental discourse around to use it to his advantage through 'strategic and accomplished performances in order to avoid narrow effeminising discourses' (Barber 2015: 446). He used several modalities, empowered and emboldened by his transcultural understanding. He chose content with clear male and female binaries. He often chose to dance the identical movements as his female partner(s) for choreographic strength, rather than doing

[18] According to Tamsin Barber (2015), 'Self-Orientalism (Kondo 1997) can be understood as an attempt to reclaim and subvert Orientalism for one's own purposes'. It is a term well-suited for Uday Shankar and many other dancers such as Ram Gopal and Madame Maneka, who seem to have claimed oriental authenticity for themselves in their own ways by marking themselves within the oriental history and geography.

[19] Barber defined auto-exoticisation for an oriental subject (Savigliano 1995) as '[p]resenting himself and other Orientals together as unique', for 'subverting Oriental stereotypes' by more positively positioning himself as an object of 'exotic' difference and desire, a process known as 'auto-exoticising' (Barber 2015: 447).

controlled movements suitable for portraying male movement stereotypes. He projected hyper-feminine bodies and movements to highlight and set off his own maleness and to counter the 'effeminising affects of Orientalism' (Barber 2015: 451).

As his career stabilised and flourished Shankar continued his representational dances from India that made up his signature repertoire. Throughout the beginning years he was torn between his adopted 'Western' identity and his status as a migrant Indian in a foreign cultural location. The audiences' reception changed from a form of curious acceptance to enthusiastic appreciation, with a specific space being created for Shankar's auto-exoticised self-representation along with his choreography. Through his choreographic experiments and his creative innovations in dance movements, he began giving shape to his somewhat limited aesthetic understanding of Indian iconography and cultural expressions, constructing a picture of his colonised homeland and the cultural diversity therein. He accepted and used the binary between his artistic identity as a colonised migrant subject while developing his professional acumen on western stagecraft and performance ethics. His choreographies used the desired idea of the Oriental male dancing body and his modern dance aesthetic together to make a mark against all other male dancers from the East. The curated projection of his neo-traditional oriental male presence ensured box-office success as well.

Shankar's childhood socialisation process may have shaped his choices as a dancer and a choreographer by creating hierarchical images in the form of men and women and also by creating means of making the hierarchies appear justified through processes of subtle or clearly instituted privileges. Such hierarchies were also fed through a socio-cultural orientation that privileged men above women, patriarchy over matriarchy, masculinity above femininity, while attributing a differential status to men from higher 'races', castes, classes, and sexuality clearly over others not from such points of advantage. At the same time, the West was changing or being forced to accept radical changes in the form of emergence of modern dance that countered gender stereotypes in the world of ballet and in the dancing bodies on the proscenium space. At that juncture the acceptance of Shankar's choreographies with all the gender stereotypes by the audience in the West is puzzling, unless one acknowledges a specific acceptance of Oriental masculinity by his audience. To enhance the appeal, the publicity, the reviews, the presentations of the Oriental and the exotic ensured a different set of expectations with regard to gender inequality, patriarchy, and exhibition.

According to Said, the West through its exposure and proximity to the East accorded a 'seat of power' to itself and handled the East as a depository of unprocessed raw wealth of 'human material, wealth, knowledge' (Said 2003: 44). It accumulated all such raw material that the East itself was not capable of processing within 'a great embracing machine' that it possessed, to process, sort, reshuffle, and convert all that it could gather and converted it to create valuable substance and power.

According to Said:

> [t]he essential relationship, on political, cultural, and even religious grounds, was seen—in the West, which is what concerns us here—to be one between a strong and a weak partner. Many terms were used to express the relation: Balfour and Cromer, typically, used several. The Oriental is irrational, depraved (fallen), childlike, 'different'; thus the European is rational, virtuous, mature, 'normal'. (Said 2003: 40)

The world of the Orient, according to Said, had its own organisation 'with its own national, cultural, and epistemological boundaries and principles of internal coherence'. But in spite of its own mechanisms and logic, it is the way that the West identified and characterised the orient that gave it, its identity and recognition (Said 2003: 40). According to Said:

> The Orient as a place of pilgrimage is one; so too is the vision of Orient as spectacle, or tableau vivant. Every work on the Orient in these categories tries to characterize the place, of course, but what is of greater interest is the extent to which the work's internal structure is in some measure synonymous with a comprehensive interpretation (or an attempt at it) of the Orient..... Every interpretation, every structure created for the Orient, then, is a reinterpretation, a rebuilding of it. (Said 2003: 158).

Shankar's auto-exoticism started pre-empting categorisation by the West. It offered its own explanation through his programme notes, his publicity photographs, and his gestural politics in the form of his public behaviour as well as his dance movements. Shankar, no longer left any room for the West to frame him, he left them no choice but to see him as proudly different. Drawing on references of kings, gods, and men of strength and valour in many of his dance presentations, he ensured an explicit and grand (rather than implicit and referential) projection of a somewhat ethnocentric showcasing. Women characters helped in highlighting this might, strength, and personality.

Dancing as Struggle

Now that I have established the grand presence that Shankar built bit by bit, from himself and his choreographic works, I would like to posit his dance journey as one that is a constant struggle to establish his identity. By visiting museums to understand India's history and by learning about his home country to validate being Indian, he managed the audiences' expectations of seeing the East in and through his untrained body and dance. He realised that the Western audience did not need to see the expertise that they expected from a trained male dancer from Western cultures, but instead they were impressed by the sincere authentic oriental male body with its alternative aesthetic that his instinctive yet artistically projected moving propagated. Barber explicates, with emphasis on place and space in studying intersecting categories of identities, that:

> The locational basis of intersecting categories has also been acknowledged by feminists who emphasise the need for a place-based analysis. Anthias (2002) pays attention to the 'translocational' constructions of identity through her notion of 'translocational positionality'. This notion emphasises how individuals negotiate identities across a range of shifting locations which contextualise social relations. According to Anthias (2002, 502), focusing on locational and translocational aspects 'recognises the importance of context, the situated nature of claims and attributions and their production in complex and shifting locales'. (Barber 2015: 442)

The idea of shifting locations and an translocational positionality (as a specifically informed and articulated choice) developing in relation to the often shifting and changing geographies in Shankar's life reached a semi-stable space in his institution in Almora. Discussed in detail in the next chapter, this shift towards a sense of culmination in terms of his dance journey was the direct result of the overlapping social and cultural connections coming together in the United Kingdom and India. The connections overlapping personal and professional ties led to a patronage of his art by people from different locations in the world and opened many avenues for artistic interactions between inspiration, imagination, and technique. Through this connection Shankar acknowledged the importance of training, his institution USICC is the proof of that. The institution for him was to be a space for unadulterated and continuous learning, not only for his students, but also for himself. Even in his developing pedagogy, he pushed for perfection in learning of traditional practices, accompanied by imaginative emersion; respect for form along with acknowledgement and experiment with self-expression; and explorations of ensemble possibilities. For him the emphasis on place and space worked as the catalysts for his growing intersectionality and eventually became central to what Barber saw as the 'processes of subject formation' (Barber 2015: 443).

Shankar grew more confident about his knowledge of the East he had hardly known anything before, and his choreographic knowledge also grew with his experience of performing and choreographing. His work showed more awareness of the power dynamics involved in the formation of vulnerable and marginal masculine identities, in the shifting economic and cultural sphere that he had to inhabit in order to survive and make a living on one hand, and also on the other hand had to transform into his committed audience. In the case of Shankar's later works one can clearly see a shift from the submissive masculinity to masculinity that is grounded and constructed by the colonial margin that it had to always acknowledge as its abode. In the post-USICC days, he finally shed his servitude and his dependence on American presenters and impresarios such as Sol Hurok and the Western audience who gave him the support that the Indian critics never provided.

In the next chapters the themes revolve the different phases of Shankar's work and struggle with institution building, choreographic experimentations, and his work with mixed media. His journey shall be mapped through his landmark film *Kalpana* and other experimental projects. The chapters will look at culture specific and location-specific understandings in his work as he looked for ways to teach and present his work 'at home', once again struggling to establish or renew his link with India. He projected his troupe as the Hindu dancers, and yet he talked of global themes on youth, work, and conflict of economic interests through his choreography. His success was always spectacular but ephemeral, never becoming truly and comfortably his in his own land. Some of his choreographies included a focus on urban space, but his heart clearly lay in the mythical representation of kings' courts and celestial representations as well as theatricalized presentations of rural community lives.

References

Abrahams, Ruth. 1986. "The Life and Art of Uday Shankar." Unpublished Ph.D. dissertation, pp. 72. New York University.

Abrahams, Ruth K. 2007. "Uday Shankar: The Early Years, 1900–1938." *Dance Chronicle* 30 (3): 363–426.

Anthias, Floya. 2002. "Where Do I Belong? Narrating Collective Identity and Translocational Positionality." *Ethnicities* 2 (4): 491–515.

Barber, Tamsin. 2015. "Performing 'Oriental' Masculinities: Embodied Identities among Vietnamese Men in London." *Gender, Place & Culture* 22 (3): 440–55.

Cho, Sumi, Kimberle Williams Crenshaw, and Leslie McCall. 2013. "Toward a Field of Intersectionality Studies: Theory, Applications, and Praxis." *Signs: Intersectionality: Theorizing Power* 38 (4): 785–810.

Coomaraswamy, Ananda. 1918. "The Dance of Siva." In *The Dance of Siva: Fouteen Indian Essays*, by Ananda Coomaraswamy, 56–66. New York: The Sunwise Turn Inc.

Coomaraswamy, Ananda K. 1937. "Uday Shankar's Indian Dancing." *Magazine Art*, 30 October: 611–613.

Coomaraswamy, Ananda K. trans., and Gopala Krishnayya Duggirala, trans. 1917. *The Mirror of Gesture: Being the Abhinaya Darpana of Nandikesvara*. Cambridge: Harvard University Press.

Craske, Oliver. 2020. *Indian Sun: The life and Music of Ravi Shankar*. London: Faber & Faber.

Erdman, Joan L. 1987. "Performance as Translation: Uday Shankar in the West." *The Drama Review: TDR* 31 (1, Spring): 64–88.

Erdman, Joan L. 1997. "Reflecting Our Past; Reflecting on Our Future." *Proceedings, Society of Dance History Scholars, Twentieth Annual Conference*, 270–274. Riverside: University of California, Riverside.

Fisher, Jenifer, and Anthony Shey (eds). 2009. *When Men Dance: Choreographing Masculinities Across Borders*. New York: Oxford University Press.

Hurok, Sol and Ruth Goode. 1947. *Impresario*. London: MacDonald Co. Ltd.

Kerensky, Oleg. 1973. *Anna Pavlova*. London: Hamilton.

Khokar, Mohan. 1983. *His Dance, His Life: A Portrait of Uday Shankar*. New Delhi: Himalayan Books.

Minh-Ha, Trinh. T. 1991. *When the Moon Waxes Red: Representation, Gender and Cultural Politics*. London and New York: Routledge.

Robinson, Harlow. USA: 1994. 1995. *The Last Impresario: The Life Time and Legacy of Sol Hurok*. New York: Penguin Books.

Rothenstein, William. 1931. *Men and Memories: Recollections of William Rothenstein 1872–1900*. New York: Coward-McCann.

Said, Edward W. 2003. *Orientalism*. London, New York: Penguin Books.

Schlundt, Christena L. 1967. *The Appearances of Ted Shawn and His Male Dancers: A Chronology and Index of Dances 1933–1940*. New York: The New York Public Library, Astor, Lenox and Tilden Foundations.

Segal, Zohra. 2010. *Close-Up: Memories of a Life on Stage and Screen*. New Delhi: Women Unlimited (An Associate of Kali for Women).

Shankar (Nandi), Amala. [1934] 2007. *Sat Sagarer Pare [Bengali]*. Kolkata: A Mukherjee & Co. PVT LTD.

Shankar, Rajendra. 1983. "Personal Reminiscences of Uday Shankar." In *Uday Shankar*, edited by Sunil Kothari and Mohan Khokar. New Delhi: RIMPA and the Uday Shankar Festival '83 Committee. 4–10.

Shankar, Rajendra. 2001. "Uday Shankar—Personal Reminiscences." *Nartanam* 1 (4, October–December): 12–34.

Shankar, Uday. 2001. "My Love for Dance." *Nartaki: A Quarterly Journal in Indian Dance, A Special Issue on Uday Shankar* 1 (4): 7–11.

Archival and Online Sources

Audio recording, Transcription of Ted Shawn's talk. 5.55 mins, Jacob's Pillow Archives.

Crenshaw, Kimberle. "Demarginalizing the Intersection of Race and Sex: A Black Feminist Critique of Antidiscrimination Doctrine, Feminist Theory and Antiracist Politics." University of Chicago Legal Forum: Vol. 1989: Iss. 1, Article 8. Available at: http://chicagounbound.uchicago.edu/uclf/vol1989/iss1/8.

Dartington Hall Records. Dartington Hall Trust Archives files [Devon Heritage Centre, Great Moor House, Bittern Road, Sowton, Exeter, Devon, EX2 7NL]. https://www.dartington.org/?s=archives.

———. LKE/IN/19: Title—LKE India 19: Uday Shankar India Culture Centre, 1932–1973.

———. DWE/A/8: Title—Dance 2, Shankar and other Indian Dancers.

———. DS/UK/843: Title—India Culture Trust; 1937–.

———. DS/UK/836: Title—Admin History Uday Shankar India Culture Centre; 1938–.

———. MC/Chekhov/S4/39: Series 4.General Files: A. Uday Shankar Play bills.

———. USIC Centre Newsletters 1939–1944 (Fortnightly), Ranidhara, Almora, U.P. Editors: Rajendra Shankar and Vishnudas Shirali (Source: Dartington Archives, Devon Cultural Centre, UK).

Legacy Alice Boner, Museum Rietberg, Zurich. https://emp-web-101.zetcom.ch/eMP/eMuseumPlus?service=RedirectService&sp=Scollection&sp=Sfield Value&sp=0&sp=0&sp=3&sp=SdetailList&sp=0&sp=Sdetail&sp=0&sp=F.

Sarkar Munsi, Urmimala. 2021. *Alice Boner Across Arts and Geographies: Shaping the Dance-Art of Uday Shankar (Alice Boner Collection, Volume 3).* Zurich: Museum Rietberg and Alice Boner Institute—Varanasi.

Scolieru, Paul. A. *Ted Shawn and the Defence of the Male Dancer*, https://danceinteractive.jacobspillow.org/themes-essays/men-in-dance/ted-shawn-defense-male-dancer/. Accessed on 23 August, 2021.

Segal, Zohra. 'Zohra Unmasked', Great Masters Series, interview by Kapila Vatsyayan, Documented by Indira Gandhi National Centre for the Arts, Part 1 and 2, DVD Material, IGNCA, Delhi. Accessed on DD Bharati, 19 November, 2012.

Simkie Paris--Delhi, Documentary on Simkie made by Documentaire de Charlotte Arrighi de Casanova. https://mezzovoce.wmaker.tv/Simkie--Paris-Delhi_v159.html. 2008, 52 mins. Accessed on 21 August 2019.

Segal, Zohra. Interview. "Zinda Itihas Zohra Sehgal", EP #01, Doordarshan National. https://www.youtube.com/watch?v=PxUD37ze-Ho. Accessed on 13 June, 2019.

Shankar, Pandit Ravi, interview on BBC Bengali Service, 1970. https://www.youtube.com/watch?v=tm8pH2ezzAk&list=RDH7GceqHJsUc&index=3. Accessed on 15 July 2019.

Uday Shankar and Simkie video footage. https://roughinhere.wordpress.com/2010/11/07/rare-uday-shankar-dance-footage-playing-on-ravis-tv-set/. Accessed on 21 August 2019.

CHAPTER 4

An Attempt at Creating a Modern Institution

The Settler is interested in the Arts of Dance and Music in particulars practiced in the East by Mr. Uday Shankar Chowdhry and is desirous of making such settlement ...

(Dartington Hall Archives, DS/UK/836, 1937: 5)

(*From the Draft Trust Deed for setting up of the Uday Shankar India Culture Centre, mentioning as Trustees—Beatrice Whitney Straight [The Settler] of Dartington Hall Totnes England, Alice Boner of Banares India, and Uday Shankar Chowdhury of Bombay India.*)

Uday Shankar's meeting and association with Dorothy and Leonard Elmhirst and his knowledge of the social and cultural experiments founded by them at Dartington Hall (in Devon, England) led to a major shift in Shankar's life and dance. His dream of a stable space for building an institution was charged and concretised as a possible venture by the Elmhirst couple and Beatrice Straight, Dorothy Elmhirst's daughter by her first marriage. Shankar was impressed by Dartington Hall as an institution, planned and started in 1925 by the Elmhirsts as an experimental educational institution and a centre for research and activism in the form of rural regeneration and the visual and performing arts. The idea was to impart an alternate form of education that would provide opportunities for the children to explore their interests freely, while helping them to develop their own personalities away from formal educational institutions.

U. Sarkar Munsi, *Uday Shankar and His Transcultural Experimentations*, Transnational Theatre Histories,
https://doi.org/10.1007/978-3-030-93224-4_4

Shankar became an important figure through whom the Elmhirsts wanted to take forward their utopic dream of helping him realise 'the educational potential of his work rather than his desire to forge a renaissance in Indian dance culture' (Vertinsky and Ramachandran 2018: 289). They already had a successful relationship with Rabindranath Tagore's institutions, Visva-Bharati University in Santiniketan[1] and the Institute for Rural Reconstruction in Sriniketan.[2] After their contribution towards building Sriniketan as a community-based sustainable rural development initiative and educational institute became one example of translocational collaborations, the couple and Beatrice Straight became interested in supporting Shankar's project of building an institution. By acknowledging Shankar's work as important but something that needed resources and a helping hand for administrative activity, they took up the responsibility as patrons and helped Shankar in fulfilling one of his most important impulses and dreams.

Shankar was, thus, able to begin and run, albeit only for a short time, an international institution for teaching and experimenting with dance, built on a hill slope named Ranidhara in Almora. The collaboration with and patronage of the Elmhirsts encouraged Shankar to experiment with a modern process in dance. He envisaged training the students to use their resources such as basic body/muscle memory and everyday movement systems to creatively develop a dance language and a pedagogical system. This system had a transcultural base acquired through Shankar's exposure to multiple experiments by internationally renowned modern dancers from all over the world. Visualised as a school where Indian aesthetics and philosophy would also be taught alongside performance skills and innovations, Shankar took help from different experts from the

[1] Visva-Bharati University in Santiniketan was inaugurated in 1923 formally. The roots of this university is in a school that Tagore had established in 1901, where he brought into practice systems of education that relied on ancient and modern modes of dissemination of knowledge. The curriculum had painting, physical education, dramatic performances, and other performing arts along with a curriculum based on mainstream learning.

[2] The Institute of Rural Reconstruction was established near Santiniketan in 1922, with Leonard Elmhirst as its first Director. It was seen as an institute that would train people and develop facilities for self-sustenance and development in rural areas. The institute continues to be one of the important places for action/development research in Eastern India.

world of dance and music to frame the teaching curriculum. His institution brought together some yet-unexplored genres of Indian performing art to contribute to his teaching and making dance.

Dartington Hall: A Model Ecology and Environment of Dance

The Dartington experiment and enterprise was started by Leonard (1893–1974) and Dorothy Elmhirst (1887–1968). Leonard Elmhirst was greatly influenced by Rabindranath Tagore and his educational institution and Tagore's belief in providing a non-interfering setting to allow a child's personality to naturally unfold. According to Larraine Nicholas, Dartington Hall had as a policy choice set itself up as following the path of 'research and progress'. She mentions that Dartington Hall School established itself as a specialised progressive school for children. As a Trust body it also established itself as a well-known and acknowledged patron of pioneering artistic institutions doing seminal work in experimental education and artistic practices (Nicholas 2007: 1). It was considered to be one of the important pioneers, according to Nicholas, in the field of dance experiments—ranging from classical ballet to modern dances inside and outside the strict realms of Western dance traditions. As per the records available in published books (Nicholas 2007; Punch 1977) as well as archival records available in the well-preserved archives of the Hall itself, it played a seminal part in bringing together and providing support to artistic endeavours spreading across many forms of performance that are dance, theatre, and music, housed both at the Hall premises directly under its own name and also for artistic journeys in different geographies other than at the Hall.

Dartington Hall's support extended to Tagore's Visva-Bharati and Shankar's Uday Shankar India Culture Centre as both were given substantial financial assistance by the Dartington Hall Trust, which facilitated transcultural conversations and cross-fertilisations possible in these two modern institutions in ways that were never experienced within the realms of the performing arts education before. The Elmhirsts along with Beatrice Straight set up the Uday Shankar India Culture Trust in 1939 with the specific intention of encouraging activities related to educational foundations, dance, dancers, films, philanthropy and so on. In the book, *Dancing in Utopia: Dartington Hall and its Dancers*, Larraine Nicholas credits 'the Elmhirsts with a policy towards dance that was unusual or even unique for its time in early twentieth century Britain.... This contrasts with the prevailing lower esteem and visibility of dance in relation to the other arts' (Nicholas 2007: 7). In Nicholas's opinion, the Hall's encouragement towards the building of a newer ecology and environment of dance was a utopic vision that dared to imagine beyond the social and the political constraints of time (Nicholas 2007: 12).

The initiative to extend help towards building Shankar's art institution in Almora was the Elmhirsts' acknowledgement of their admiration for the cultural significance of a colonised country such as India (Fig. 4.1). The patronage extended by Elmhirsts' aided Rabindranath Tagore and Uday Shankar among others to dream of a newer ecology for dance within India. Larraine Nicholas mentions that 'Dartington's open window

Fig. 4.1 Dance demonstration by Madhavan, October 6, 1936, with Shankar and Chekhov standing on the right, Dartington Hall, Chekhov Studio (Photo by Vishnudas Shirali. © Dartington Hall Archive)

on the world was in part founded on an imperial power's confident tendency to absorb and appropriate. Dartington's cultural programme from 1934 until the outbreak of the war did just this by supporting not only Shankar but also a number of European artists displaced by political events (Nicholas 2007: 94). The Dartington Hall papers mention that the Elmhirsts heard about Shankar from Margaret Barr[3] in 1933–1934. The Devon archive records:

> Uday Shankar (1900–1977); Activity- Dancer. Invited to Dartington in 1933 (date possibly 1934) to perform and for a limited period, taught and gave demonstrations before returning to India, where with the assistance of Beatrice Straight, by 1940 he had founded the Uday Shankar India Culture Centre at Simtola, near Almora in the Himalayas. The Centre specialised in training the dancers in the art of concentration, observation, imagination, improvisation, composition and choreography. He devised course for training of a dancer in various related aspects of the performing arts. (Dartington Hall Archives, DS/UK/836, Dates. 1938–)

As per the communication preserved at the Dartington Hall Records, Uday Shankar wrote to Dorothy Elmhirst for the first time in March 1933, requesting her to come and see the performance at the Arts Theatre in London. Shankar also asked in his letter for her advice and help in finding an impresario who could arrange for his performances in other larger public theatres for a larger audience. To this Dorothy Elmhirst's prompt reply was regarding the organisation of his future performances at the Globe Theatre, which she mentioned as one of the largest and best venues in London. Shankar visited Totnes (Dartington Hall) on 1 April 1933, Saturday. As partners in their jointly owned company 'Compagnie Uday Shankar-Danses and Musique Hindoues', Shankar and Boner kept in touch with the Elmhirsts, especially Dorothy and the next few years saw several trips of Shankar's troupe to Dartington Hall. Boner was the manager as well as principal support behind Shankar's endeavours till his introduction to the Elmhirsts.

'Uday Shan-Kar and his Hindu dancers' gave an Open-Air Theatre performance that was illuminated by firelight, on 26 May 1934, on the way back from a world tour, while returning home to India. Shankar's

[3] Margaret Barr, the well-known dancer/choreographer (1904–1991) was born in Bombay (Mumbai). She studied with Martha Graham in New York. In 1930 she joined Dartington Hall as the Dean of Dance.

positioning of the performance by his company of dancers and musicians as traditionally Indian and his already famous status brought a large number of people who were taken by the performance. Shankar's urban cosmopolitan awareness of the Western audience and stagecraft and his ability to incorporate indigenous/regional art practices along with the iconographic representations of the artistic sculptures from the Indian temple art were significant representations and appropriate cultural representations of him as a 'symbolic carriers of nationhood' (Nicholas 2007: 93). His choreography was suitably appropriate for Dartington Hall with its references to the 'authentic' Indian aesthetic, with appropriate and controlled open-ness of choreographic applications of forms that were stylised to be creative and yet remained grounded in a culture-specific impression of the colonised country of reference. The relationship between the Elmhirsts and Uday Shankar grew over time and he returned with his troupe of dancers on 2 June 1936. This time he rented a property named Redworth House from the Arts Department Hall for a month and gave a performance at the Barn Theatre on 14 July 1936. He was invited to Dartington Hall again in 1937 for a series of performances at the Barn Theatre.

Michael Chekhov,[4] the celebrated actor and director of the Chekhov Theatre Studio at Dartington Hall was impressed by the way in which movements that Shankar created were deeply informed by his vision and the interrelationships between the imagery his mind had absorbed from motifs all around him, from existing dance forms, from sculptures, from mythological tales, as well as from the beauty and reality of his surroundings (Sarkar Munsi 2008: 89). After one of Shankar's performances at the Hall in October 1936, Chekhov mentioned that he wished to steal three things from the dancer: First, his rich culture which informed him in whatever he did to create a new dance. Second, his technique, where each point in his body seemed to be permeated with the appropriate emotion and feeling even as he constantly tried to create a new technique of his own for expressing and communicating through movements. Third and

[4] Beatrice Straight had a big role in bringing Michael Chekhov, a political refugee from Moscow and the nephew of Anton Chekhov, to Dartington Hall. His studio opened in 1935 and was active at Dartington Hall till the year 1938 before he relocated to the USA. During Shankar's visit, when he was almost always accompanied by his younger brother Ravi Shankar and his troupe of dancers and musicians, a lot of interactions are noted between Chekhov and dancers such as Zohra Segal, Ravi Shankar, and others.

last, Chekhov wished to steal from Shankar his music, for music permeated his own and his dancers' bodies, and it would be worth the attempt for the Dartington Hall students to have music in their bodies just as Shankar did (Vatsyayan 2003: 97–99).

Shankar's assimilation, processing, and representation of different cultural and social spaces in India created a confluence that brought diverse community performances, ritual celebrations, festivities as well as myths and beliefs together that were communicated through his creative as well as aesthetic representations. His creative flow made the most of the bodily and intellectual capabilities of his dancers. By demonstrating the freedom accorded to each of the individual dancers in the workshops at Dartington Hall, Shankar could emphasise the possibilities of creative ideations and imaginative explorations. During his visits to Dartington Hall, Shankar offered classes and workshops on his creative process in dance. After his first year's successful performance, he travelled with Madhavan, a Kathakali dancer, whose solo dance items as well as his class presentations became extremely popular.

Students were taught eight sets of hand movements, then the permutation and combination of those with head, shoulder, elbow, wrist, arms, torso, waist, and feet, thereby aligning the whole body with the preliminary hand movements. Each possibility was explored in isolation or as an individual structured movement first and then expanded or complicated by recognising and involving other parts of the body. Much later, it seemed like mathematics when we were taught these processes, with us having the right to add individual inputs in the creative dance classes of USICC in Kolkata later, without feeling guilty about mutilating or disrespecting any pre-existing movement. The practice of having the whole orchestra present and innovating with live music in the improvisation classes, also added a boost to the creative process. The clear distinction between reproducing, creating, recreating, and acknowledging the original, was part of the movement making and learning.

Shankar's dance programme consisted of his solo and duet *Shiva-Parvati* with Simkie, and his new choreography *Nritya Dwanda*, in his 1935–1937 trips. His Dartington Hall experience, especially his exposure to Chekhov's technique of teaching theatre classes influenced Shankar heavily. He absorbed Checkhov's pedagogic processes and realised the need for developing his own teaching method. This was also the time that Shankar seems to have started learning a specific dance technique. He met his Kathakali teacher Shankaran Namboodri in 1934, at Kerala Kalamandalam, he invited the Guru to Kolkata and formally started learning from him. It was there that he—in consultation with the Kathakali expert Namboodri, experimented with his solo dance piece *Kartikeya*, and his ballet *Nritya Dwanda* in 1935. The dance vocabulary that developed during and after his Dartington Hall visits finally was formalised into a movement vocabulary. By the time USICC in Almora began its classes, Shankar's basic movement vocabulary had gotten a polished structure, tried and tested in Shankar's experimental workshops and lecture-demonstrations in and outside India (Fig. 4.2).

Those times at Dartington Hall provided clarity to Shankar regarding his pedagogy. At that time he was not seeking concrete finished outcomes or products but revelling in the ability to identify the interim stops in the journey through the movement creation process. Through such exposures and conversations, such as the ones at the Chekhov Studio, one may locate the birth and development of the desire and ability to create

Fig. 4.2 At Dartington Hall Open-Air Theatre, 1936 (Photographer B. Mukherjee. Photo © Legacy Alice Boner, Rietberg Museum. Zurich)

not only a dance grammar but the synthesised idea of creative dance-making. In Zohra's autobiography she writes about the troupe's visit to Dartington Hall in 1936, 'Our hosts, Mr. and Mrs Elmhirst, their beautiful daughter, Beatrice Straight (then a well-known actress in the States), left nothing to be desired. Our whole troupe was installed in a children's school, vacant due to the holidays, and we felt like Goldilocks and the three bears when using their tiny beds, tables and chairs' (Segal 2010: 72).

In Ravi Shankar's recently published biography, Craske writes about this five-month long residency as well, where the troupe worked on new choreographies. He writes, 'Dartington fostered a fertile creative atmosphere. Also present were the modern dance pioneers Kurt Jooss and Sigurd Leeder, who had been given safe haven from Nazi Germany by the Elmhirsts…' (Craske 2020: 65–66). In 1936 Rudolf Laban's dance pageant, choreographed especially for the opening extravaganza of the Berlin Olympic Games at the Dietrich Eckart Stadium, was banned by Goebbels for being insufficiently Nationalist-Socialist in spirit. In 1938 he came as a political refugee to Dartington Hall, as a visitor on several occasions with short term visas. Politically his acceptance by the victims of the Third Reich remains a matter of great speculation. But through all this, Dartington Hall remained a beacon of artistic confluence, trying to continue with its artistic activities and internationalism and transcultural conversations through the years, while world politics grew more toxic with the rise of fascism in Germany and associated socio-political developments.

During this time, Beatrice Straight grew very fond of Uday Shankar. She played a crucial role in creating the funding possibilities through her consistent efforts to establish the India Culture Trust in 1937. Beatrice travelled to India and the Far East, studying dance and drama, at times joining the Uday Shankar Company of dancers and musicians on their tours. She was fourteen years younger than Uday Shankar and was besotted by his charisma like many other women in his life.

Craske describes the tumultuous time it was for Europe. Shankar's troupe was touring many countries in the continent before travelling to America to perform at venues such as the Carnegie Hall in what would be their last coast to coast tour before World War II. On the last day of the American performance season, 12 March 1938, the German army annexed Austria (Craske 2020: 69). The open access to world stage was closing up fast and it was time to explore different experimental methods and material to access the multicultural, multi-locational possibilities. Shankar's institution had the aspiration of becoming his window to the world torn apart by the war. The turn towards developing a pedagogic structure for creative dance at home was something Shankar had been exploring already, and the Dartington Hall and its trustees made it possible.

According to Zohra Segal, Shankar had composed a number of new dances in 1936, during their time at the Dartington Hall, which housed extraordinary talents at that time. She specifically mentions her exposure to the 'Stanislavsky method' in the classes conducted by Michael Chekhov. This and the Mary Wigman technique of Modern Dance, according to Zohra, helped her in formulating the syllabus of the Uday Shankar India Culture Centre in Almora in 1939. The plans for Almora seem to have been born amidst this atmosphere of cultural and political cosmopolitanism, where transcultural conversations were the norm. Shankar was greatly influenced by the range of invitees and activities at the Hall that continued from 1934 till the beginning of the World War II in 1939 (Segal 2010: 72–73).

Towards the Realisation of a Dream: A Modern Institution in Dance

The Dartington Hall played a major role as a patron that offered space to not only Shankar and his company of dancers and musicians, but also to Margaret Barr and her School of Dance-Mime (for a short while), Kurt Jooss and his company, and Michael Chekhov for teaching theatre in a dedicated studio space. From Shankar's first visit there in 1934 with his troupe till the formal opening of the USICC in Almora, Shankar's assignment as a teacher at the Dartington Hall dance school was the precursor to his returning for several years to the Hall to plan for the Centre he wanted to set up as well as for creating dance choreographies and performing for the niche audience that the Hall ensured. Most writings on Shankar's tryst with Dartington Hall and the imagination of his dream institution concentrate on the failure and short-lived experiment with USICC. Reports and letters between the Elmhirsts and Boshi Sen,[5]

[5] Boshi and Gertrude Sen, are important links between the Elmhirsts and Indian cultural developments in the late colonial times. Closely connected to Jawaharlal Nehru, Indira Gandhi, Rabindranath Tagore, and Uday Shankar, he acted as the link between the

an agricultural scientist, who was the point of contact for financial as well the administrative links between the two institutions in the UK and India, have been referred to by most writers. Interestingly, the Dartington Hall archives also store a priceless collection of crucial reports, newsletters, and letters that note the non-administrative side of the USICC, Almora, that offers a basis for analysis of the curricula, ensemble work, and Shankar's pedagogy of creative dance. The Hall's commitment to alternate forms of education as well as the Elmhirsts' reputation, in my opinion, needs more of a discussion in and for itself, rather than being dismissed as 'elite fascination' (Vertinsky and Ramachandran 2018: 294). It may be easy to group together Shankar's patrons and audiences from multiple countries over fifteen years as uninformed enthusiasts from Europe and America, but is problematic to describe this reception of Shankar's performance from the mid-1920s till the time in the late 1940s when he created his film *Kalpana*, as just a singular form of reception i.e. naïve admiration, from an audience in search of 'exotic popular entertainment' (ibid.).

As the writer of recent and detailed documentation of the USICC, Almora, Sonal Khullar in her essay on Almora sums up the seriousness of the endeavour as:

> *The Rhythm of Life* and *Labour and Machinery* addressed contemporary political and social issues, and departed from the 'Hindu ballets' for which Shankar had become famous in Europe and the United States during the 1920s and '30s. They marked not only a distinct phase of his career, but also a turning point in the history of the performing arts in India. Drawing insights from everyday life, folk and tribal performances, and modernist art, the Uday Shankar India Cultural Centre expanded Shankar's repertoire beyond Hindu mythology and Orientalist fantasy and laid the foundation for modern and contemporary dance in India. (Khullar 2018: 15)

Shankar's process of dance-making and pedagogy travelled a long way during his lifetime. Almora is perhaps one of the ways to understand the effort that went into this journey. It would also be helpful to understand the collaborative effort contributed by the collective of

Elmhirsts and many of the efforts they funded in India in the first half of the twentieth century. The couple were greatly influenced by Swami Vivekananda's teachings and had established an Agricultural research institute for sustainable farming in the hills of Almora, in the Himalayas, that later became the Vivekananda Parvatya Krishi Anusandhan Sansthan (The Vivekananda High Altitude Agricultural Research Centre).

musicians, vocalists, dance masters, and the students and professional dancers of the troupe apart from Shankar himself. The collaborative planning and development of the institution-building project with the owners of Dartington Hall appears to be one of the most important stages in Shankar's life. In this stage one sees the consolidation of his teaching process along with the development of a method of transmission of his ideas that he wanted to imbibe into his dancers/students through his own institution. This period is markedly different also in terms of Shankar's choreographic experiments. His focus clearly shifted from his earlier fascination and obsession with the reproduction/aestheticisation of community dances and choreographies influenced by temple sculptures, myths, and celestial figures. From the list of choreographies that were created post-1935, it is clear that his dance began to respond to real-life imageries and different human conditions. His movement repertoire became nuanced with socially constructed references that were based on class, caste, and gender on the one hand, while becoming increasingly politically nuanced through the expression of experiences of power relations as well as the understanding of work and labour on the other hand. In the years preceding the finalisation of the plans for the USICC, Uday Shankar was invited often to perform with his troupe of dancers and musicians and teach at Dartington Hall. The Hall records mention shows at the Barn Theatre on 14 July 1936 and 22 October 1937. The business contract between Shankar and his business partner, manager, and one time mentor Alice Boner was dissolved in 1939, after which Beatrice Straight, and Leonard and Dorothy Elmhirst began funding the activities of the USICC in Almora via the Elmgrant Trust with a contribution of £25,000. The Dartington Hall papers (No. DS/UK/836) mention that:

> The school's aims were to train young Indian dancers and musicians in the traditions of folk forms of Indian culture. It was successful for five years until Shankar became interested in making a film, which the Elmgrant Trust[6] did not fund as it was considered to be outside the interest to the original agreement. In February 1944 Shankar closed the school without consulting the Trust. A reorganisation committee for the school was set

[6] The Elmgrant Trust was established in the November of 1936 by Dorothy and Leonard Elmhirst and Dorothy's daughter, Beatrice Straight. This new charitable trust was intended to further the objectives of the Dartington Hall Trust by making grants to individuals and organisations whose work and institutions were supported by the Dartington Hall Trust. One of its first projects was to extend funds to the USICC, Almora.

up in 1944 with Uday on its board in the hope of re-settling the school elsewhere. In 1954 LKE[7] persuaded Uday to resign as a Trustee.

The Grand Plan: The Uday Shankar India Culture Centre

One review of Shankar's performance at the Majestic Theatre, by John Martin[8] on 14 February 1937, in the New York Times, is yet another glimpse of the multiple ways in which the west itself saw these dances in connection to the artistic practices that it was familiar with. Martin writes:

> When the final curtain falls tonight, if indeed it should actually prove to be final, he (Shan-kar) will have succeeded in this his third American season in drawing virtually capacity houses in fourteen performances. But he will, no doubt, have little inclination for such backward glances as this, however, for he has something to look forward to which makes such passing success seem picayune. (Martin 1937: 8)

This particular piece of writing by Martin is important as it actually gives us another bit of news about the discussions around the establishing and patronage of the Uday Shankar India Culture Centre that seem to have been underway when this was written. Martin also wrote about Shankar's plans for opening the Centre, supposedly, in Varanasi. He wrote:

> He is to abandon his schedule of world tours and establish in Benares an all-India Center of Hindu Arts.... A staff of Hindu teachers will be engaged for the school, which will admit Occidental pupils and expeditions will be formed to travel to untrodden parts of India with sound and motion picture equipment for gathering regional dance and rhythms...
>
> The building which he hopes to obtain for the Center is a Maharajah's palace on the outskirts of the city, which has never been occupied except

[7] Leonard Elmhirst (LKE) held Uday Shankar's creative abilities and his capabilities at a very high esteem. Even after the disappointment that Shankar's whimsical and irresponsible act of leaving Almora Centre in 1944 brought to this family who had put their trust on him. Shankar left without making any arrangements or informing anybody, yet Leonard Elmhirst's file records show that he waited for Shankar to again start the Centre at some new place.

[8] John Martin's reviews create a documentation of Shankar's dance journey diligently through the 1930s and even later, especially at tours organised by Sol Hurok.

> for private performances and has been abandoned for even that purpose for several years. It was formerly known as Palace of Pleasure, a name which Shan-kar will change into Temple of the Dance… (Martin 1937: 8)

The review also mentions the involvement of the Elmhirsts and their already ongoing patronage of Kurt Jooss and many other important companies of dance and music. A strong backing can be sensed in the way Martin portrays Uday Shankar's efforts to revive and restore 'Hindu' art, in spite of the way he has been 'damned by certain purists among his fellow country-men, who would rather see the art die out entirely than be adapted to theatrical changes' in the article published in the *New York Times* on 14 February 1937. This rather disturbing and repeated reference to 'Hindu / Hindoo' art, and 'Hindu' dance without almost ever mentioning the colonised country that Shankar belonged to, seemed like either an uninformed or a deliberate reference to Shankar's religious identity (to continue with the Oriental othering) used interchangeably with the geographical space and name of the country that was home for the dancer/choreographer. One needs to note that Shankar's choice to move away from the specific mention of 'Hindu' was evident for the first time when he chose to name his Centre 'Uday Shankar India Culture Centre' while its registration, discarding the 'Hindu' tag finally.

John Martin, also sure of his readers in the dance world of the West, further wrote that Shankar had not brought 'pedantry and dryness into his stage material' but 'there is ample testimony from eminent Hindu scholars that he can meet his purist antagonists in their own ground and defeat them'. In the concluding section of the review John Martin expresses concern over lack of similar patronage for American dance and throws a question at the readers, 'An all-America Center of the dance arts, why not, indeed!' (Martin 1937: 8).

This and many other press coverages and reviews published in different parts of the world (*The Penang Gazette–The Strait Times* of 27 August, 1938; *Western Morning News*, Plymouth of 22 November 1937; *The Illustrated Weekly of India* of 29 May 1938) that talk about the USICC through the time of its planning and materialisation need a specific discussion on the far-reaching impact of the vision of the institution in the colonised land of India. This vision clearly was energised by the idea of engaging with pedagogy, restoration, and documentation; with traditional knowledge systems as well as modern explorations of the arts in general and dance in particular. The enthusiasm around the Centre seemed to have been marked by a possibility of a practice-based intervention in the Indian embodied practices that would be significant for the world of art internationally, especially with the involvement of the British/American patrons as well as entrepreneurs. The Centre may have been proposed to project, encourage, and teach Indian art, but it brought to the world a certain weightage to the idea of supporting the survival, restoration, experimentation and transmission of knowledge both for traditional and modern arts. Thus, the idea of the USICC, often under-acknowledged and summarily dismissed as an over-ambitious, insignificant, and short-lived grand plan only, may be seen as one of the key areas of the consolidation of Shankar's idea of transnational artistic collaborations that opens our analytical frame to his modernist understanding about the transmission of knowledge.

The decision on the finalisation of space for the Centre seems to have happened in consultation with Beatrice Straight, within the period between 30 August 1938 (according to a *Times of India* report on the arrival of Beatrice Straight on that date titled 'Proposed Indian Art Centre') and 22 September 1938 (according to a report published in the daily newspaper *The Hindu* titled 'The National Art Centre at Almora: Mr. Udai Shankar's Appeal to the Govt'). Beatrice Straight's role as a well-wisher and patron did not waiver even after the waning of the romantic involvement between Shankar and her that began with her introduction to Shankar around 1936 and lasted only for a few years but gave birth and life to the idea of the Centre. Zohra Segal, in her autobiography *Close-Up: Memoirs of a Life on Stage and Screen* (2010) writes about travelling to Almora with Beatrice and Shankar one autumn morning in 1938. According to her, they were charmed by Almora's quiet beauty and the visibility of Mount Kailash from the slope where the proposed Centre was going to be built. Govind Ballabh Panth allotted ninety-four acres of land at Simtola in Almora for Shankar's Centre. To begin with, Shankar rented a number of cottages from the owners of the estate named Ranidhara on the designated slope. A large room was built as the Assembly Hall and the main classroom which had a panel of glass on one side. One side of this room could be turned into a stage with the help of Hessian curtains. The audience would sit on the ground for many performances that would happen in this space. This convertible studio theatre was built on a slope, levelling it to make dressing rooms and class rooms below (Segal 2010: 76–90).

The publicity brochure containing the announcement for the starting of the Almora School is available at the Dartington Hall Records. The brochure titled 'Uday Shankar's Project for an Art Centre in India' begins with a well-known letter from Rabindranath Tagore, where Tagore welcomes Shankar 'home', while acknowledging the laurels he has acquired around the world. Tagore sends this letter as an acknowledgement of Shankar's artistic capability and his achievement as a dancer. He writes:

> Before you bid good-bye to the ashram, there is one thing I would like to tell you. There is no bounds to the depth or to the expansion of any art which, like dancing, is the expression of life's urge. We must never shut it within the bounds of a stagnant ideal, nor define it as either Indian or oriental or occidental, for such finality robs it of its life's privilege which is freedom. You have earned yourself rich praise from the connoisseurs of the art in many lands and yet I know you feel deep within your heart that the path to the realisation of your dream stretches long before you where new inspirations wait for you and where you must create a limitless field of new forms of living beauty. Genius is defined in our language as the power that unfolds ever new possibilities in the revelation of beauty and truth. It is because we are sure of your genius that we hope that your creations will not be mere imitations of the past nor burdened with narrow conventions of provincialism. Greatness in all its different manifestations has discontent for its guide in the path to victory where there is triumphant arches, but never to stop at, but to pass through.
>
> There was a time when in the heart of our country, the flow of dance followed a buoyant life, Through passage of time that is nearly choked up, leaving us bereft of the spontaneous language of joy, and exposing stagnant pools of muddy impurities. In an unfortunate country where life's vigour has waned, dancing vitiates into catering for diseased mind that has lost its normal appetites, even as we find in the dance of our professional dancing girls. It is for you to give it health and strength and richness. The spring breeze coaxes the spirit of the woodlands into multifarious forms of exuberant expression. Let your dancing, too, wake up that spirit of spring in this cheerless land of ours; let her latent power of true enjoyment manifest itself in exultant language of hope and beauty. (Khokar 1983: 75)

What makes the letter significant is that it also records Tagore's acknowledgement of Shankar's work, which may also have been the main reason behind a subsequent offer from Tagore to bring Shankar to Santiniketan to consolidate the pedagogical structure for teaching dance and movement there. In a preserved article at the Dartington Hall Archives, named 'Reawakening of India's Classical Dance' by Uday Shankar, published in the *Illustrated Weekly of India* dated 30 June 1935, Tagore's son, Rathindranath Tagore's handwritten note on the margin of the article says, 'Couldn't this Centre be established at Santiniketan? I shall also try to see him and induce him to do it, Rathi'[9] Incidentally this Article published in the *Illustrated Weekly* is available as a documentation of Shankar's vision of an all-India centre for dance after his introduction to the Elmhirsts of Dartington Hall. One finds further elaboration and finally, a detailed structure proposed for the Centre that got planned with the promise of support from Dartington Hall in another article by M.H. Brown titled 'Save India's Dances from Decay: Need of All-India Centre' in the *Illustrated Weekly of India* dated 29 May 1938,[10] which actually mentions concrete plans for the Centre in Almora by Shankar indicating the consolidation of the plans after over three years of negotiations between the Elmhirsts, Shankar, and the other concerned people. The article says:

> There is, however, a crying need for an all-India organisation with a leader known to the whole country; a man who can also enjoy powerful support for his schemes.
>
> Such a person is Uday Shankar, whose work I have already quoted and who is due to return to India after his visit to Java and Bali. His company has already returned. He has proved by his own work and his capacity to draw a crowd in any town in India, that he has now both the experience and the popular support essential for such a job as an all-India dance centre. (Brown 1938: 16–17)

From M.H. Brown's writings it becomes evident that Shankar had at this point explored all possibilities as well as requirements for setting up such an organisation. Brown wrote that along with the teaching of dance there would also be documentation and research facilities at the Centre, as there was an urgent need for creating an archive and a documentation Centre that would also archive information on music, musical instruments, costumes, ornaments, mythology, drawing, and painting. Brown continues to say that:

[9] Part of Leonard Elmhirst's papers, Dartington Hall Collections, Devon Archive.

[10] Part of Leonard Elmhirst's collection, Dartington Hall Collections, Devon Archive.

> The plans that Mr. Shankar has considered would produce a much more accomplished type of dancer than is common today. For example, he believes that a dance student should have a thorough knowledge of literature and art, as well as of music. A musician should be able to make his instrument as well as play it and a dancer should be able to paint and draw. Of course to study dancing thoroughly, it would be necessary to send researchers about the country, to study local dance forms, collect legends, obsolete musical instruments, and other material which would throw more light on the evolution of this art. (Brown 1938: 16–17)

Principally put forth as the larger aim of establishing a centre like this, these ideas helped plan the curriculum of the centre, but did not mean to deviate the centre's goal from its main aim of teaching the pure forms of dances from different parts of India. The initial plan was that Shankar would establish a residential centre that would offer courses for three to ten years. Shankar's vision was put forth by Brown to highlight the additional idea to provide patronage to the best dance companies of excellent and well-trained individual dancers who would tour within and outside India. This plan took for granted both the coming of students from within India and different foreign countries to USICC, Almora, and also the possibility of then reaching the audiences in the East and the West with the dance productions that the performing troupe would be creating in Almora. Nobody can say what would have happened had World War II not started when it did. Though Shankar's utopic dreams were given a shape and also got to be seen as a solid physical as well as conceptual endeavour, one of the reasons for its inherent instability was the situation of the world at that particular time.

According to the biographical book on Boshi Sen and his wife, *Nearer Heaven than Earth: The Life and Times of Boshi Sen and Gertrude Emerson Sen* (2007), Boshi Sen introduced Shankar to the Elmhirsts when he approached them with the idea of the institution that was in his mind. By then Beatrice Straight had fallen in love with Shankar and was hoping to marry him one day. She was already an established actress of some repute and had become impressed by Shankar's stage appearance and his artistic vision. The Elmhirsts and Beatrice Straight sought contributions from people who would become associate members of the centre by making payments of certain fixed membership fees. From what is quoted as a section of Boshi and Gertrude's letter to the Elmhirsts in the same book, their expectations from and their understanding of the institution become very clear. Overawed by the scope of a near-utopic idea Boshi and Gertrude Sen wrote, 'There, among the eternal snows, is the home of Siva, India's god of dance. And it is within sight of the snows that India's premiere dancer of today, Uday Shankar, has lately founded at Almora, a school of dance and music, known as the Uday Shankar India Culture Centre' (Mehra 2007: 533).

The prospectus for Almora was finalised two years after the actual opening of the USICC. The document stored at the Dartington Hall Trust Archive mentions the illustrious patrons and support group for this centre as a varied group of people, starting with the Principle Trustees of Dartington Hall in Devonshire, Mr. and Mrs. Leonard Elmhirst. Alice Boner continued to be a part of this endeavour, as well, till 1939. Also among the prominent patrons were Mr. Whitney and Daphne Straight, Sir William Rothenstein, Rabindranath Tagore, Romand Rolland, Leopald Stokowski, Sir Chinubhai Madhavlal Ranchhodlal, Michael Chekhov, Jawaharlal Nehru, Sir Firozkhan Noon, and John Martin. Brown's article, on the other hand, identifies the source of principle support to be from:

> .... the great company of people of India; men and women who over and over again have encored the Shankar company. The Men and women who have proved that their country's dances are near their hearts and have thus demonstrated that the time is ripe for putting such dances on a permanent basis so that they may be inherited by their children and their children's children'. (Brown 1938: 16–17)[11]

The Vision and the Structure: A Multi-Art Institution

The Centre got the name the 'Uday Shankar India Culture Centre', and not the 'Uday Shankar India Cultural Centre', as it has been mistakenly mentioned in some articles in the past.[12] Dartington Hall's publicity

[11] M.H. Brown 'Save India's Dances from Decay: Need of All-India Centre' in the Illustrated Weekly of India (May 29, 1938: 16–17).

[12] A very common mistake that has been recurrent is getting the name of the Centre wrong. The correct name is 'Uday Shankar India Culture Centre' and not 'Uday Shankar India Cultural Centre' as is mentioned in Sonal Khullar's recent article 'Art and Life at the Uday Shankar India Cultural Centre' (2018), in the journal MARG. This article is a very important addition to the documentation on Shankar with all its photos and sketches from a private collection.

brochures announced Shankar's imminent return from his second tour of America in 1938 and his opening of a unique organisation that would be equipped to carry on explorations and research in music, costumes, mythology, stage craft, scenography, lights, sound, props and other performance aids, along with dance, to encourage young people to learn performance practices as philosophy, work, and profession. The choreographic processes that had shaped his experiences in different parts of Europe and America now were incorporated into the curriculum that was developed in consultation with his chief patrons at Dartington Hall.

Reproduced below are sections of the text from the brochure carrying the date October 29, 1941—as it gives us important insights into the actual format of teaching, along with the means and aims of artistic education. The brochure also strengthens our argument for an evaluation of Shankar's vision as a modernist one. The endeavour involved an international collaboration, detailed and prolonged trans-local planning, and a well-developed and ambitious idea consisting of different levels of expertise. The brochure was signed at the bottom by M. G. Hallet, Governor of United Provinces, signifying clearly the interest and involvement of the state administration, at least, at the inception of this modern institution. The beginning of the three paged document (Brochure of Uday Shankar India Culture Centre, October 29, 1941, Dartington Hall Records, LKE/IN/19) reads:

> ***Uday Shankar India Culture centre - Almora, U.P.***
> *After two years of work with the students, the Centre has been able to test and verify the method of instruction and to readjust, where necessary, this method to the requirements for achieving the ideals and aims to which it aspires. The student performance in Naini Tal last summer, and their praiseworthy work in the Ram Leela shadow-play during the Durga Puja celebrations at the Centre, their experience in helping to make masks, costumes, clay models, artistic articles of various kinds for our exhibition, substantiate the belief that a dancer becomes a better dancer if his or her background consists of music, painting, sketching, theoretical study combined with actual practice and work on the stage.*

The document also includes a section on the newly added Manipuri curriculum under Guru Amobi Singh mentioned as 'one of the few remaining exponents of the old school who still preserves the true tradition in this style of dancing':

> ***First Year:*** *Angabhangi*[13] *– exercises and correct movements of the fingers, hands, neck, eyes and body.* ***Second Year:*** *Dance with songs, depicting the meaning in gestures and mudras*[14] *with full facial expressions.* ***Third Year:*** *Revision. Lasya*[15] *style; dances of the Gopinis; Rasa.* ***Fourth Year:*** *Tandava*[16] *Dance: Dance of Krishna.* ***Fifth Year:*** *Leharoba, Naga Dance, Sool Dance*[17] *etc. Final polishing of the whole technique.*

The brochure acts as a report as well as a vision statement in reporting about the newly staged shadow play *Ram Leela*:

> *Episodes from the Ramayana were first staged at the Centre in September 1941, and presented in the form of a shadow-play, projected on a huge white screen. The Puja and the performances take place in the open, on the mountain slope just outside the Centre grounds, where nature has provided a large amphitheatre amidst wonderful surroundings.*
>
> *The success of the Ram Leela was great and the attempt to bring art through this form of celebration to the masses proved most gratifying. The words of the story sung in the background and amplified by means of a loudspeaker made it possible for everyone to follow the play.*

[13] A range of movements of the body, for increasing the mobility and coordination between different body parts.

[14] Mudras are specific hand gestures used for aesthetic enhancement or expressive narrations of specific meanings in dance. Often acting as symbolic and codified patterns of communication specific to particular dance forms, mudras are the gestural language that is an intrinsic part of dance grammars. Neo-classical dances, have developed a set of mudras as a process of classicisation in which a certain amount of similarity is now noticed between totally different dance forms from different parts of India. This is though to be the result of the overarching importance given to Natyashastra as a driving text that has acted as the principle structure of formalisation for all the dance forms that are now included in the list of classical dances.

[15] Lāsya is the form of dance associated with women. It is believed to have been danced by Siva's consort Parvati, and then taught by her to Usha, the daughter of a sage.

[16] According to the Natyashastra chapter 4, *Tandava* refers to a specific rigorous form of dance that is believed to have been created by Taṇḍu after receiving instructions from Shiva.

[17] Different regional dances.

The vision of the centre clearly propagated an inclusive secular approach, specifically mentioning the multicultural atmosphere with many nationalities and castes (Fig. 4.3). It also emphasised on building of a centre for Research and an archive:

> *In order to make it possible to inaugurate a fully equipped department to work in the near future on music, costume, history and development of dances, the practical interpretation of texts on dance, drama, music, and allied subjects, the Centre has started collecting materials to form a museum, a picture gallery and a well equipped library. Any donations of books, art objects, manuscripts, and costumes, will be deeply appreciated. The cooperation of societies and private individuals working along similar lines, will also be gratefully welcomed.*

The document provides an idea about the interest it generated in the new institution in the cultural elite of India:

Fig. 4.3 An outdoor movement demonstration by the members of performing troupe including Zohra Segal and Narendra Sharma USICC, Almora (© Narendra Sharma Archives)

> *Many important persons have visited the centre in the past two years.... a few of them may be mentioned: His excellency Sir Maurice G. Hallett, Governor of the United Provinces, His Highness the Maharajah Gaekwar of Baroda, Sir Harry Haig, the former Governor of the united provinces, pandit Govind Ballabh Pant, Seth Jamnalal Bajaj, Mrs Vijaya Lakshmi Pandit, Sir Chinubhai Madhowlal Ranchhodlal, Mr. K. M. Munshi, Mr. N. C. Mehta, and Dr, Panna Lal.*

The brochure ends with a message from Sir M. G. Hallett, Governor of the United Provinces, who noted the presence of at least ten thousand people as audience.

> *GOVERNOR'S CAMP, United Provinces, October 29, 1941.*
> *'During my visit to Almora this year I have once again had the great pleasure of seeing performances at the Uday Shankar India Culture Centre.... They [students] have all reached a very high standard, and there were several of the pupils who will be worthy successors of their master. On the second occasion we saw a story from Ramayana depicted as a shadow-play.*

Glimpses of Activities at the USICC

The *USIC Centre News*, dated 13 May 1940, carried an Editorial titled 'Creative Urge'. It read:

> Creative act emerges out of the casual, ordinary and humdrum life of ordinary existence. Independent of the social, logical and the political laws, it stands out as a marvel, a tremendous force of spontaneous urge, resplendent in its originality....
>
> The Centre supplies the stimulus by its regulated and studied method of training, to afford scope for the creative urge to function; it equips the body with the language through which the exuberance of emotion can be brought to aesthetic fruition. (USIC Centre News, Vol. 2. No. 13. 13 May 1940, p. 1)

One of the descriptions regarding the classes that Shankar conducted at Dartington Hall comes from Ravi Shankar's Bengali article 'Amar Dada: "Kalpanar" Raja', meaning 'My Brother: the king of imagination' (Ravi Shankar 2000: 44–53). According to him, each hour-long class was filled with enthusiastic students. The musical improvisation along with the same in dance, on themes, techniques, and ideas made it a space for creativity and also inter-art dialogue. These classes were started as one of the most important parts of the daily schedule in Almora. One of the best imaginative and experimental classes by Shankar was described by Ravi Shankar, where Shankar had asked all the students to close their eyes and feel the ground with their hands. Instead of simply feeling the hard floor under their hands, he asked them to imagine the floor as water and then slowly to think that the hands were immersed in the water, which was sometimes cold and sometimes hot. Introducing the dancers to the world of imagination, he then asked them to imagine different paces, surfaces, and circumstances in which their bodies needed to move in and react to. Ravi Shankar emphasised that Shankar's work with the students would never start with imitation of the movements he created for them to follow, instead he was always pushing them to react to some ideas, or imageries, all the while trying to create an understanding of weight, speed, and proximity in them. Ravi Shankar's acknowledgement of this method in the words 'Oh, it was so mesmerising' (Ravi Shankar 2000: 53), is also repeated in some of the commentaries by the guests, whose writings were published in the *USIC Centre News*.

Ravi Shankar as well as Zohra mention an encounter with romanticism as well as harsh everyday reality in Shankar's works. Similarly simplistic and stark realism as well as magical surprises were parts of his stagecraft. While Ravi Shankar stressed the presence of classicism in his choreography, Amala Shankar talked about an artistic temperament alongside a grounded professionalism in his approach towards dance and dancing bodies, both on and off stage. A detailed review of Shankar's classroom techniques at the USICC would give us the opportunity to prove this point. He consolidated his technique using the knowledge he had acquired from his personal experience of choreography, performance, technique, stagecraft, and showmanship. He also drew from his experiences with Michael Chekhov of Dartington Hall and Zohra Segal (who had acquired her expertise from Mary Wigman), as well as from traditional forms of dance that he had become acquainted with in the course of his journey though India. There were music classes and classes on Indian art traditions, in addition to compulsory training for students in classical dance. The routine followed at the Almora Centre, given below, provides us with an interesting insight into Uday Shankar's legacy. It also provides us with the academic tools needed to describe the trajectory of the development of Shankar's dance technique in the history of modern dance in India.

A daily routine, rigorous and innovative at the same time, was followed at the Centre:

> The day started with breakfast at 8:00 a.m.
> **8:30 a.m.** General class—walking, rhythm, musical consciousness, clapping, general body awareness for concentration and coordination. Attendance to this class was compulsory for students and all troupe members.
> **10:00 a.m.** A class on Technique—Dance and Music.
> **11:30 a.m.** Classical dance—Bharatanatyam, Kathakali, Manipuri.

Post lunch:

> **3:30 p.m.** Theory—Aesthetics, Psychology, and Literature
> There was a break for games in the evening after which the classes resumed at 7 p.m.
> **7:00 p.m.** Improvisation/Composition—attended by all teachers, students, and troupe members. This was the time when Uday Shankar sat with a drum in the centre of the class, and played different rhythms, and the participants had to improvise. Zohra, Narendra Sharma, Amala Shankar recalled this part of the classes extremely fondly as this was a space where many new individual experimentations and ideas could be shared.'

For the troupe members all day long rigorous rehearsals and other work such as costume-making were mandatory. The Centre conducted classes for eight months in the year and the troupe travelled all over India and abroad with its repertory for four months in the winter. The training was essentially meant to teach students how to develop their own system of bodily movements and evolve their own dance aesthetics, rather than teach them complete dances. At the end of each month, students would present a programme that comprised of twenty to twenty-five items. The Centre had one annual performance in October. Throughout the training course, a lot of emphasis was laid on the all-round personality development of the performer through cooperation and teamwork.

The archival records, anecdotes of Amala Shankar, the autobiography of Zohra Segal (2010), her recorded interviews and writings of Narendra Sharma (2004) were helpful for me to understand life and work at

USICC. Of great help was of course Mohan Khokhar's writings (2001) as an administrator at Almora. My analysis is also aided by the embodied understandings (both strength and weakness) of the form and its pedagogical structure. Sonal Khullar's article, 'Almora Dreams: Art and Life at the Uday Shankar Indian Cultural Centre' (2018), the video recording made by Chandroday Ghosh (2003) at a Workshop on Uday Shankar's style facilitated by Amala Shankar, Narendra Sharma and Anadi Prasad, (with many of us from USICC Kolkata as participants) at the Paschim Banga Rajya Sangeet Academy[18] are also the sources I have referred to for the reconstruction of the classes and techniques.

Classes and Pedagogy[19]

The USICC brought together traditional master teachers, such as Guru Kandappa Pillai who was also Balasaraswati's teacher (from Tamil Nadu for Bharatanatyam), Guru Amobi Singh (from Manipur, for teaching dances from Manipur), and Guru Shankaran Namboodiri (from Kerala for teaching Kathakali) at Almora. Ustad Allauddin Khan, the renowned Sitar maestro was in charge of the Music department. Among many musicians who came together at the institution were Ali Akbar Khan (Ustad Allauddin Khan's son), Vishnudass Shirali (who was one of Shankar's music composers for a large part of his career), and Ravi Shankar (youngest brother of Uday Shankar) who became a world-renowned sitarist, in his own rights, later. About the beginning Zohra wrote:

> When the school open in March 1939, it had about ten students: Indian parents being wary of the stigma attached to dancing, most of them were on scholarships. But as the year went by and we toured India with our second ballet *Labour and Machinery* (Depicting the hold of Machine over Man) the Culture Centre gained great popularity. We had dancers from all over India, belonging to the most illustrious families, flocking at Almora, despite its inaccessibility, including two of Mrs. Vijaya Lakshmi Pandit's daughters. We also held short summer courses for teachers and college

[18] West Bengal State Academy for Dance and Music.

[19] Shankar's classes on improvisation were remembered by Narendra Sharma (Personal interview, Delhi, 2004, and Video documentation of the Paschim Banga Rajya Sangeet AcademyWorkshop on Uday Shankar's Style with Amala Shankar, Anadi Prasad, and Narendra Sharma, 2003) in vivid details.

students who are otherwise unable to attend the schedule of classes. (Segal 2010: 89–90)

Zohra also recorded the presence of a large number of female students that made the Centre a very different place than the Kerala Kalamandalam and more similar to the liberal modern educational institution, Visva-Bharati founded by Rabindranath Tagore. Zohra Segal's accounts of the Centre included several specific names, among them Amala Nandi (later Shankar), Zohra's sister Uzra Mumtaj (later Butt), Lakshmi and Saraswati Shastri, and Simkie are the prominent female names. As mentioned elsewhere, each of these women, including Zohra played a very significant part in the teaching or troupe activities or both. Looking back, the very idea of the notion of a residential institution, specifically imagining such an art-based curriculum and training, far away from the cities, and not banking on the traditional Gurukul[20] systems that Indian informal artistic education knew and was familiar about seems like a completely utopic space, and something much before its time. The USICC was definitely not aspiring to project or adhere to a completely traditional learning system though it was built with the structure of Kerala Kalamandalam, an institution established in 1930 following the model of the Gurukul system, in Kerala. Shankar saw Kalamandalam[21] as one of the successful role models but wanted the USICC to focus on a rather idealistic synthesis of traditional art-based education and modern institutions such as Visva-Bharati University. The uniqueness of Shankar's institution soon made it popular and new students, both male and female, joined from different family backgrounds, with different mother tongues, and religions.

Students came from different regions within South Asia, and there were a few Europeans among them as well. The idea of an inclusive

[20] Many of the traditional art practices and their learning process involved a constant commitment from the master teacher (guru) as well as the student (shishya). In this system widely known as guru-shishya *parampara* (tradition), the learning process required the student to stay with the teacher at his/her residence, or a monastery or a specifically designated residence by the Guru and offer services to the household and do other work while learning the art. In Gurukuls knowledge was transmitted orally. This education system was available for higher caste male students, with very few exceptions.

[21] Kerala Kalamandalam was started in 1930 by the Poet Vallathol Narayana Menon as a public institution for teaching the traditional performing arts of Kerala Kathakali, Kutiyattam, Mohiniyaattam, Thullal, and Panchavaadyam, in a Gurukul based educational system. Till date it continues to be one of the premier residential institutions of international repute.

institution, of multiple religions, languages, economic classes, and educational backgrounds was concretised. As discussed earlier in this chapter, the finalised name of the institution suggests Shankar's distancing himself and his art (as a pedagogue) from the complexities that were inherited through the previous history of simplistic use of terms such as 'Hindu'/ 'Hindoo'. Orientalist implications that suited the marketability of Uday Shankar's touring company from the late 1920s, possibly got over-written due to newer secular consciousness and aspirations. I would want to read a certain conceptual re-adjustment in this clear shift. The claim to the geographically specific cultural space rather than an ethno-religious identity helped create a secular environment that he wanted for his Centre, as a place to encourage and initiate a range of modernistic artistic expressions.

Shankar's pedagogy was in itself a training in experimentation, rather than a fixed grammar, and, therefore, it could be fashioned by and for each student. Shankar himself told Narendra Sharma and his other students time and again that they were learning the technique for imagining movements of dance in still images, daily work, the shape of a cloud, a sudden rhythm, and all things that we are surrounded by. It is this imagination of kinaesthesia that Shankar was imbibing or at least trying very hard to encapsulate in his pedagogy. And that certainly did not die with him. Many of his followers carried this in their teachings in their own ways. But of course, when the pedagogy cannot come up with a structure of alphabets, grammar, and identifiable and imitable segments, it has almost no hope of surviving. This expectation of a fixed technique and the construction of a fixed grammar that can be packaged could most probably have been identified as Shankar's grammar of dance, but it would have destroyed his experiment with the human ability to imagine ways of creating and pushing his students into building upon everyday experiences that would help them express ideas through their own kinaesthetic negotiations. The expectation thus cannot and should not be the same as from classical dances which think of perpetuation through a strict grammar. For Shankar, that was never the aspiration. Instead, maybe Almora's experiments need to be seen as exactly what was important for Shankar to teach, if not movement grammar. Zohra summed up the achievement of Shankar as a teacher in her words, 'His own classes were fabulous. It was as if years and years of an artist's visions had come to life, and he was suddenly able to explain his theories about art giving form and articulation to his dreams' (Segal 2010: 86). She mentioned that she and Simkie assisted Shankar in his classes and rehearsals, because of their experience with his particular style of dancing. Zohra was 'given the task of compiling the five-year course' as she had trained in modern dance at the school of the well-known German dancer Mary Wigman. Zohra felt that the training at Wigman's school was very useful, and Shankar told her that he watched her classes to get ideas about teaching. Zohra conducted the classes on basic exercises to activate different parts of the body with specific instructions on beats and steps, neck movements, activities for corrections of postures, with movements around the shoulders, spine, waist, hands, elbows, wrists, and fingers. Often regulated through directions, unlike in classes on innovations and improvisations, Simkie's and Zohra's classes prepared the beginners' bodies for the next stage of learning. Simkie's classes were also to create awareness and connection between rhythms and emotions.

According to Zohra Segal, Shankar taught instinctively. In his own classes he gave structure to a process of creating images of moving by relating to particular moments from everyday lives. This is supported by Shanta Mohan's notes which were used in Khullar's article. Shankar's method was distinguished by his instructions as recorded by Shanta Mohan, 'how to control many movements at the same time, how to relax your mind, how to be active in your mind, and how to feel all the parts of your body. How to rehearse for show—how to imagine yourself and be one of the public and see the effect you are creating—to rehearse with a feeling of the show' (Khullar 2018: 26).

The improvisation classes held in the evenings had a large section on imagining the movement structures and sometimes included 'pieces of pure mime' (Segal 2010: 87) on given themes such as is mentioned by Khullar:

> You are very happy. Dance as you like. Or You can imagine yourself to be M. Gandhi or one of the people who sat around him—you may be a firm believer of non-violence, a hypocrite, a journalist, or a coward, a sneaky sort of man and so on. Act it individually, in duets or in groups if you like. Be very sure of what you do. On another day, Mohan remembers: we were supposed to listen to the music and dance accordingly. (Khullar 2018: 26)

Shankar's discussions on art, and artistic experiments in the west, his own experiences of dance and audience across the world, his ideas of scenography and stagecraft, and also the invited lectures by distinguished guests at the Almora Centre are well documented in the *USIC Centre*

News. The strong reference and respect for the traditional dance idioms in Kathakali, Bharatanatyam, and dances from Manipur were constantly taught simultaneously with a strong emphasis on experimental vocabulary and movement responses to new impulses that Shankar continued to supply in his instructions in his class. The teachings of the three traditional forms mentioned above were compulsory for even the troupe members. The idea was to learn them from the best of experts, to push boundaries of existing vocabularies, and yet not compromise in the renditions of a particular repertoire at all while dancing a particular item from any form.

Zohra also recalled that 'Dada maintained that once a dancer had been trained in his method, he would be able to follow any technique with ease because his system provided the basic technique for all actor-dancers. He invented a whole set of exercises based on the years he had spent in teaching his group-members' (Segal 2010: 86).

In her opinion, Shankar's class exercises were designed 'for complete relaxation and suppleness' so that the body of the dancer became aware of the natural movements that it was capable of producing by pushing the boundaries of each part of the body. For example, one of these realisations began with concentrating on walking normally and then slowly with more stylistic emphasis on different parts of the body, such as with exaggerated hip movements, or by using a larger swing of the hands with the walk. Another example is that of sitting on the ground with the spine straight but loosening the neck muscles and the torso. The instructions then would lead the dancer to move the torso from one side to the other, without stiffening the neck. It takes a totally relaxed torso and a relaxed neck to achieve the natural way the neck actually bends the opposite way of the direction of the torso first, before it follows the torso to the side it has already bent. Instructed grammars of dances, are usually much more rigid, they instruct and expect imitation as the way of imbibing and learning, and remembering each exercise as the base of every experience. Shankar's teaching introduced, like many of the modern forms, the process to move in a certain manner, and left the outcome to a large extent on the dancer to arrive at. Sharma also emphasises Shankar's insistence on developing one's own movements in that experimental space.

Shankar's institution seems to have been built as a space with equal opportunities for both genders, though it did not continue long enough for us to be able to comment on the gendered nature of institutional practices. Following Tagore in his institution building ideas, Shankar built his

Centre away from all the large cities wanting to shape it as a modern institution. He was confident that the already established artistic institutions such as Kalakshetra[22] in Chennai and Kalamandalam in Kerala will have also helped the increase in public confidence in his culturally grounded agenda and parents would allow their wards to join and stay at the residential Centre. His training structure saw a significant role for the women teachers/instructors such as Zohra.

Shankar's consciousness about the gender codes of movements becomes evident in the fact that he used Kathakali as the base for building the repertoire of male movements while drawing heavily from Manipuri for the female ones. Difficult though it is to imagine women from educated upper and middle class families joining a performance troupe in a professional capacity as a dancer, Shankar's troupe had women dancers even before the beginning of his institution in Almora. The institution in Almora saw many women joining the school. It even saw the mother of two sisters, Saraswati and Lakshmi Shastri, coming to stay near the institution to keep an eye on her daughters. Later she joined the Centre in the capacity of Matron, in charge of the women students. As I have already observed in my writings on women dancers in the institutions established by Shankar, the thematic content though never chosen with the intent of portrayal of a strong woman, had great opportunity for female participation. By establishing a troupe consisting of male and female dancers and musical accompanists he contributed significantly in what Tagore had started in his own way, the more or less, non-judgemental acceptance of the new woman professional dancer who does not need the excuse of any religious sanction to be present on stage. These were women who mostly came from middle-class family backgrounds and almost none of them were from traditional performers' families. It is important to mention that a series of marriages took place within the first three years at the USICC, with Shankar marrying Amala, Zohra marrying Kameshwar Segal, Simkie marrying Prabhat Ganguly, Rajendra Shankar marrying Lakshmi Shastri, Debendra Shankar marrying Krishna, and Ravi Shankar marrying Annapurna (Segal 2010: 90).

[22] Kalakshetra, later named Kalakshetra Foundation, was established in Chennai in the year 1936 by Rukmini Devi Arundale and her husband, George Arundale. Kalakshetra specialises in teaching Bharatanatyam and facilitates the research and performance of fine arts.

Walking and Other Techniques

According to most of the people who have had direct experience with Shankar's teaching technique, most of his classes started with a walking exercise. For all his students and members of his troupe, this remained an important technique to introduce dancers to the form that later came to be known as the Uday Shankar style. Zohra wrote that Uday Shankar believed that the aspiring dancers needed to walk properly before they started dancing, and he believed that walking revealed personalities. The walks always started with a natural gait, that would be confident, unaffected, rhythmic (Segal 2010: 87) and the participants were asked to always be mindful of their fellow walkers. One whole hour of any class would be dedicated to these walks that would challenge the dancers in different manners on different days. There were some ground rules to these walks—starting with one's own rhythm and with any one of the foot first, the group of dancers would form a circle, and slowly and steadily work towards following the same rhythm, and coordinate the steps, while maintaining the distance and the circle at the same time. The instructions would be given by Shankar, and the dancer would have to keep on listening and complying. The complicated coordination between the control on rhythm, size of steps, maintaining the distance, and the line in the group, and slowly adding to these steps other movements, hand gestures, body movements, and so forth would turn the walk into a complex movement set, perfectly coordinated as an ensemble movement but not actually taught as such. Such an exercise has been described by Narendra Sharma, as the backbone of Shankar's training, whereby a dancer first learnt to become aware of his/her responsibility as a group member, even before he or she learnt to be a dancer. This process continued as a signature process for Amala Shankar's classes with us after we became teenagers. She also started with the same walking exercise, and one of her main reasons was that this simple process made dancers realise how similar human bodies are in their original movement systems and how similar the movements are when one is taught to pay heed and respond to the impulses of moving, rather than being taught or forced to move by imitating. Zohra Segal described the one hour spent on walking round and round the Studio Hall by all members of the troupe as well as students to the beats of the giant drum as:

> The rhythmic walking would evolve into simple dance steps, reverting once again to natural walking. This would be done alone, in pairs and in groups till the student felt no inhibition in facing a big crowd or occupying a large space. The additions to this walking exercise were always new, keeping the students keyed up to see what would follow. And woe to him who was not all there! For Shankar had an eagle's eye and a psychiatrist's judgement of character. (Segal 2010: 87)

Sonal Khullar's article mentions details from the notebooks of Shanta Mohan, where Mohan had recorded the exercises using the WALK. This excellently documented notebook of Shanta Mohan we get a sense of the exact words that Shankar may have used. As a student of Amala since childhood, in the second life of the USICC (established by Uday and Amala Shankar in Kolkata), I have grown up hearing similar instructions. Therefore, Khullar's contribution in bringing Shanta Mohan's daily notes from the classes is of huge additional importance and historical value, where Shanta Mohan in her diary, has notes she wrote during her class hours in Almora. These detailed instructions given are from classes that used walking as the primary tool. Her diary entries describe steps such as the beginning of the class where all participants had to begin walking naturally in a circle, slowly falling into a unified rhythm. The class then progressed gradually with the instructor adding tasks to the walk, such as adding hand movements, changing rhythms, changing direction of the walk, using hand movements—all the while following instructions keenly.

Amala Shankar gave similar descriptions of classes in Almora, saying that every day there was a surprise waiting for the students and the troupe members in this class. Some days they would be asked to walk as if they were really tired, progressively becoming slower. The hands would have to hang in front while the head hung down with the tired weight bending the body forward from the waist, due to lack of energy. Even while walking so slow, all the participants had to follow the same rhythm, and match steps. This would go on till there was a real sense of tiredness that everyone could portray. Dragging their feet all members of the group put one foot in front of the other. And then there would suddenly be an instruction to slowly change the mode of walking as well as the mood, brighten up, look up as if there was something to hope for. Following instructions, the participants had to act progressively energetic, walk with joy, make a determined sound with their heels and slowly increase the rhythm and pace, always carefully matching steps and rhythm with other fellow participants. Some days the students would be asked to introduce a hop-in-between-steps on a count of 4, clap on one and three, or two and four etc. They would be asked to do specific hand movements to express the lightness that they were walking with and show the feeling of joy in their expression as well. The class would end with very high energy after having started with enactment of dejection and tiredness.

The idea in these classes was to feel individually, self-reflexively, and yet always consciously working at being a part of a group. This was an ensemble-building work, that anticipated movements of the others as dancers learnt to walk, move and react together. The process was to achieve a range of movements that came from the walking itself but were energised by different corporeal states of being. The role of the instructor was crucial. Even while being static and observing he/she was in anticipation and being in the same mental realms with all participants, in a way how the group worked depended on his/her being attuned to them and enabling their concentration. Group feeling was the goal, and it was referred to, again and again.

Describing a progression of movements in a similar class through an entirely different enabling process, Sonal Khullar writes from Shanta Mohan's diary entry dated 9 August 1941:

i. Walk naturally—let the hands work freely—no sound of the heels.
ii. Same rhythm, same step, no sound of the heels, concentrate and keep a smile on your face at all times.
iii. Now keep that and imagine that you have something in your palm, maybe a book, a ball, something to stitch, eat or anything and do accordingly.

Don't forget to concentrate on rhythm, smile, and sound of heel.

iv. Now you have to exchange your things with each other—you have to stop face to face, exchange, tell the person what you are giving him or her, hearing what the other one is giving and then quickly imagine what to do with the thing you got and do accordingly.
v. Now take back all the things that you have given to people—try to remember what thing you exchanged and with whom—take them all back. Return the things which you got from others (Khullar 2018: 25).

Shanta Mohan wrote in her diary, 'Calculate well, be free with your step' (Khullar 2018: 25–26). The training in the Centre indeed was about developing a thinking relationship with every step or body movement or hand gesture that one used or assimilated to create a movement. Not imitating, but actively engaging in constructing and taking charge of the hand gestures, facial expressions, footsteps, covering of space, rhythm, constantly through a repeatable movement segment that one creates in class, is a lot of work and it involves a lot of thinking, calculating ahead, and remembering so that one can create, retain, as well as improve while one repeats what one has created as his/her own movement segment. It requires a different sort of engagement, from a class where one learns to follow and recreate/imitate a movement segment taught to him or her as an unchangeable pre-constructed vocabulary of a classical dance. Khullar mentions that 'Feeling, or expression, was a hallmark of Shankar's pedagogy at the Centre'. She also mentions that according to an entry in Shanta Mohan's Diary on August 16, 1941, Shankar's aim was to reach students: '1. Judgement of spaces'; '2. Balancing the body'; 3. 'Training the eye'; 4. 'Heroic and comic bhavas/expression' (Khullar 2018: 26).

In light of the teachings of Amala Shankar many years later at USICC, Kolkata, this note by Mohan regarding the 'judgement of spaces' signifies one of the first things that one would learn in her class that has stayed with me all my life. Developing an instinct of continuous assessment of allotted space, light and shadows, keeping to one's own allocated zone while doing different body movements, as well as maintaining designated distance or closeness within the ensemble choreography, demanded a lot of coordination. These two ideas of space in the training were both equally important and varied according to the performance venue or medium such as proscenium or shadow performances behind a curtain (see Chapter 5 for details).

Between moving and stopping there are hundreds of micro-moments that one takes care of. Such movements push the boundaries of control or balance while mostly looking effortless or controlled by the dancer at the same time. This dichotomy between reaching the limits of each possibility while being in control and remembering all the micro-moments in the sequence of moving, is possibly what Shanta Mohan's second point of 'balancing the body' means. Another important lesson from Shankar's classes mentioned above, was to 'train the eye' of the dancer. This meant that one needed to become one's own critic or self-reflexive. Observation and reproducing a fellow dancer's innovation was as important as being able to discern critically the problems with someone's (including one's own) movements.

Learning to express a range of different bhavas/expressions was the other important element mentioned by Khullar above. In these sessions, Shankar gave tasks of representing different situations such as a village festival (eventually made into a popular performance item) or a class room (continued to be a part of Shankar's repertoire and eventually was included also in *Shankarscope* in the 1970s). Creating skits and producing performances continued to be a part of Shankar's repertoire, and also was included in *Kalpana*. Some of the popular dance items that were created at the Almora USICC were based on actions and emotions related to a particular kind of work such as village celebrations, harvesting, fishing, hunting, and workers in a mechanised setting of a factory, and so forth. From the imaginations of the class settings, such movement expressions seem to have travelled through many layers of improvisations to finally be choreographed as dances that remained important as Shankar's choreography.

The Centre followed a schedule of a monthly performance as a sum up for the monthly activities of the institution. These performances usually had a big audience present and all the students as well as troupe members looked forward to these events. Zohra mentions, 'Once a month the students prepared a concert all by themselves. Along with some hilarious skits and burlesque items, some remarkable dance pieces emerged from these concerts, namely Narendra Sharma's *Crane Dance* and Kameshwar Segal's *Kathputli* or *Puppet Dance*' (Segal 2010: 87). Zohra's writings give us an idea about the heightened creative atmosphere that led to the choreography of Uday Shankar's first full-length ballet, *Rhythm of Life*, before the winter tour of 1938–1939. This is also the first choreography by Shankar that was not on a mythological theme. It was instead based on an individual's emotions 'symbolically placed in a sociological theme'. The ballet was acknowledged as 'a new experiment on a contemporary theme, that centred around his reactions about the ongoing political situation and his critique of it' (Segal 2010: 88–89). Zohra's writings and the reviews mentioned in the *USIC Centre News* claim this ballet as one of the most popular ones of the decade. The thematic inclusion of the modern concerns of society and the reflections on the times was a new way of engaging with social concerns through dance.

In the second year, *USIC Centre News*, Vol. 2, No. 20, 1940, reports that the troupe had started working on its new performance *Labour and*

Machinery (see also Chapter 3 for details) that was being set to music. As discussed earlier, this landmark production brought in movement explorations that were generated to suit the machine-like movements to depict de-humanised contemporary labour and the embodied tussle between emotive human actions and mindless mechanised moving. The innovative movements created in the experimental space of USICC brought immense praise and accolade to Shankar. It is this production that signified a completely changed movement exploration, where Shankar moved completely away from accepted balletic representation into symbolic mechanised movements of multiple machines working simultaneously in a factory. Besides *Labour and Machinery*, Shankar also worked on two other his choreographies as per the *USIC Centre News* report titled 'Studio News', which were *Kirat Arjun* and *Kama Dahanam*. The report also stated that the troupe was rehearsing four hours a day (*USIC Centre News*, Vol. 2. No. 20, 1940).

The same newsletter also reported the celebration of *Janamashtami*, celebrating the occasion of Krishna's birth. It reads:

> A special feature of the celebration was constituted of speeches on different religions. Vijesekara spoke on Buddhism, Sardar Mohammed on Islam, Sangal on Jainism, Segam on the Radhaswami Sect and Joshi read a few chapters of the Gita. Shanta read a poem eulogising the divine love of Krishna, while Sharma and Sardar Mohammed sang devotional songs. Guru (Shankaran Namboodiri) gave a scene from *Kamsa Vadham*,[23] in the Kathakali style, without costume or make up. Shivaram and Panikar helped him by taking parts in the story. (*USIC Centre News*, Vol. 2, No. 21, 1940, p. 2)

The *USIC Centre News* maintained as a record of the secular and modern structure of the USICC of the Centre's overall emphasis through the pedagogical process. The editorial of *USIC Centre News*, Vol. 2, No. 22, dated 30 September, marks the completion of six and a half months of the Centre's beginning of its teaching course for the first batch of students. It also records in its editorial, the large number of applications seeking admission at the Centre. Though it does not provide details, there is mention of a stringent selection process. The editorial also mentions that as many of the students could not pay the fees, some

[23] The Kathakali episode around the story of killing of *Kamsa*.

of them were chosen on the basis of merit for scholarships that were generously donated by different well-wishers. The first batch of the Centre, thus, had seventeen students out of which five were studying without paying fees, nine students were paying half of the designated fees, and 3 students were paying the full tuition and boarding charges. The editorial also records that there was marked progress in the way the students had started understanding the importance of holding a posture, and could also walk on rhythmic beats. They had also started being able to concentrate and divide their attention to multiple things that they were instructed to do simultaneously in their dance movements. Rajendra Shankar, mentioned the progress of the students in the following words:

> Now they were good at fairly complicated movements, have learnt to be aware of their own mistakes, and during the last two months they have actually given two performances, unaided and all by themselves. They organised rehearsals, thought out the subjects, designed the costumes, supplied the musical accompaniments, and managed the stage and curtains. These performances, which are organised by the "Centre Club" form a part of their training in helping them to create dances, dialects, songs and tunes, appropriate for their needs. They are advised to undertake easy subjects and the results have been much better that was expected of them. (USIC Centre News, Vol. 2, No. 22, 1940, p. 1)

The same newsletter mentions that after each show the students themselves discussed the merits and demerits of the performances as a self-evaluation of their efforts. This contributed to the understanding of audience reception and helped the students immensely as peer review was one important part of the learning process. At the end Shankar himself commented on the performance, giving a detailed review of all the important elements, such as stagecraft, lighting, props, costumes, musical accompaniment, theme, choreography, and of course, the dance movements and each dancer's performance. The newsletter highlighted this performance-making process as one of the most exciting events in the ongoing routine of classes, as the students learnt to take responsibility, got actual experience of stage and light related skills, experienced teamwork and coordination, while the artistic involvement stirred their imagination and made them confident and less self-conscious.

Shankar's dream institution did not last beyond 1944. World War II made international enrolment of students impossible. Transfer of funds from Dartington Hall became difficult. The funds dried up. The cultural and social rubric of the country was deeply affected by the simultaneous struggle of the South and South East Asian countries—as Burma and parts of northeastern India were occupied by Japan. Calcutta was bombed as well. 'Quit India' movements against the British administration saw mass mobilisation and protest at the call of Mahatma Gandhi. Many national leaders were jailed, and there was large scale repression and violence. Shankar produced a full-length ballet at Almora and named it 'The Rhythm of Life' on the theme of national freedom struggle, almost as a last-ditch effort to keep the energies of creativity alive.

Meanwhile at the Centre in Almora, growing distance between Shankar and his troupe members, a series of student unrests, and disciplinary actions led to Zohra and Kameshwar leaving the Centre in 1943. Shankar lost interest in teaching. In Shankar's letters to the Elmhirsts, towards the end, Shankar was already talking about a new excitement and sending out appeals for funds for making a film. Lacking suitable plans for sustainability, and also a dearth of professional, pedagogical, and disciplinary understanding required in the running of an institution caused a series of crises. Boshi Sen and the Elmhirsts exchanged letters expressing helplessness about Shankar's problem with a long-term goal. Finally, Shankar left the administrative people at the Centre in the beginning of a series of new admissions. He also did not inform the Elmhirsts about his decision to leave. Shankar's shift of interest to film-making has been blamed by some for the untimely demise of a perhaps untimely experiment—a modern dance institution in the hills of Almora. Shankar is remembered for his effort at making a significant contribution to dance education and as an artist who was not able to make a success of the institution he built. There is ample reason to mourn the closure of the USICC, Almora as it was a significant loss to marking of space for modern dance in India. While Kalakshetra, Kerala Kalamandalam, and Visva-Bharati continue successfully, the Uday Shankar India Culture Centre is only a nostalgic memory of an utopic attempt at institution building (Fig. 4.4).

Fig. 4.4 The announcement of closing of the USICC, Almora, Picture Post London, 13 January 1945 (@ Dartington Hall Archives, UK)

References

Brown, M.H. 1938. "Save India's Dances from Decay: Need of All-India Centre." *The Illustrated Weekly of India*, 29 May: 16–17.

Craske, Oliver. 2020. *Indian Sun: The life and Music of Ravi Shankar*. London: Faber & Faber.

Khokar, Mohan. 1983. *His Dance, His Life: A Portrait of Uday Shankar.* New Delhi: Himalayan Books.

Khullar, Sonal. 2018. "Almora Dreams: Art and Life at the Uday Shankar India Cultural Centre, 1939–44." *Marg* 69 (4): 14–31.

Martin, John. 1937. "The Dance: Hindu Center; Shan-Kar to Preserve Indian Arts." *The New York Times*, 14 February, 8.

Mehra, Girish N. 2007. *Nearer Heaven Than Earth*. Delhi: Rupa & Co.

Nicholas, Larraine. 2007. *Dancing in Utopia: Dartington Hall and Its Dancers.* Hampshire: Dance Books Ltd.

Punch, Maurice. 1977. *Progressive Retreat: A Sociological Study of Dartington Hall School 1926–1957 and Some of Its Pupils.* Cambridge: Cambridge University Press.

Sarkar Munsi, Urmimala. 2008. "Boundaries and Beyond: Problems of Nomenclature in Indian Dance." In *Dance: Transcending Borders*, edited by Urmimala Sarkar Munsi (Ed), 78–98. Delhi: Tulika Books.

Segal, Zohra. 2010. *Close-Up: Memories of a Life on Stage and Screen*. New Delhi: Women Unlimited (An Associate of Kali for Women).

Shankar, Ravi. 2000. "Amar Dada: 'Kalpanar' Raja (in Bengali)." *Desh*, 10 June: 44–53.

Vatsyayan, Kapila. 2003. "Modern Dance: The Contribution of Uday Shankar and His Associates." In *New Directions in Indian Dance*, edited by Sunil Kothari, 20–31. Mumbai: Marg Publications.

Vertinsky, Patricia and Ramachandran, Aishwarya. 2018. "Uday Shankar and the Dartington Hall Trust: Patronage, Imperialism and the Indian Dean of Dance." *Routledge Journal of Sports in History* 38 (3): 289–306.

Archival Materials

Dartington Hall Records. Dartington Hall Trust Archives files [Devon Heritage Centre, Great Moor House, Bittern Road, Sowton, Exeter, Devon, EX2 7NL. https://www.dartington.org/?s=archives.

———. LKE/IN/19: Title—LKE India 19: Uday Shankar India Culture Centre, 1932–1973.

———. DWE/A/8: Title—Dance 2, Shankar and other Indian Dancers.

———. DS/UK/843: Title—India Culture Trust; 1937–.

———. DS/UK/836: Title—Admin History Uday Shankar India Culture Centre; 1938–.
———. MC/Chekhov/S4/39: Series 4.General Files: A. Uday Shankar Play bills.
———. USIC Centre Newsletters. 1939–1944 (Fortnightly), Ranidhara, Almora, U.P. Editors: Rajendra Shankar and Vishnudas Shirali (Source: Dartington Archives, Devon Cultural Centre, UK).
———. DS/UK/836. 1937: 5—(From the Draft Trust Deed for setting up of the Uday Shankar India Culture Centre, mentioning as Trustees—Beatrice Whitney Straight (The Settler) of Dartington Hall Totnes England, Alice Boner of Banares India, and Uday Shankar Chowdhury of Bombay India).

CHAPTER 5

Beyond the Proscenium with Dance, Magic, and Film

One of the characteristics of the transmissions brought about by the rise of the digital and networked media, Wolfgang Ernst (2013) observes, is that the traditional separation between transmission media and storage media becomes obsolete.

(Maaike Bleeker 2016: XVII)

Exploratory Projects and Reflexive Quests

This chapter searches for a way to understand the in-between-ness of the art-based creativity that pushed Uday Shankar to search for something beyond a unidimensional exploration of dance-creation for the proscenium and the standard methods of communicating to a particular type of audience. It also becomes imperative to write about this almost unexplored urge in Shankar, where he is obviously experimenting with the co-evolution (Bleeker 2016: XIX) of physical thinking as a choreographer and transmitting of the same through creating multiple manifestations. He used variations of the same thoughts and movements for specific yet different forms of reception. In his chosen projects of producing a shadow play, a film, and a mixed-media performance, Shankar made evident his thinking ahead of the times. He also took monumental chances with his career by not letting go of his vision to experiment beyond his expertise. A lot of letters and doubtful comments can be found on record

U. Sarkar Munsi, *Uday Shankar and His Transcultural Experimentations*, Transnational Theatre Histories,
https://doi.org/10.1007/978-3-030-93224-4_5

in different archives showing that many of Shankar's individual decisions were viewed sceptically and some waited for him to fail. Depending on how one looks at the outcome, Shankar is seen as an experimenter and a somewhat impetuous adventurer moving from one project to another, by some. By critics, he is seen as a person who never stuck to any project for long, shifting from one experiment to another, leaving behind a trail of unfinished projects at times or even discontinued partnerships. In order to place Shankar's quest in the context of Indian modernity and individual freedom, Avijit Pathak's argument in 'Feasibility of another Modernity' is important:

> The process of modernity implies the process of individuation: Individuals can rediscover themselves, unfold their potential, and evolve their own life projects. Nothing can be imposed on then simply because of their birth in a caste, clan or identity. In other words, modernity means a radical shift: from fatalism to active agency, from ascription to achievement, from passivity to meaningful choice. (Pathak 2006: 16)

Shankar's works, in this particular chapter, will be seen as the outcome of his journey as the individual artist/dancer/choreographer/thinker in a civil society that is still undecided about its negotiation with the closed traditional systems and a 'vibrant public sphere' (Pathak 2006: 19). I see Shankar's move beyond proscenium spaces as an endeavour to engage through dance-related tools with the public sphere instead of taking the safe way of continuing standard choreographic processes.

The three experiments that I shall take up for study in this chapter are the shadow play technique used and perfected by Shankar, his sole 'educational' (Shankar's letter to Beatrice Straight, dated October 28, 1943) film *Kalpana* (1948), and his multimedia exploration *Shankarscope* (1971). Shankar's engagement with the medium of shadows was to move beyond the simple choreographic creations on stage and into the realm of using two dimensional shadows created with the help of a screen behind which the performance unfolds. It challenged the idea of the imagination of the scope of bodies that had to now become image representations. He introduced a whole new set of techniques with regards to *Kalpana*, which unleashed a new meaning for spaces, bodies, and props in a creative conversation between dance and film. *Kalpana*, a box-office failure, but considered a landmark in dance films shows dance, human bodies, scenic interplays, props, and social arrangements in combinations that could not be possibly created on the proscenium. *Shankarscope*, yet another experiment in mixed-media techniques, brought together experimentations using stage presentation, dance on screen and magic in a nostalgic retelling and re-presenting of older dances.

There is no writing on Shankar's work behind the screen with shadow-based choreographies such as *Ramleela* and *Life of Buddha* (later re-choreographed and restaged as *Mahamanav* by Amala Shankar in 1983 and 1993). *Kalpana* has been written about more from the angle of studying it as a film rather than as an outcome of an experiment with dance on camera. Some writings, including mine, address the socio-political angle in his choreography. For me though, *Kalpana* as a film may be taken as the first film that uses methods that were already being identified in the West as 'dance for the camera', and this needs to be explored with specific analyses of scenes where the camera becomes one of the actors alongside the dancers/actors and the props. As for *Shankarscope*, the analysis is far more complex, and there is neither any documentation nor any academic writing on it. The production, for which Shankar was criticised severely as someone who did not know what he was doing, is a coming together of stagecraft, choreography, theatre, film, and magic, and is a path-breaking combination of all of the above. I shall be relying on my experience as a very young member of the audience, scant written material, and recorded interviews of a few of the performers who were part of this production. For me Pathak's framing of the modern individual remains the reassuring frame of reference as it asserts the dynamic character of modernity as that which creates space for individuation. The importance of breaking away from traditional forms of practice is, thus, a choice and part of an active agency that leads to experimentations that may venture out of the boundaries set by the commitment and bindings of the traditional. This chapter is centred around a discussion on Shankar's experimenting with traditional as well as new vocabularies of dance (influenced by modern European dance pedagogy). It also highlights the beginnings of Shankar's experiments, the mixing of proscenium with extra-proscenium presentational possibilities, and using of mixed media for students' and his troupe's productions way before it became common in Indian films and stages.

Shankar's position may also be understood in the light of his upbringing, his training and association, however brief, with the J. J. School of Arts and his exposure at the British institution of the Royal Academy of Art. Sarkar's assertion that 'Most Bombay artists produced by the J. J. School of Art, as we have seen also remained loyal to the earlier art traditions' (Sarkar 2015: 427) strengthens this argument. Most of Shankar's experiments may also be understood as his response to the changing scenario that he was encountering in the world and in the particular spaces of traditional as well as modern dance. His experimentations began in the period of intense political sensitivity between the two World Wars, and continued till the period of turbulent political unrest in Kolkata[1] in the 1970s. His awareness of the different possibilities of experimentations at once links him to far eastern traditions of shadow puppetry as well as the Bauhaus movement and the revolutionised technologies in films such as Metropolis (1927), which is seen as a predecessor to Uday Shankar's film *Kalpana* (1948) by many film critics. But his silence regarding the contemporary developments in the local, national, as well as the international front is disturbing and shall remain unexplained in this book due to a politically strategic silence that remained normalised around the Shankars. Sumit Sarkar addresses the scenario within India by saying:

> Post-Swadeshi debates were occasionally suggestive of modernistic values that helped to contribute to the sea change in Indian art from around the 1920s. Upendrakishore Raychaudhuri, inventor of improved methods of half-tone reproduction, argued that there was no necessary contradiction between patriotism and critical receptivity to external values and methods. Patriotism needed to combine 'legitimate and affectionate pride in all that is noble in our national life and traditions with 'sincere regret for our shortcomings and eagerness to remove them ... (Sarkar 2015: 427)

In Shankar, we consistently see the above dilemma. To continue to be the celebrated dancer/choreographer that he had become by being the Ambassador for Indian culture , or to give in to the instinct of experimentation was a dilemma, that gets manifested in the three distinct forms that emerge as his negotiation of 'critical receptivity to external values and methods' mentioned above.

[1] Shankar was based in Kolkata during the turbulent times of the 1970s, when the far-left led Naxal movements in Kolkata as well as national emergency imposed by the then Prime Minister, Indira Gandhi, saw a lot of political violence and unrest in the city. He was separated from his family but continued his choreographic work during this time.

Shadow Play Based on *Ramayana*

The not so common artistic genre named shadow play may be defined as a show in which shadows of puppets, flat cut-out figures, or live actors are projected onto a lighted screen. Commonly known are the shadow puppetry performances common in the South East Asian countries where elaborately decorated three dimensional or flat puppets are used for storytelling against a scenography. Live human actors also use shadow technique using specialised lights, telling stories through the actions behind the screen.

In her diary-like autobiography, Zohra Segal described the setting of the play in the following words:

> After we completed our two all-India tours, dada planned an open air shadow-play depicting the story of the *Ramayana*. For this Ramlila epic, he had had a huge white screen made, to be stretched across an open air stage at the bottom of a slope Near the cottages. The dance-drama unfolded itself in a shadow-play by dancers moving in front of a single high powered lamp placed on the floor in the centre, far back on the stage. The audience was seated on the floor in front of a white screen somewhat in the manner of a Greek Amphitheatre. (Segal 2010: 91)

According to the descriptions of Zohra Segal (2010) and Amala Shankar (Personal interviews, 2003), the first ticketless presentation of *Ramayana* became a unique and popular attraction for people from near and far. Each person coming to see it would bring a handful of grain that in an agricultural community was not hard to contribute. It ensured a symbolic community participation. A large number of performers were required to perform in all the roles, including a large group of monkeys who made up Rama's army to fight Ravana and rescue Seeta. Shankar's fascination with the use of shadows in performance became evident quite early while he was working with his dance troupe in Almora. The scenic beauty of the mountain slope in Almora became his backdrop for *Ramayana* (1941), which became his signature production and has continued to influence many dancers in India since then. The performance site, specifically chosen to expand the possibility of multiple levels and elements of the visual, utilised the multiple levels of the natural scenic elements of the mountain slope and the paths that led down to the stage at the specific location of Ranidhara for the premier performance. Shankar, thus, expanded the whole area of the performance space both in terms of the total scenographic scape and the imaginaries of reception for the audience. Site specificity, much before its hype in contemporary dance performances in the West, thus, became one of Shankar's achievements that have not been acknowledged at all (Figs. 5.1 and 5.2).

A section from *The Hindustan Times* review dated November 3, 1941, with the heading 'Ramleela in Almora' by Saudamini Mehta was reprinted in the Brochure of Almora. It read:

> Nearly ten thousand people had gathered to see the performance (Ramayana in shadow-play), hardly anyone in Almora had probably remained indoors. Even from the surroundings, men, women, and children had walked long distances to attend the show and return at midnight. Almost all present there knew the story of Rama Chandra and yet the entire

Fig. 5.1 During the rehearsal of *Ramleela* at Almora conducted by Shankar, Hanuman's shadow is being projected on screen (Photo © Narendra Sharma Archives)

Fig. 5.2 The shadow play Ramayana showing Jatayu's attempt to stop Ravana from abducting Seeta (© Bharat Sharma and Narendra Sharma Archives)

> audience was spellbound by the performance.... He (Shankar) is seeking to rouse the inner consciousness of the masses and regenerate their latent aesthetic sense through modern technique; indeed he is endeavouring to achieve a synthesis between our cultural heritage and the spirit of the age.[2] (Brochure of USICC, Almora, 1941)

Experimenting for the first time with shadow techniques, with Amala in the role of Rama, Shankar configured ways of expressing ideas, expressions, and gestures behind a screen. Sonal Khullar in her article (2018)[3]

[2] A Brochure from the Uday Shankar India Culture Centre, Almora, from the Dartington Hall Archives, Devon, advertised Chekhov's studio, performance by Shankar's troupe at the Hall and the news about Shankar's dream institution in India.

[3] The article incorporates excellent material from the notes, diaries, and photo collections of Shanta Mohan (née Goel), an erstwhile student at the Centre, though it mis-spells

refers to the diary records of Shanta Mohan (nee Goel) to describe the movement training that led up to the performance. She writes:

> Leading up to the Ramlila, the Centre's most famous production, staged as a monumental open-air shadow-play in October 1941, he tasked students with creating movements that were 'animalish, devilish, ghostly or god-like, anything but unhuman-like' and actions associated with particular professions: 'a dhobi, a dyer, a doctor, lawyer, sweeper, water-carrier, or anything you like.' On some days, his instructions were minimal. On others, they could be quite elaborate. All the while Shankar exhorted his students to 'concentrate hard and imagine well' and encouraged them to 'choose simple things and drown yourself in the feeling of that'. (Khullar 2018: 26)

Shankar in one of his very few writings explains his interest in the use of shadows in a very short paragraph in an article named 'Fundamental Approach to Indian Dancing' that was published after his death by the West Bengal Dance Group Federation.

> the shadow-play seen in Malabar and Indonesia, had always lingered in the sub-conscious mind. Here I created the gigantic shadow-play that could be watched by over 6,000 people in the amphitheatre formed by the nature in the hills. The artists performed before a powerful source of light and their shadows in a white screen 40 feet square gave all possible means of creating dramatic effects. The subject chosen was Ramayana and with light movable sideways, fore and aft and artists working with great precision and coordination, it was possible to create vast distances, tremendous speed and army marching ahead! (Shankar 1998: 10)

An article titled 'Ramayana in Shadow-play' published in the stencilled copy of *USIC Centre News* on Monday, October 20, 1941, written by an anonymous writer identified only as 'A visitor' is important in this context and therefore has been included here, keeping the unknown author's articulation unchanged as this text is difficult to access. The article is one of the very few descriptions available of *Ramayana*. The article talks

Ramleela as Ramlila and also more importantly records the name of the Centre in Almora, which in reality according to the deeds available in Dartington Hall Archives was 'Uday Shankar India Culture Centre'.

about the coming together of proscenium presentation as a site-specific performance. The report reads:

> The slopes on the hill-side had been cut and a natural amphitheatre had appeared to the north of the Culture Centre. At the foot a huge stage had been erected in such a way that from the top and the sides everything on the stage could easily be visible... Tier upon tier rose the natural seats hewn out of the rocks facing the stage and the distant snow, skirted by a forest to the left and hemmed in by the Centre buildings on top, in front and to the right.... and no less than ten thousand people would have gathered.
>
> Near the studio on the top rose a cry and about fifty flaming torches were visible. A murmur rose from the crowd, but before anyone could leave the place, a voice on the loud speaker explained that a procession would start and requested everyone to keep the place. The procession started with loud pounding of drums and a shriek of the Dhudka. Ravana and Mandodari were leading with Vibhisana, Kumbhakarna, Indrajeeta, Kabandha, and lesser demons following. Passing through the crowd along the tortuous paths, roaring and gesticulating in keeping with the character assumed, they arrived to the left of the stage and went below to the dressing rooms. Soon after rose another cry from the office of the Administrator which served as Ayodhya. From here started Rama, Sita, Lakshman, Hanuman and all the followers, and passing through another path, they went in by right side of the stage.
>
> The entire opening of the stage had been covered by a white screen 45 feet by 35 feet and speculations were rife as to the way in which the shadow-play would start. But music soon starts and the curtain is lit up. In a forest sits Sita with Rama,[4] while Lakshman mounts guard. The golden deer comes springing, and Sita sets her heart on getting it. Rama is thus decoyed, and soon Lakshman goes to help him leaving Sita unprotected,

[4] The shadow play, Ramleela, was choreographed on a section of the story of Ramayana, based around the fourteen year-long exile of Rama during which he was asked by his own father, Dasharatha, to leave his father's kingdom on the eve of his coronation to go and spend this period in the forest. Rama left accompanied by his wife Sita and his brother Lakshman to obey his father and his step mother Kaikeyi. The shadow play gave Shankar the chance to experiment with the images that could be used to show movements such as flying of the large bird Jatayu, the crossing of a sea by the monkey companion Hanuman by jumping across it, the large scale war preparations for Rama's attack on Lanka that are commonly known stories in India.

> but within a magic line out of which she is advised not the step. Ravana appears in his mighty form which he transforms to that of a puny beggar and approaches Sita. Her heart melts with pity, but as soon as she steps out of the circle, Ravana grasps her and takes her away. On the way Jatayu fights and is mortally wounded. This fight is exhibited in a masterly way, giving an impression actual flying on the part of Jatayu.[5]
>
> Rama becomes desolate when he finds Sita gone. Soon in his search for her he meets Hanuman and makes friends with Sugriva. Bali is killed, monkeys are mobilized, work is carried on of building a bridge over the sea, and in the meantime Hanuman jumps over the sea to Lanka. In the leap hanuman actually is seen shooting up the sky and then landing in Lanka.
>
> The scene then shifts to the Asoka garden where Sita sits desolate, hanging her head down in grief. The demons and demonesses sing and dance to amuse her. A more weird and fantastic scene could hardly be imagined of. But soon they go to sleep and Hanuman appears and delivers his message of hope and speedy deliverance to Sita. The scene again shifts and we see two armies arrayed to battle. But in the end Ravana is slain by Rama and there is a great jubilation in the camp of the monkeys. Sita is restored and the party now moves to Ayodhya. The brothers again meet. At this time the huge curtain is mysteriously moved away, the lights appears in the front and the full stage is exposed to view. Finally comes the coronation which looks like a picture from the other world. The whole play took about a hour and a half and how the time passed no one realised… (*USIC Centre News*, October 20, 1941: 1)

The anonymous author further continues, ‘As I sat, I realised what an influence it has over the people. Such a huge crowd sat and watched as one person with rapt attention’ (*USIC Centre News*, October 20, 1941: 6).

The anonymous author’s praise of *Ramayana* mentions it as an attempt at establishing a new format of presentation for the Centre through such works of art, play, pageantry, drama, and dance, while Rajendra Shankar writes about Shankar’s influence on Ravi Shankar’s ‘training in stagecraft, lighting, set-design and general showmanship’ and Amala Shankar’s acknowledgement of having learnt a ‘new vision of life and art, creation and presentation’ (Rajendra Shankar 2001: 25). The

[5] Such references to the use of techniques that can be utilised in shadow play are the only descriptions one gets.

Ramayana of which one scene was revived by Amala Shankar in 1983 during the Nehru Utsav in Delhi gave some of the USICC, Kolkata students a chance to experience some of the techniques of the shadow play as presented by Shankar.

Lord Buddha/The Life of Buddha[6]

This shadow play was staged on the occasion of the twenty-five hundredth birth anniversary of the Buddha in 1953. Shankar explained his idea of continuing with the shadow play in this sketchy and almost casual explanation about his later production on Buddha and the techniques it required. Shankar wrote:

> In the next shadow-play, on the life of Buddha coloured shadows were used. The success of the shadow-plays is encouraging because it provides a great medium for outdoor entertainment, cutting down price of admission so that more people can see there. It was also during the working out of the shadow-play that I realised what a great power the mere movement of the body and limbs can provide, for in here in the shadow it is not possible to use any of the linear movements and expressions of the face. (Shankar 1998: 10–11)

The programme note reprinted in Mohan Khokar's article (Khokar 2001: 58) mentions that *Lord Buddha*, the shadow play, was performed in three parts. The first part was on stage and consisted of a village scene twenty-five centuries after the birth of Buddha. The next two sections were about Buddha's life as the young prince Siddhartha, and the renunciation of Buddha. It created a precedent for coloured shadow plays (as Shankar claims himself in his interviews and writings) as the background for the shadows of the moving bodies was a colourful screen that had been created with (now primitive) hand-painted coloured slides, projected to create the changing backdrops. Uday Shankar explained in his programme note that the background was projected from small slides painted by Amala Shankar, using her nails (Fig. 5.3).

[6] This shadow play on Gautam Buddha's life is mentioned in Shankar's own words quoted in the Bengali book, *Shankarnama* (2019) and his biography, *His Dance, His Life*(1983) as *Lord Buddha* and in the book Uday Shankar released in 1983 after his death, edited by Sunil Kothari and Mohan Khokar, as *The Life of Buddha*.

Fig. 5.3 A scene from *Mahamanav*, of Siddhartha's mother queen Mahamaya on a palanquin (both the palanquin and the figure of the queen are cut-outs being carrying by dancers) (© Collection of the author, who is one of the shadow palanquin bearers)

Behind the Screen—*The Life of Buddha* Recreated as *Mahamanav*

Mahamanav, the recreated shadow play on Buddha's life is an important first-hand experience that I attempt to use to reconstruct the idea of using shadows instead of proscenium performance to tell a story. The performance premiered in an open-air auditorium in Kolkata and ran full house for ten days in 1992. This recreated work was the last of the major presentations of Amala Shankar.

Guru P. Raghavan[7] helped Amala Shankar recreate the Shadow play in 1993 with the cast from USICC Kolkata troupe members. Amala Shankar herself played the role of Siddhartha (young Budhha) in the story, with me as Siddhartha's wife Yashodhara. Rejecting the possibilities of using the available digital facilities in the early 1990s, *Mahamanav* used much of the older techniques for projections. Amala Shankar had asked well-known composer, Dipak Chowdhury to create the music for the choreography first, explaining to him each of the scenes and their musical requirements down to the minutest of details.

The performance created an unique experience for the audience. While training for the shadow play all the dancers had to learn to work without the help of facial expressions or abhinaya, a tool that is commonly used in Indian theatrical dances, where dramatic story-telling engages the movements, hand gestures, as well as the facial expressions simultaneously. The participants had to learn an essential set of skills for this performance. The memory of the six months long rehearsals is filled with the efforts of shifting the focus from direct stage appearance as a dancer to becoming a shadow representation. A shadow is a stark presence in which movements become highlighted due to the monochromatic mass of the images. The images therefore need to have identifiers for the audience to be able to understand who or what they are representing. Props, head gears, ornaments, clarity of gestures need the most careful attention to become specifically and consistently identifiable. Since faces could not be seen, the same person could engage in every scene using different costumes as per the requirement of the roles. I was one of the crowds in the first scene, an attendant of Prince Siddhartha's mother queen Mahamaya before and during his birth in the next scene, and then again part of the crowd in the third scene. From the fourth scene onwards, I was Yashodhara. In the next scenes off and on, again and again, I camouflaged my special headgear worn to identify Yashodhara, so that I could join in with the dancers or help in the scene changes by carrying or replacing props. In the scenes of Buddha's renunciation, I was the temptress who tried to disrupt the sage's concentration by appearing in the camouflage of his wife Yashodhara. In the final scene multiple lamps of different colours came on and multiplied

[7] Guru P. Raghavan joined Shankar before his film, *Kalpana* and continued with the troupe as a true and devoted troupe member. He later took up the responsibility of teaching Kathakali at the USICC in Kolkata when it restarted in 1965. He remained with the Centre till he retired due to old age and ill health in the early 2000s.

the shadows of the human figures on the screen. While the screen was filled by these figures signifying the increase in the number of disciples of Buddha, I walked with all the others behind the screen to be a part of the procession signifying the spread of Buddhism in different geographies.

One of the most striking memories I have is around the huge white curtain, vitally important for the projection of shadows and specially made for the performance. All of the senior dancers who were part of the production were mobilised in this process[8] of tying the white curtain to the hanging rod lowered on the stage, before the beginning of the final technical rehearsal. As the main prop on which everything depends for a shadow play to be successful, the curtain had to be hung in a manner so that there was absolutely no crease. In most auditoria the stage crew could not be depended upon and we all sat on the floor tying and adjusting the knots and the folds after which the rod would go up stretching the white screen without crease. Often this could take hours if the technology available in smaller auditoria was not helpful, but this was an essential work before we could start the work of adjusting the lights behind the curtain. As participants we were taught to carry out the technical and dance responsibilities simultaneously as per the specific requirements of the shadow play technique. We all worked with costume changes, making and arranging of props, scene changes, besides doing two to three roles each. One of the most commonly used techniques in shadow choreographies is to regulate the size of the shadow. The more important the role, larger the figure of the person needs to be. Thus, highlighting of important figures could be achieved through the placement of characters or props nearer to the source of light to make them look larger on screen. Shadow plays, as I learnt, need very specific dresses and ornaments which have no resemblance to those used during proscenium performances. There is no requirement for a beautiful ornament or an intricately patterned or a colourful saree. The attire's draping to highlight figures, and the ornaments and head gears that would have enough ways of creating a design in the shadow were conceived keeping in mind the play of light through the material, and design which would aestheticise the figure of the dancers. For example, an illusion of a *anga-vastra* (a

[8] As a specialised performance, the cast and crew were specially hand-picked and trained from people who were senior members of the regular Uday Shankar India Culture Centre troupe. It always was clear that Smt. Shankar was keen on holding this re-choreographed and recreated performance as her last contribution in the form of a complete dance work.

decorous cover for the upper body) would be created by draping a long strip of a lacey border giving an illusion of the imagined drape, rather than actually using a drape of any sort. One could wear a half skirt and not a full saree but in a manner so that it looked like a designed attire while enhancing the body's portrayal in the shadow form. Special head gear was created to enhance the visual representation of the figures in the shadows. The idea was to create a sense of dimensions in the shadow. A crown that would look beautiful in its shape and in its detailed embossed design when viewed on a proscenium might look like a flat mass from the front in a shadow representation. In other words it would simply fail to be the crown in representation unless carefully designed in a manner so that the light and shade interplay can give it its new presence in the shadows.

Dance and any other movements always had to negotiate the body's representation in the form of a shadow. Some of the movements had to be performed adjusting to the shadows and the way the images were appearing vis-a-vis other bodies, so unlearning and reorienting the ideas of the presentational contours of each of the smallest of gestures and movements was as much a part of the training as the perfection of dance movements and choreographic necessity. Clusters or crowd configurations could never be the same as on stage. They had to be created using light and shade in a way so that each of the bodies were outlined and yet would represent a crowd when viewed as shadows by the audience.

Lights, Props, and Slides

Shadow performances work on an entirely different logic than the proscenium performances. The principle source of light needs to be only a single one to avoid multiple conflicting shadows that would defuse clarity. We all learnt the way to help with the major source of light behind the scene. Setting up of the lights in a particular manner so that the human figures could be viewed from head to toe without any distortion of the image for the audience was a skilled task that some of the dancers were trained to handle. This meant raising the light to a certain height from the ground depending on the depth of the stage. Since the production was heavily dependent on the clarity of the shadows, a lot of time was spent on adjustments of the light arrangement. A thousand watt bulb placed at the centre of the stage behind the screen about thirty feet away from the screen would throw a triangular source of light on the ground and also light the screen so that the full figures of the dancers could be seen.

Mashima's hand-painted and nail-etched colour slides were created for different backdrops for different scenes. Each scene had specific slide. The slides were mounted two at a time on a primitive slide carrier which was fixed in front of a second light that was placed beside the major light source, mentioned before. The technique of using the slides required the principle one thousand watt bulb to be switched off and the slide light to be put on simultaneously. Any distortion due to a small change of the source of light had to be kept in mind while creating the choreography and also by each of the members of the cast, as the proximity of the shadows differed according to the source of light and that altered gaps and placements of characters. The moment the colourful slides projected the image on the screen, the story-telling took another special dimension where the dark black shadows gained life through their coloured backdrops. Most often, Amala Shankar's favourite colours were earthy a range of yellow and browns and Lapis Lazuli blue. Through the changing slides the scenography acquired an impressionistic idea of intricate details of forests, palaces, and courts adding to the descriptive element of a dialogue-less story-telling process.

Many handmade and easy-to-carry props were created and used. Making of the props was great fun, as we would work like the parts of a well-oiled machine creating shadow stories. Card board cut outs were used to create the impressions of intricately designed furniture and also head gears and crowns. The different festive properties such as flags, chandeliers, and festive lights were created for the procession that gave the impression that thousands of people were walking across a long distance to reach the festivities after the announcement of the birth of Siddhartha. The chandeliers were created by putting a single stick through the centre of three bamboo baskets placed upside down, with the largest on top and the other two gradually smaller ones arranged below according to size. The baskets, the edges of which were decorated with decorative lace that had small ball-like trinkets hanging on them, gave the total shadow a beautiful intricate chandelier.

A prop resembling a dead body was prepared for the important scene, where the young prince Siddhartha left his palace for the first time and experienced life outside. He saw aging bodies, poverty, and death. To create a prop which would give the impression of a body being carried by four people on their shoulders, a long stick and a soft but heavy saree were used. The cloth was folded and tied along the stick and filled with more of the heavy material in between its folds. The stick was long enough so that it could be carried by two bearers in the front and two at the back. The long bag-like cloth—approximately of the same length as a human figure, created the impression of a dead body being carried. A figure in front would walk with an earthen pot that is seen commonly even now during the last rites in villages in India. The mourners would follow with a stooped gait, with a choreographed and similar movement setting the mood and emotion of the scene. Shadow play as a genre and a technique remains inimitable and rare till date in India.

A constant source of mirth and giggles was the way the shadows sometimes embarrassed us with the representation that the audience would be seeing as the final image—created as a result of our actions behind the scene. In stage choreographies one is accustomed to be consciously adjusting and maintaining the places that one was allotted. By the time we were rehearsing for the shadow play, many of us were seasoned proscenium performers. But we were unprepared for the surprises shadow representations could spring by the images that fused on the screen. We could be standing at a proper distance from each other, but unless we had rehearsed with the shadow lights on, it was impossible to know if a sword held by one dancer would look as if it was poking the dancer in front right at the back or some even more awkward place. Such incidents could fill one book but the takeaway I guess is that the shadow presences are negotiated with a set of very minute scrutiny of the representations that finally reach the audience. The upside to this is that the shadows give the performers a sincere mirror and an instant feedback to see and attend to. It is like a rehearsal studio behind the curtain, which facilitates adjustments.

Producing the Image/Pushing the Imagination

Uday Shankar's film *Kalpana* remains one of the path breakers in Indian dance films. The fascination that Shankar nurtured from the very beginning of his dance journey for interartistic creativity, was given a free rein in the production of this film. Shankar's wish to make a movie is documented in a number of letters written by him to the Elmhirsts at Dartington Hall. He wrote these letters both for appealing for funds for the film as well as for highlighting the creative urges he felt at that particular moment.

In my published essay 'Imagi(ni)ng the nation' (2011) I have used the two words—imaging, and imagining, as closely related wishes, for telling a nation's story as well as imagining a future direction for it, at the same time. The image and the imagination run closely and parallel to each other, where a celebration as well as a critique are both housed in a somewhat indirect melodramatic story-telling endeavour. Shankar's *Kalpana* shows us in ample ways how both the words could mean two different and often parallel trajectories that the film audience is led to and through. Shankar in his interview to Shambhu Mitra[9] mentioned that he did not know anything of film making and yet worked on his artistic instincts. For Shankar images and choreographic imagination often were dependent on each other for creativity, but at other moments they functioned completely independently of each other.

In *Kalpana* the moving images record different points of his actual as well as imaginative journey. At the same time, an image is often used by him to present the real within the reel and to curtail or limit uncontrolled imagination.

Amala Shankar noted in her interview (Ghosh 2019: 128) that the idea of *Kalpana* was born at Almora. Shankar had started his centre with a zeal that waned after a few years as he increasingly became more and more immersed in the plans for his next project of making a film. According to her, there was some opposition to the idea of making a film among the students, faculty, and members of the performing troupe.

The story of the closing of the USICC and the beginning of Uday Shankar's experiment with films is available through letters between the Elmhirsts and Boshi Sen, who noted in many of their concerned correspondences that Shankar was no longer very invested in the idea of the institute of dance education that had seemed to be his principle interest in the recent past. The Dartington Hall records noted:

> the Elmhirsts set up, alongside Beatrice Straight, funding via the Elmhirst Trust to support the 'Uday Shankar India Culture Centre' a school in Almora, India in 1937. The school's aims were to train young Indian dancers and musicians in the traditions of folk forms of Indian culture. It was successful for five years until Shankar became interested in making a film, which the Elmgrant Trust did not fund as it was considered to be

[9] Interview of Uday Shankar by Shambhu Mitra, https://www.youtube.com/watch?v=JHq-uBio5vE, accessed on 25 January 2018.

outside the interest to the original agreement. In February 1944 Shankar closed the school without consulting the Trust. (Dartington Hall Records, file no. DS/UK/836)

Shankar's enthusiasm regarding the making of the film was acknowledged even in the earliest years of the Almora days as has been documented in various letters and Boshi Sen's biography by Girish N. Mehra (2007). Thus *Kalpana* is in many ways a post-script of the USICC, Almora. It is also a continuation of Shankar's next stage of experiments. The film was not only about a collage of images and memories revisited but also a layered set of imaginations. Some of those were presented in the form of a story line, but others delved deeper into the utopian dreams of the protagonist of the film script, and indirectly of course the dreams of Shankar himself. Referring to the unfinished business of institution-building that he had taken on, Shankar was possibly trying to provide himself and his critics with a valid reason for having moved on, leaving his patrons, associates, troupe members, and the students without an anchor. Film scholar Philip Lutgendorf wrote,

> *Kalpana* is perhaps best appreciated as a long dance performance similarly interrupted by a quasi-autobiographical storyline that, unless one is familiar with Shankar's life, can be confusing to follow, as well as by satirical and allegorical set-pieces that comment (often obliquely) on then-contemporary events and trends. The acting is, at best, highly mannered, and Shankar's flat delivery of lines and static poses seem especially awkward. Although Amala Shankar, as his main love interest, is more spirited, it is clear that neither of these talented artists was really comfortable expressing feelings through verbal language. It is dance that is lifeblood of this film. (Lutgendorf 2017: 2)

Kalpana did not do well in the box office, but it won critical acclaim, from the international film critics. A large number of the Indian audience and critics remained sceptical about it. There was a sharp polarisation between those who admired it and those who criticised it. Over and above, a dispute regarding ownership of the film, that still goes on in the form of a court case, pushed the film into oblivion for a long time. A very poor quality print of *Kalpana* was available for the students of USICC and admirers to see. The film remained in semi-oblivion for over fifty years. Satyajit Ray, the well-known Oscar winning film director from

India remained a diehard fan of the film among many others and watched it repeatedly.

But *Kalpana* is in the news again. Quite recently the well-known film director, on Martin Scorsese's initiatives, The Film Foundation—World Cinema Project has restored the film and as a result the world is looking at *Kalpana* with renewed interest. Amala Shankar was invited to walk on the red carpet in 2012 at the showing of the restored version at the Cannes Film Festival. On the occasion, Scorsese in a short video clip before the movie, promised the audience that they will themselves see that the great work of hallucinatory, homemade expressionism and ecstatic beauty does not just include dance sequences… but whose primary physical vocabulary is dance (sic).[10] Scorsese's description necessitates linking the idea of the image of the nation that Shankar creates in his film to what Homi Bhabha mentions as narratives of the nations in the 'Introduction' of his book, *Nation and Narration*. He writes 'Nations, like narratives, lose their origins in the myths of time and only realize their horizons in their mind's eye. Such an image of the nation—or narration—might seem impossibly romantic and excessively metaphorical…' (Bhabha 1990: 1–7). I propose that we place *Kalpana* in the group of those films from the post-World War II era of internationalism when nations were not trying to wipe off their differences and create a 'global' world of cultural universals but were trying to establish a phase of international exchange of ideas, and the projection of a distinct and modern national identities. *Kalpana* (presently available in different versions on the internet),[11] the film that Uday Shankar wrote, directed, and starred in, was completed in the year 1948, and is now recognised as a product of the heightened creative surge of his modernistic endeavour in dance. Acknowledging the somewhat hyper-emphasised nationalism portrayed through the medium of dance theatre in the film within Indian dance history, I had underlined '… the importance of viewing Shankar's work academically in the context of the dual discourses of colonial and postcolonial development in performance, and the trajectories of development of dance in India' (Sarkar Munsi 2011: 127).

[10] See https://www.dnaindia.com/lifestyle/report-a-dream-uncanned-uday-shankar-s-1948-film-kalpana-1691196, accessed on 09 September 2021.

[11] See *Kalpana*, the movie at https://www.youtube.com/watch?v=S6hnsycStbY, accessed on 30 October 2019, or https://www.facebook.com/NARTHAKI/videos/359372408830378 accessed on 25 August 2021.

In the next section, *Kalpana* and its structure shall be read through the framework suggested by Ashish Rajadhyaksha, where he sees the time period from 1895 to 1990 as creating a culture of engagement with the moving image:

> This is a particular kind of public: one that celluloid not only exemplifies but, in hindsight, may have fabricated largely on its own, and narrativized primarily as a mix of text and social action through the twin regulatory mechanisms of containment and excess. 'Containment' is a formal requirement of the film frame and a social requirement of perhaps the most crucial institution of the public domain in our time of celluloid: the movie theatre. Its inherent structural instability, notwithstanding – perhaps exacerbated by –its fantasy character, has real public consequences that it does not apparently share even with sequel technologies such as, say, video. (Rajadhyaksha 2009: 7)

Both 'containment' and 'excess' were part of the proscenium-to-screen shift for Shankar. On the one hand he was dealing with (not very successfully all the time, as is evident in the acting styles of the principle protagonists in *Kalpana*) the issues around speech and text, and on the other hand most of the actors/dancers needed to adjust their performances to the requirements of the screen. Over-acting and over-dramatisation both are a constant, therefore, in the film making it difficult for the audience to shift its own position and gaze from those required for a stage performance to a cinematic one. Choreographically, Shankar's task seems to have been easier. Since he had the vision of an artist, the scenes depicted through choreographed compositions were spectacular and exciting. The representational movements had to be supplemented with a large degree of physical theatre, especially in the whole section on life and mechanisation in the factory. Shankar often gave an example of the sets that come across as elaborately crafted and constructed mentioning that they had run out of money, and had to make do with 4 feet by 4 feet wooden boxes and some other boxes of different geometric shapes that were made by carpenters. These light props could be rearranged within 20 minutes for different requirements of film scenes.

Shankar's changing relationship with his country, his audience, and his art was also quite different at the stage when he was filming *Kalpana*. After spending years designated as an Oriental entertainer, his work with young dancers and experienced dance and musical master teachers in Almora seemed to have added a pedagogically conscious engagement with the ongoing negotiations in pre-independence India around the idea of nationhood and its possible structure.

Filmed at a time of immense social, cultural, and political changes in India, *Kalpana* makes its narrative into a combination of a dance-theatre production and an experiment of 'Dance for Camera'.[12] In the process, its narrative oscillates between being a projection of the range of socio-political conditions within the country and an artistic and idealistic imagination of the future. What makes it significant is the inclusion of ongoing debates of that time, around revival, reform, and restoration of cultural practices that were going on in the space of policy formations for the soon to be independent country. Planning for opening of the Sangeet Natak Akademi (1953) and other such government departments, encouraging and pushing for establishment of art institutions (i.e. Kalakshetra [1936], Kerala Kalamandalam [1930]) and passing of acts/laws (i.e. Devadasi abolition Act of 1947) as well as the success of Tagore's Visva-Bharati University (1921), seemed to push Shankar towards an internal reflexion on the failure of his own institution USICC in Almora. One of the dominant commentaries that emerges on this issue is the connection between patronage and the vision of institution-building that becomes presented in forms of group dialogues at multiple times in the film. Shankar uses scathing remarks as dialogues by the protagonist Udayan at parties of elite acquaintances, where tokenistic expressions of sympathy for the poor, or the loss of human lives during the Bengal famine invites his anger at the elite upper class. He also used these social spaces to symbolically strike out against the rich and yet uninformed people and the lack of interest or care for the future of the nation, and its cultural and social upliftment. The camera in *Kalpana*, becomes the medium through which Shankar manipulates the audience reception of the danced theme.

Amala Shankar recalled that one day Shankar, she, and Guru Dutt were sitting together when Shankar asked for a Bengali word for *Imagination*. As soon as Amala translated the word, he asked Guru Dutt to write down the name of the film, and that is how the name *Kalpana* came into being. According to Amala, Shankar wanted to capture his artistic imagination

[12] Dance for camera is a genre of dance that is projected through the camera to reveal the central themes of the film. Used mainly in experimental films, creation and choreography typically is only for use in films and videos. The camera becomes a major stake holder along with dance and the dancer(s).

of the Almora Centre in the form of this film. Often valued as the detailed documentation of his choreographies, the film remains in an uneasy realm of reception even now, with film critics expressing quite contradictory thoughts about it. The Bombay film industry's commercial productions *Chandralekha* (1948) and *Kismat* (1943) were released around the same time, and they became popular and box-office hits, doing much better than *Kalpana*.

The Nation Captured: Film as the Medium of a Dance Artist

Many people have found similarities between some parts of *Kalpana* (1948) and *Metropolis* (1927), a silent film considered to be a pioneering futuristic science fiction movie, filmed for seventeen months in 1925–1926. The film was made in Germany during the Weimer times and was centred on the idea of labour, class-divide, and exploitation. There were mixed reactions to the film. Clearly influenced by Bauhaus and communist ideology, *Metropolis* was described as simplistic and trite. Meanwhile, *Kalpana* remains a path-breaking experimental film for both the dance and the film scholars. For many, the dances in *Kalpana* are pieces of existing choreographic work put together in a story that seems autobiographic, simplistic, and weakly enacted. For some film critics, *Kalpana* is too long and scattered and for many of its admirers it remains a wonder in terms of scenography and presentation that has something new unravelling every time one watches it. Randy Martin's words, 'While dance is neither language nor politics, it is clarified and qualified through these means' (Randy Martin 1998: 4) provides a lead towards understanding Shankar's work through the layers of socio-cultural collages that he created in *Kalpana*.

In *Kalpana* Shankar makes intermittent political statements as a part of the portrayal of the real life of Udayan, while his utopian dreams cross over frequently between completely imagined dream sequences and harsh realities of the country he is dreaming for. Though the film chooses to engage in a limited and controlled manner with ongoing debates, the issues of class, caste, and religious hierarchies and social exploitations become forceful in their representations.

In a previously published chapter on *Kalpana* (Sarkar Munsi 2011: 124–50), I described scenes from *Kalpana* as a montage of dance sequences strung together by creating a story about an artist's dream of building a dance institute. Shankar himself describes it as 'a propaganda for art and culture' in his interview to Shambhu Mitra.[13] The combination of the real and dream sequences provided Shankar the freedom to move in and out of a linear narrative structure and also use unrelated dance pieces in a modernist abstract manner. Over the years the film has started having a different conversation with the current times. As India changes its relationship with its citizens in the twenty-first century, the film can now be seen as a post-colonial marker of near-utopic aspirations for social and cultural change that took shape in the newly independent nation.

There are three distinctly identifiable strands in *Kalpana*. Firstly, it is successful in creating lasting impressions of everyday realities of India in the 1940s. Images of bodies affected by hunger, the famine, and social inequalities on the one hand and the representation of people from the privileged classes and castes, the life of excess and comfort, the exploitation of the working classes on the other hand were presented in a narrative that exists parallelly with the choreographed dance sequences. There were clear similarities with the performance themes popularised by Indian Peoples' Theatre Association (IPTA),[14] with concrete references to Bengal famine of 1943, exploitations of the poor, religious fundamentalism and discontent of the farmers among others. Throughout the film some issues related to gender, education, and social hierarchy appear repeatedly in many scenes. Often not related directly to a linear script—these important issues run through the film as a thread of social commentary, reiterating its commitments to social justice.

Udayan's quest for a sustained system of patronage for an institution for art and wholistic learning is the second strand that is developed side by side through the film. This section shows rehearsals and the struggle to build an art institution and the life therein. A lot of dance sequences became part of the activities and festivals of the art institution within this strand.

[13] See Shankar's interview by Shambhu Mitra at https://www.youtube.com/watch?v=JHq-uBio5vE.

[14] IPTA performances were created with clear political messages such as *Bhukha Hai Bangal* (by Bengal Cultural Squad, used to collect relief funds for the Bengal famine in 1942), *The Spirit of India* and *Amar Bharat* ((by Central Squad IPTA), Dharti ka Lal (film, 1946), between 1940 and 1946. Many of Shankar's students and troupe members joined IPTA after the Almora Centre shut down.

The third strand is a documentation cum showcasing of Shankar's repertoire. This strand also weaves itself into the story but is valuable as unconnected documentation as well. In this section there are solo, duet, and ensemble choreographies by Shankar that make the film a dance-filled spectacle. The film takes them on a journey through the experiences and imaginations of the principle protagonist, using multiple languages of words, dances, and dramatic enactments.

At the time of planning his film, Shankar already was disappointed by his patrons. He had been refused fundings for establishing his performance troupe in 1930 by many princely states in India, the heads of whom knew his father personally. He had to close down USICC at Almora after his funding from Dartington Hall had stopped. The funding for *Kalpana* was not coming as planned. *Kalpana* began thus with a strong critique of the figure of the patron and the power that is wielded by any agency or individual that controls artistic creativity by controlling the finances. Udayan is seen trying to get a financier to read the story he has written for a film. He encounters the message 'Box office is our god' from the financier he approaches and the film moves in and out of his real life and his script/dream. The dreams and wishful imaginations of the author remain de-texted deliberately—projecting many urgent and political conversations as well as his older choreographies in a seemingly floating montage. Thus, *Kalpana* stops short of making any strong political statement, but the fractured images drive home the immediate and important issues that the soon to be independent nation needs to attend to—in order to move forward. Beginning with a over-dramatic projection of a familial structure of control and heteronormativity, the first few scenes are about Udayan's childhood where he is growing up in an atmosphere of strict and autocratic control.

His limited but significant engagement and exposure to works of IPTA may have cross-fertilised both the spaces. His students i.e. Ravi Shankar, Narendra Sharma, Shanti Bardhan, Sachin Shankar, Zohra Segal, and many others who were working for IPTA, created theatre and dance productions. Some similarities in movement principles and the reflection of thoughts around the nation and its relationship with its citizen-subjects can be traced between Shankar's choreographies and the work of the

IPTA, and remain captured in the two movies *Kalpana* (1948) and *Dharti Ka lal* (1946),[15] both of which released around the same time.

The powerful language of critique the film uses from the beginning, projects itself in a handwritten note on the screen signed by Uday Shankar, which asks the audience to be alert so that they do not miss any 'vital aspect of our country's life in its Religion, Politics, Education, Art and Culture, Agriculture and Industry' (from film *Kalpana*, 2.29 mins). The note continues to say that the director does not want to deliberately criticise any particular group of people or institutions, but has tried to be honest in his representational narrative. He ends the note by writing, 'It is my duty as an artist to be fully alive to all conditions of life and though relating to our country and present it truthfully with all the faults and merits, through the medium of my art' (from film *Kalpana*, 2.42 mins).

Beginning with a dramatic projection of a familial structure of control and heteronormative socialisation the first few scenes of the film are about Udayan's childhood where he is growing up in an atmosphere of strict and oppressively autocratic control. Shankar's protagonist Udayan's dream/film script sets itself in a undefined rural space to begin with. His torturous experience at the school, his love of art—painting and performance and his experiences with contrasting figures of incompetent and vicious versus kind and generous teachers—who bring out the worst and best in young Uday, gives a logical explanation for Uday Shankar's wish to establish an ideal inclusive institution where art will be taught to one and all along with subjects. His own somewhat negative experience in school may be the reason for him to create an engagement with the theme of means and ends of education, that starts at the very beginning of the film and continues to surface intermittently—intertwined (if a bit haphazard fashion) with issues of caste based discrimination, gendered socialisation, and questions of power and hierarchy.

The first few scenes establish a stark contrast of the protagonist's everyday experiences to his dreams. His experience of fights with his

[15] *Dharti Ka Lal* (1946) is a film made by Khwaja Ahmed Abbas, based on the stories, *Nabanna* (The Harvest), *Jabanbandi* (Confession) by Bijon Bhattacharya, and the story *Annadata* (The provider) by Krishan Chander. The cast of the film was made up of mostly IPTA actors. Using operatic form as well as theatre, it portrayed the severe political crisis through the plight of a family during the Bengal famine of 1943.

classmates, beatings received from his teachers and family are in contrast to his dream world where he encounters oppositional socially defined qualities of gentleness/ruthlessness, unkind/compassionate behaviour, non-violent aesthetic movements as against deliberate physical assaults that hurt, symbiotic and ensemble practice in contrast to fractious individualism. One of the scenes in his dream directly deals with the idea of good and evil through a popularly enacted episode of Kathakali around the killing of the demon Hiranyakashipu by Nrisingha Avatar to rescue Hiranyakashipu's son Pralhad from his demonic father.[16] The oblique reference to oppressive control that children face in the name of discipline within family setups, cannot be ignored, especially as one sees Pralhad being violently attacked by his father Hiranyakashipu in the shortened episode in Kathakali style.

The Regional Space and the National Identity

Uday Shankar's vision of India as a multicultural, multi-ethnic, multi-caste, multi-religion, and multilingual country is put forth forcefully in *Kalpana*, through several choreographed sequences. Several community identifications are made possible for the viewers through specific regional references, such as different dialects, dresses, head gear, and ornaments. Shankar seems to have applied a curatorial choice whereby he chose some stories that he wanted to tell while not mentioning others. His choice is clearly highlighted in the film, as it concentrates on social and cultural commentaries on the diverse people and their cultural practices, while taking forward his socio-cultural commentary through the story of the protagonist, his love of dance, and his dream of building an institution for modern inclusive education. It is clear that the idea of making a movie had been there in Shankar's mind for some years. His dissatisfaction as an artist and a pedagogue made him write the story of Udayan, who is an artist and a dreamer, weaving his dance creations in a story which reflected, often simplistically, the images of a colonised, shackled country.

Joan Erdman writes:

[16] Nrisingha Avatar is an incarnation of god Vishnu, who is known for his ability to protect his devotees. *Hiranyakashipu Vadh* (Killing of Hiranyakashipu) is an episode where Pralhad—the son of the demon, is rescued from his own father by Nrisingha Avatar. Nrisingha's iconic representation is that of a lion in the upper half of the body and claws, while he has a human torso and lower body.

> Nationalism and colonialism are not mere external contexts for Shankar's dance and success; they are the context in the midst of which he performed, was reviewed, met his patrons, and created his repertoire.…Recently, viewing Uday Shankar's *Kalpana* in Madras (now called Chennai), I sat amongst a dance audience from the Sri Krishna Gana Sabha, which presents an annual dance conference every December. An Italian practitioner of *Bharatanatyam* and scholar of Indian culture exclaimed while watching Shankar's dances, 'This is new, it's post-modern, it's Indian! Everyone needs to see this now'. (Erdman 1997: 273–74)

Shankar successfully establishes the contrast between the rural and the urban environment as well. As the protagonist moves to the city—a space is differentiated by his scenography, contrasting lifestyle and aspirations. His old and new friendships, his efforts towards the formation of a performance troupe, and eventually a show that ends up in violence between the promoter and the protagonist of the film—reflects some of Shankar's disillusionment as an artist in real life. Uday's experiences are shown through his trials and tribulations around his performances, his relationship with troupe members, and his growing involvement with dance-making. All through these episodic and often unconnected sections the difference between the real and the dream remains a constant, sometimes blending into each other through the dance on the screen.

Throughout the film he remains deeply critical of the city elite he is introduced to. It is highlighted through the clothes, aspirations, and obvious references to sharply different privileges that people get used to. His encounter and scepticism of token references to Indian nationalism is often shown as synonymous with a majoritarian—upper caste/class Hindu nationalism. Though never clearly criticised—the modern state and its invisiblisation of major social inequalities is either critiqued or countered through scenes showing unity in diversity in a rather utopian manner. The role of the state in the modernisation of the society and the strong defence of the state's sovereignty and secular principles remain vitally important throughout the film. In the case of Kalpana, the showcasing of the Nehruvian theme of 'unity in diversity' and the national identity as a secular and multi-ethnic one comes through as one of the most clear and uncompromised message, thus, carving out a space for people's expressions in and through dances and festivals in a colourful and syncretic array of living traditions that refer to the history of the geographical space that was soon going to be part of an independent nation. Regional dances that remained an important part of Shankar's image and identity of India's people and their calendrical cycle, become the texts through which he puts his images and imagination across (Fig. 5.4).

Shankar's changing relationship with dance languages from different parts of India and his introduction and growing respect for dance forms such as Manipuri, Kathakali, Bharatanatyam, and Kathak that eventually became designated as 'classical' soon after Indian independence also left their mark on the film. A section in the film that starts with a variety programme from his Academy, weaving in images of costumes, musical instruments, and embodied aesthetic expressions from different parts of India. The choreographies include dances from Manipur with Guru Amobi Singh beginning the performance, followed by Amala Shankar performing Raas and a group performance by many men and women dancers. Shankar's fascination with Kathakali, of course, makes him explore movements, expressions, postures, as well as facial make-up and costumes all through *Kalpana*. He also invited a large number of Kathakali dancers to be a part of the team of dancers/actors in the film. A solo kathak performance was included adhering strictly to the grammar of the soon to be classical form.

Fig. 5.4 Screenshots from *Kalpana*: top left to right—the factory, Uday and Amala Shankar in a duet, oppression of the worker by the factory owner and Katrikeya. Below left to right—'Head-less' dance, the on scene education and graduation; a scene that depicts a performance (© Screenshots are taken and collated by the author)

A Commentary on Socio-economic Transition

The film recreates Shankar's stage production *Labour and machinery* (see Chapter 3 for details) as a complex narrative on human labour, the agency, and ownership related to the means of production. The questions around the farmers and their sustenance, land rights, human conditions under feudal/industrial systems, and the emergence of the exploitative class of middle-men and money lenders are taken up directly or indirectly. Most of the sections dealing with labour remain realistic in the film's main story and the protagonist's dreams. The issue of the ownership of means of production and human labour are brought into focus in the theme of industrialisation in a section that starts with a model of a factory being proudly displayed by a man with an aspiration to open a factory. Using the film space, Shankar creates an oppressive space which activates the whole community of villagers as machines that they were operating, to become parts of factory production mechanism. They are subjected to severe exploitation and surveillance. The set of the interior of the factory becomes intriguing with different mechanical operations going on at different levels simultaneously. The different geometric boxes, human bodies, and a complex arrangement of light and shade, engage the imagination of the viewers in a space that transforms into a giant multi-facetted factory in operation. The camera enhances the affect of labour showing in minute details the complete mechanisation of human bodies, that have seized to think, and are driven by impulses of control exerted by external agencies. The controller of the human machine is seen activating one of the four bodies standing in a line, to generate and thereafter add different movements in all four bodies that move in complete unison.

This re-choreographed scene from a stage production *Labour and Machinary* (choreographed first in Almora) becomes one of the most striking sections of the film. The later part of the same scene includes a lament for the lost village life and the loss of the agricultural land and a subsequent revolt by the workers. The violence that follows clearly projects the divide between the owner and the workers. Noteworthy in the factory sequence are close-up as well panorama shots of real-life movements in portraying actual human effort of the sweating, toiling bodies in the various working moments, such as carrying huge iron rails, putting coal into furnaces, and bodies shackled together by ropes and chains moving in unison. The synchronised collage of moving bodies captured on camera turn the united human effort into a cinematic spectacle.

In another section of *Kalpana*, artistic labour and ensemble practice become the focus where the activities of the performing troupe of the protagonist is seen rehearsing. The importance of dedication, hard work, and sharing of goodwill and group synergy are projected through the scenes in this section. As the director of the film, Shankar seems to take the liberty of bringing in the real experiences of USICC, Almora, to loosely refer to this theme by enacting and representing the real process of rehearsals and hard work necessary in the production process of a performance.

Gender(ing) in *Kalpana*

Women characters in *Kalpana* are created from a space of ambiguity that may have been the result of the nation's ideation of women as well as Shankar's (and possibly Amala's) biographical inputs.

Erdman writes that some of the critics and audiences especially in the West were troubled by the story, where the story's principle women characters are openly fighting for Shankar's attention, and quarrelling and trying to cause harm or sabotage each other's lives. 'It was a pre-independence narrative, and contained reminders of what was alleged to tarnish Uday's reputation. In brilliantly creative dance scenes and less scintillating dramatic ones, *Kalpana* satirized Indians who tried to retain lost power after independence and showed women in competition for his favors' (Erdman 1997: 272).

I have analysed the roles played by women in *Kalpana* and been concerned about the loosely framed patriarchy that creeps in every now and then into the thematic underpinnings of the film in my article Imagi(ing) the Nation:

> The nationalist discourse has always fixed the 'ideal' role for its women citizens, thereby, creating separate standards of social/cultural behavioural practices for the male and the female subjects. On yet another level, women are portrayed as the symbolic embodiment of the nation as a gendered entity, the eternal mother who absorbs all the hurt, disgrace, and calamity directed towards her children and who is pained when the children quarrel among themselves and create disharmony (Sarkar Munsi 2011: 141).

The storyline has two principle women characters: Uma (played by Amala Shankar) as the good/selfless dancer; and Kamini, a complex entity with selfish, spoilt, and jealous traits. There are frequent clashes between the two women that are perpetrated mostly by Kamini's jealousy and possessiveness over Udayan. The melodramatic scenes of two women fighting for Udayan's attention, and eventual closeness between him and Uma, repeatedly play out heteronormative stereotypes of women and their emotions—going against the strongly formed narrative of equality and emancipation of the dream sequences.

The portrayal of Mother India, a common metaphor applied to signify the plight of the colonised nation, along with other social evils such as child marriage, find place in *Kalpana*, through balletic representations using elaborately choreographed dance movements.

In Kalpana there are sections where the protagonist states that without women's emancipation there cannot be any hope of creating a modern nation. He also ridicules orthodox male ideas about gendering in several scenes. In some other scenes, women characters are determined, ambitious humans, travelling and staying far away from their families to follow their interest of becoming performers. There are a number of scenes where a group of confidant women walk down a ramp-like set of pathways—looking ahead and walking tall in a symbolic stride towards equal and just future. In that sequence the women are dressed in everyday attires, without head cover. The fitted kurtas and salwars worn without any scarf covering the upper body, are powerful visual statements of women claiming their rights to public spaces. The walking here is rhythmic, with the heads held high and eyes looking forward. The women's bodies project a fearless public presence with a controlled sway of the torso, that projects self-assurance and confidence that challenge social strictures and yet keep the walking women's bodies grounded within the danced language of the film. This scene continues into the next where these women are shown to be confronted by a group of traditionally dressed older males, who dance a set of movements signifying a number of rules and regulations, delivering strictures to the women regarding social do's and don't do's. This scene becomes important as the camera catches the above-mentioned actions of the men and the defiant reactions of the women in breaking into loud laughter and dismissing the strictures in choreographed unison. The liberating gestures of questioning, defying, ridiculing, and resisting patriarchy create a completely opposed and contradictory space against the hypergendered themes, gestures, and dance movements that are clear signifiers of Shankar's dance repertoire included within *Kalpana*.

In yet another resistive narrativisation, one sees anger and disappointment in Udayan as he sees lust and patriarchal dismissal in the eyes of moneyed patrons while interacting with the women artists of his troupe. He clearly understands the women dancers' stereotyped reception as available and easy women—instead of talented dance specialists. Through this continued thread a simplistic but strong and resistive message is framed.

Education as a Theme: Towards a Conscious Nation

One of the recurrent themes that needs specific attention is the education policy of the independent nation that may have been rooted in Shankar's childhood experiences within a deeply problematic draconian primary education system. This significant and interventionist articulation begins with a group of graduate students proudly celebrating receiving their degrees on a segregated podium, while all around them the scene is filled with the top of umbrellas covering the heads of the crowd standing on the lower ground, signifying an unbridgeable gap between the educated within formal modern education system and the unlettered section of the society. Soon after the new graduates emerge in two separate lines of males and females with the degrees clasped in their hands, and walk with a rhythmic gait across the stage while a number of parents are seen waiting for their sons and daughters to receive their degrees at the graduation ceremony. The parents are heard congratulating their offspring and also discussing the dowry that the male graduate would now bring. The fragile gender equality that was seen for a few seconds, disappears within their social/familial space. Shankar clearly projects a hope for a social space without hierarchy and equal opportunities as the graduates point to a large question mark on the screen and seek answers regarding the uncertainties regarding their future. This powerful scene reaches a climax when all female students are seen demanding a standardised national education system and throwing away their degrees by protesting in their own regional languages. In another scene, Shankar's dream experiment with wholistic education at the USICC Almora, is recreated where through the story-telling mode of balletic representation of the daily classes and dance-related activities.

A Satirical Take on the Cultural Policies and the Patrons of Art

As stated earlier, *Kalpana* refers to the issue of art-patronage time and again. Shankar's concerns over the political and cultural consequences of the growing trends of capitalism and consumerism are repeatedly visible in the encounters of Shankar's protagonist Udayan with such individuals and their attitude towards art and artists.

The culmination of the quest for support for the dance academy is shown in a long segment around the preparations and the final event of a dance festival organised by the Udayan Kala Kendra modelled on the real life and activities at the Uday Shankar India Culture Centre. The build-up to the festival is shown through rehearsals and preparations in the form of costume-designing and making, handling and structuring of props, and finally setting up of the stage, sets, and lights. Amidst the easily identifiable reproduction of backstage atmosphere, the announcer introduces the evening. The audience is made up of men, women, and children of all ages and from all classes and creed. Some of them are dressed in attire from different parts of India, while many are wearing Western clothes. Indians wearing Western attire are refused entry while others are welcomed in. Everyone regardless of his/her social position, is asked to crawl through low doors, in order to recognise and value the space of artistic creativity as a place that demands respectful experiencing and understanding.

As a part of the very same scene a number of heads of princely states are seen arriving at the festival venue. Some walk in, others come in palanquins and special carriers. All of them are asked to enter through the same low entrance hole, much to the chagrin of the heads of states. The satire and the comedy of the scene is simplistic, but relevant in its timeliness in the pre-independence scenario in India. As a choreopolitical choice, this part of the film displays concerns regarding the debates around the integration process of these small kingdoms, whose status and loyalty vis-a-vis the soon-to-be independent democratic country were sharply in focus at the time as is explained by Partha Chatterjee in State and Politics in India. He writes that during the partition there were 565 princely states that were under British paramountcy, without them being actually ruled by the British rulers in India. Through a series of political negotiations the terms of transfer of power were set to give the rulers of these princely states full sovereignty after 'the lapse of British paramountcy', unless they chose to join either Pakistan or India (Chatterjee 1997: 1–2). The British policies of difference towards these feudal states, helped the rulers maintain the severest form of feudalism, while the British took advantage of the despotism and policies of subjugation these rulers functioned with. Shankar commented on that in the performances within the festival programme. The rulers in their representations are ridiculed and called out for their arrogance and ignorance. I describe some of the dialogues in my writing:

> There are constant dialogues, narratives, and songs which raise questions like: 'who does this nation belong to?'; 'what is the way in which all people, male/female, old/young, poor/rich in India will have equal rights as citizens?'; 'what is the end of education?'; and so forth. These questions are raised along with slogans and statements like: 'The land belongs to the ones who toil in it'; 'there cannot be a nation without national education'; and 'be selfless for the mother-nation'' which are projected in the context of dramatised storylines portraying the dream. (Sarkar Munsi 2011: 145)

Kalpana for Shankar becomes a storyboard where he records all his concerns in often-scattered form of compilation. This particular segment creates an important conversation on accumulation of power and money in the hands of certain sections of the population and the impunity accorded to them because of their class status.

Two songs from this section of *Kalpana*—'Hum naach rahe Kathputli jeise' (meaning 'we are dancing like marionets') where the critique of the unthinking ways in which religious, caste, and gender divisions are perpetuated is expressed, and 'Bharata jai jai Bharata jai jai, jagrata Bharata jai jai jai' that celebrates India as a conscious and enlightened nation are important. They highlight two parallel and almost clashing threads of thought that are important in relation to the future vision of the independent nation that is projected through the story around which *Kalpana* consolidates itself. In the first song, the lament is for the ways in which people are comfortable living the life of a marionette, not choosing the path of emancipation. In the second song, he portrays the emergence of unity and national consciousness through the movements of a large number of dancers in an unending procession where a message for the new nation as a united and active one is put forth powerfully.

Kalpana in the Context of Indian Dance History

Kalpana is a documentation of dance movements as well as a prominent choreographic work by Uday Shankar. It also is a documentation of a range of Indian dance forms. Some of the film clips that exist of past dance practices from different ethnic communities in India can be found in the records at the Anthropological Survey of India, Royal Anthropological Society (UK), archival material existing at other colonial archives all over the world, scattered personal archives including filmed dances preserved at the Jacob's Pillow archive, and a short assemblage of film clips showing celebrations and dancing made by Uday Shankar and Alice Boner. *Kalpana* significantly captures the ritual and social space where dance has been a part of life in India. In an almost conscious anthropological choice and stance, the dance forms of the nation were portrayed as representatives of multiple identities made up of differences in language, religion, caste, class, gender, and geographies. These were portrayed through complex choreographies of bodies in space with identities stamped through musical instruments, costumes, ornaments, dance movements, and gestures. These scenes had a particular motive behind their compositions, they wanted to segregate according to types of dances, but they also wanted to create a garland like togetherness. Such complex and conscious ensemble-based choreographic productions were unknown before the USICC, Almora started training not only dancers but also choreographers in 1939.

In *Kalpana* one experiences the possibilities held within all embodied forms of knowledge such as dance and martial forms of art. While the neoclassical dances (formally declared as 'classical' in the post-independence times) and their presentational formats remain largely distanced and divorced from everyday life, the dance artist in Shankar brought together the ornamental classical/mythical representations through the figures of Shiva, Parvathi, Kartikeya, Indra, Gajasura, Pralhad, Hiranyakashipu together with figures of the farmer, the landless labourer, the factory worker, the famine affected emaciated people of Bengal into same visual scape. The human figures in different dances—from all over India, from everyday realities to characters of the dreams of Udayan, share the screen through the story. In the process, dance gained legitimacy of a powerful language, much beyond the ornamentality accorded and affixed to it as a form of high art. *Kalpana* therefore is a modern endeavour, an endeavour to imagine a world in the process of change and existing in between reality and hope for an ideal future.

All exploiters, oppressors, and elite are shown to be of upper class/caste groups from different parts of India. The commentaries that are on policies, education, work and labour, capitalism and mechanisation, agriculture, gender, and politics, seem to be situated in an independent India, at a time when the colonial handover of responsibilities has already happened. The questions asked or the resistance shown seems to be directed towards the planners and leaders of the newly independent nation. Shankar's Brahmin, upper class upbringing and his extensive exposure to the West did not make him very different from many of the policy makers who also came from the similar backgrounds. But his critique of the direction that the national policies were taking placed him on the opposite side of the turf from the planners of the nation.

The surprising absence of the references to the figure of the coloniser as the oppressor is an important point for discussion here. This film was planned at a time when India was in the last leg of its existence as a colony. The coloniser was very much of real presence. The figure of the colonial oppressor in the form of an exploiter, a violent administrator, or official that was commonly seen in the Indian theatre and films of those times is totally absent in *Kalpana*.

Dance and Art in *Kalpana*

The dance movements range from well-defined and grammatically immaculate neoclassical vocabulary to casual everyday gestures. Some of the dances—as discussed earlier—are almost exact reproductions of stage productions, while others are scenes developed for furthering the themes of the film. None of the pre-choreographed dances, i.e. *Kartikeya*, *Snanam*, *Grass Cutter*, *Astra Puja*, *Ras Leela*, *Indra*, *Shiva Parvati*, are longer than 1.5–2 minutes except for *Labour and Machinery*. A montage of community dances mostly with some changes made to the forms by Shankar help the representation of the image of the nation.

Often criticised for his borrowed Western eye and aesthetics, Shankar, from the beginning of his choreographic journey had two distinct elements in his choreography and choice of narrative. On the one hand, his projection of an imagined India that came alive through popular Hindu myths and portrayals of gods and goddesses, with costumes and jewellery carefully crafted and often chosen from the different adjacent cultures of Bali, Java, and so forth created an extended 'Indian'-ness that was beyond the everyday 'real'. And on the other hand there was a glorified, exoticised presentation of life and dance in India. This element is abundant in *Kalpana* as Shankar chose to weave in the most popular of the dances into the main narrative of the film. Inevitably, he danced as the principal male character in all these dances. In the reclaimed and restructured 'classical' dances like Bharatanatyam, gods and goddesses were the main elements, but in Uday's productions the themes around gods assumed a grand dimension with the use of group choreography.

In the course of Shankar's journey then, *Kalpana* also is a proof of the distance covered by Shankar himself as he travelled from his youth to maturity, from an untrained instinctive mover with a strong sense of artistic arrangements on stage to a man who trained himself to respond to the modern moment in his own culture. This modern moment was not only to create an Indian modernity but also to explore the vibrant world of dance that existed beyond Indian borders and to create and open a path for future transnational conversations. *Kalpana* is full of such joyous celebrations, often chaotic in arrangement. It is a space that Shankar seems to wish to fill with documentations from his memories of dance, nostalgia of success, his exposure to various cultures, his travel, dance collaborations, his methods and material for choreography, important moments of learning, disappointments, and also small references to his personal life. Like many artists of that time, Uday Shankar seemed to have been relating to his story in *Kalpana* through its interartistic interweaving of story, music, lyrics, dance, theatre, and scenography. He appears as an artist as well as a patriot, channelling creative urges to perform his duty to the newly independent nation and its society, politics, and culture. This time also stands out in terms of the consolidation of multi-art endeavours and the spectacular growth of the film industry in India. In that particular time frame, it was as if he was looking back and making sense of all that he enjoyed, learnt, and detested from past experiences.

Shankarscope

Uday Shankar's work with the production of *Shankarscope* started in 1970, right after he recovered from his second heart attack. By then Shankar had chosen to move away from his family and had chosen to embark on a new journey that he had become excited to start, both in terms of his professional as well as personal choices.

Regarding his artistic choice of using this form of multimedia experimentation, Shankar wrote about the thoughts behind *Shankarscope* in his introduction to the production, in the publicity material:

> From the beginning of my journey as an artist, I have never ever wanted to repeat any performance. I have always been excited by the thoughts of creating something new and special regarding the glory and traditional culture of India. Luckily most of those new productions have been received with a lot of love and appreciation all over the world. In the beginning of the 50's I had undertaken the work of producing the large and elaborate shadow-play '*Ramleela*' – a new form of performance on proscenium space, which was appreciated by the audience across the world. After that I produced *Lord Buddha* (Life of Buddha), a shadow-play in colour – which again got lauded for its innovative and creative potentials. I have also produced '*Shamanya Kshati*'[17] and '*Prakriti Ananda*'[18] which have been received with a lot of enthusiasm by the audience in India, Europe and the Americas.
>
> But I have been planning an experimental and exclusive variety programme for last twenty years or more, which nobody else could have even imagined then. I had not been able to produce it due to the lack of monetary support, but now am happy to be able to do so. I have heard that there are a few productions of this kind that have been successfully created in different parts of the world now. I am really happy that my dreams have come true now. This is a variety show that brings cinema as a part of the stage performance. This magical show brings together proscenium and cinema techniques… (Ghosh 2019: 249, Translation mine)

True to Shankar's claims, *Shankarscope* uses camera footage and images to extend thoughts beyond bodies, giving them a larger space, easily moving between the proscenium and the screen. The scope of using the camera to extend a stage dance in and out of a dream sequence was utilised to bring together the presence of the choreographer as well as the camera as co-creators. Shankar as a choreographer used his dance-making

[17] 'Shamanya Kshati' meaning literally 'a small loss' is poem by Rabindranath Tagore which was the idea behind this production by Shankar.

[18] 'Prakriti Ananda' is based on a dance drama written by Tagore by the name 'Chandalika'.

process as a conversation with directorial imagination, whereby the mediation was through his dancers and his images, which sometimes spoke together and at other times spoke to each other. Sequences blending the stage with the film projection established the two different mediums at the outset. Portions selected from Shankar's film *Kalpana* and from some of his stage productions, such as *Prakriti Ananda* moved in and out of the film to the stage and back (Fig. 5.5).

N. Adajania's note prepared for the Serendipity Art Festival 2019 (as displayed with the exhibits on *Shankarscope*), contained a publicity leaflet of two showings (performed on 8 October, 1971) at the Mavalankar Hall, Delhi. It records Bharat Sharma's comments:

> I have vivid memories, especially the magnificent beginning of excerpts from his film *Kalpana* on a giant net/screen upstage, and dancers dancing behind it. The narrative thereafter was sketchy but the techniques applied/invented were thrilling and often magical.
>
> Film projected on film had same dancers as on stage. It created an illusion of dancers coming upstage and then receding into the screen into abstract spaces. (Adjania's note for exhibition on *Shankarscope* at Serendipity Art Festival 2019)

One of the lead dancers of *Shankarscope*, Sharmistha (nee, Polly) Guha, in her interview,[19] described the rehearsal and creation of *Shankarscope* as 'very different from any other productions'. She said that the rehearsal started like all others with Shankar describing the mixed-media choreographic arrangement. Guha said that she and the other dancers were in awe of the idea and could hardly understand the design that Shankar was imagining. The rehearsal continued for six months at the well-known art space in Kolkata, named the Academy of Fine Arts, before the production was ready.

The Stage

For Shankar and the camera man Mahendra Kumar who helped him produce his last innovative production, in *Shankarscope* the 'challenge was to make onscreen characters and objects 'move' seamlessly onto the

[19] Sharmistha (Polly) Guha was one of the principal dancers in *Shankarscope*, a popular photograph of her eyes dominated one of the programme pages of the publicity brochure, from a scene from 'Prakriti Ananda'.

Fig. 5.5 Brochure for 'Shankarscope'—October 8, 1971 (© Urmimala Sarkar Munsi)

stage. Actors or objects had to move through a flap in the screen at the very moment their onscreen images appeared. The images also had to be life-size' (Suman Layak 2016: 4). The stage had a net/screen for the film projection that was made of a specific material of cloth that is used for cross stitch embroidery, named cellular cotton. This screen was used for the projection of pre-shot film elements that were an intrinsic part of the production. The special character of the screen was that it had 4 or 5 slits that could not be seen by the audience but created entrance and exit points for the cast to move on to the stage and vanish behind the screen without the whole screen moving at all. The stage had a raised platform of approximately eight feet height with stairs on both sides was right along the cloth screen. The cast was trained in the magical appearance and disappearance using the raised platform to walk on and off stage, always playing on the element of surprise with the help of a specialised stagecraft throughout the story. The lower or the dance stage, the raised platform, the space behind the screen, and the screen itself were all different spaces for performance utilised to the full for a magico-real experience. The utilisation of multiple performance spaces consistently were put in dialogue with each other by placing the bodies of the dancers in different spaces simultaneously. That allowed a conversation or coordinated choreography with each other.

Shankar's programme note for *Shankarshope* at the *Mavlankar Hall* programme consisted of a variety of items, seemingly put together for the purpose of showcasing the multimedia experiments, that gave a different aural and visual quality to many of the dance pieces included in Shankar's previous performances or in his film *Kalpana*. The list includes:

> *(1) Introduction; (2) Announcer Introducing himself; (3) Announcer and the Mikeman; (4) Drum Dance (Uday Shankar and others—from Kalpana); (5)Prakriti Ananda (a fantasy based on Tagore's dance drama Chandalika); (6) Announcer upside down; (7) Announcer and the Singer; (8) Dream of rhythm (Uday and Amala Shankar's Duet from Kalpana); (9) Jyotiswaram (Bharatanatyam); (10) Eternal Song (a contemporary piece); (11) Carpet; (12) Naga (a choreography from 'Kalpana'); (13) Dance Mad (a contemporary choreography); (14) Announcer and Belly Rolling (where Santi Bose would show the manipulations of stomach muscles); (15) The Beauty Competition (contemporary piece using dance and mime); (16) Epilogue (A concluding group performance); (17) National Anthem.*

Almost all the dance pieces from *Shankarscope* were dependent on multiple media and performed on screen, stage, or both simultaneously. In absence of detailed written material, the following section is consolidated on the basis of my memories and what have been shared by Sharmistha Guha (better known as Polly Guha, a well-known dancer/choreographer/ instructor from Kolkata), and one of the principal dancers in *Shankarscope* in a prolonged set of interviews from 2019 and 2020.

Sections from *Kalpana*: A number of items were recreated from Shankar's film *Kalpana* and represented by using the stage and the screen together, perhaps reflecting Shankar's nostalgia of the film production and his desire to create a conversation between dancing bodies across the barriers of different mediums. While the original dance was projected on the screen, the dancers performed the theme on the stage to produce an on and off-screen synchronisation of affect. Polly Guha mentioned that the scene banked on the revival of the nostalgia and memory of Shankar's heydays in the minds of the audience.

From *Prakriti–Ananda*: The programme note for *Shankarscope* mentions 'A fantasy based on the original "Chandalika" of Gurudev Rabindra Nath Tagore, depicting the vices and curse of untouchability'. The scene began with a young man falling asleep while reading a book, and then dreaming of somebody calling him by name[20] (Khokar 2001: 64). As the young man got up from his bed, he was transported from the real world to the world of his dreams on the screen as the eyes of the mother of Prakriti beckoned him and started telling him the story of the daughter (Prakriti), whom she has lost. The story told by her on screen was enacted on stage 'through a unique Corps de Ballets of Shankar's School of Dancing' (Brochure, 1971).

[20] The scene brought Chandalika, out of its original context, to be a story by Tagore being read by a member of the contemporary society, implying thereby the ongoing presence of the phenomenon of caste system and untouchability.

The two eyes of the dancer Polly Guha, were filmed and used on screen as the haunting/haunted eyes of the mother of a girl-child, who wanted to challenge patriarchy, caste hierarchy, and social marginalisation. The references to Tagore's story, Chandalika, according to Guha, was clear to those who were familiar with the story already, but otherwise, the sequence in and for itself was a mixed-media presentation of a story of traversing a real and a dream world.

Eternal Melody: A newly engaged young couple died in a tragic accident on a bike after their engagement ceremony. In spite of their commitment to each other that they promised to carry out, they found themselves challenged in the post-death world, as they could not keep their promises. Nothing they thought to be eternal seemed the same. Their realisation that neither the elements such as earth, sky, wind, forest, ocean, and nor the human qualities such as vice, virtue, or divisions such as gender, caste, nation, religion carried any eternal significance brought them to the realisation that nothing is ever-present but faith in god (Khokar 2001: 64).

The screen became vitally important in depicting the couple's last journey on screen and the falling of the bodies on the stage through the screen. The use of the screen to project the filmed sequence was followed by a section on and off-screen.

Lady and the Thief: This short sequence was based on an episode around the life of a urban household. It was constructed as the events of a theft in a woman's house, where she had left her old mother-in-law with a trusted watchman. The story revolved around a thief's experience in that house as he entered the house and tried to escape with some valuable ornaments. The audience as well as the thief were shocked at the ability of the old lady, who managed to catch the thief by trapping him in the gunny bag that he had used to entrap the lady. The comical elements of this performance used on the screen and the stage also carried some elements of magic.[21]

Dance Mad: Is described as 'A melodrama of love affairs of modern Romeos, composed with dance and music' in Shankar's programme note published by Mohan khokar (2001: 64). Polly Guha remembers her role as the lady love of a man who was ready to leave for his office. This

[21] Sharmistha (Polly) Guha, during her interview date 28 January, 2010, at her house in Kolkata described the skilled actions the cast needed to learn in order to include magical acts.

sequence had Guha dancing with a circular movement to slowly disappear through the split curtain after the man left for office. The audience was spellbound when the man returned once to take his hat and again to ask for his bag that he had left behind and got both these items as they were handed to him through the screen. Such use of simple but timely and coordinated magical moves along with artistic techniques of mimes, music, and dance, created a multi-sensory effect and forced the audience to open up to the idea of inclusive multimedia reception.

Beauty Competition: According to Shankar's publicity material, the Beauty Competition was a colourful and entertaining satire on the beauty competitions. According to Guha, Shankar wanted famous actresses like Chandrabati Devi, Chhaya Devi, and Renuka Devi to participate in the Beauty Competition sequence in *Shankarscope*, but as none of them agreed, the cast was used to create that sequence. It was a satire on the fashion industry and the beauty competitions that had just started as events showcasing the fashion world. A mingling of the stage cast and the filmed characters created a visual made up of a successful merger of on and off-screen activities that became a meaningful sequence through the bi-medial choreography. The scene used the split screen through which the competitors came out to the stage one by one.

The last scene of *Shankarscope* consisted of a group composition performed by all the members of the cast, where shadows, stage, and films came together in creating a sensational ending. Polly Guha described the details of the smooth manoeuvres through the screen, the constant organising, and handling different levels of stage, props, and also operating the dimmer lights as and when needed. She mentioned that the training was not only on dance and coordination between screen and stage presence, but also helped in expanding the meaning of participation to include showmanship, split second adjustments, and the use of smooth and timely moving, stealthy shifting of positions, and completely controlled and manipulated ensemble time and movement sharing.

Shankarscope was not very successful, though it was appreciated by art makers as a 'multimedia' presentation. At the same time this new experiment by an iconic dancer was not accepted favourably by many. A popular political weekly *Shankar's Weekly* published a review on 24 October 1971 that mentioned *Shankarscope* as an experiment and a 'gallimaufry of unrelated forms of performing arts'.

It continues the review, critiquing and praising the presentation, saying:

> Uday Shankar's latest venture '*Shankarscope*' leaves us wondering what the renowned artist is trying to achieve at this point of his career. He has had his days of glory and awards. But the urge in him to do something new has taken shape as *Shankarscope*. Shankar's eagerness to explore the multimedia possibilities at a time when such mixing of mediums were limited by technologies as well as examples of other such works is lauded by some of the people who went with an expectation of the reappearance of Shankar's choreographic 'magic' for the proscenium, but at the same time echoed the disappointment about the medley that *Shankarscope* seemed to become for many of them. At the same time, the people who participated in the performance still express a great thrill and amazement at the experiments that they witnessed and were a part of as participants. (*Shankar's Weekly* 1971: 27)

The review concedes that it must have been quite thrilling for the participants and Uday Shankar himself to 'manage this kind of off-and-on stage effects and moves almost at the click of a switch'. The review indicates a refusal to accept Shankar's wish to move beyond the stage productions:

> .... one would be wasting his time if he were to look for the 'art' for which Uday Shankar is known. His transcending of barriers of stage and screen could only establish beyond doubt the fundamental difference between the two forms.... There is a lot of scope in *Shankarscope* for Uday Shankar the technician.... Quite certainly this is not the work of a master which we know Uday Shankar to be. (*Shankar's Weekly* 1971: 27)

Shankarscope is remembered by many as a great wonder using stage and screen. But it is remembered by many others as something that did not make any sense, even though it came across as an interesting experiment. Shankar's active life as a choreographer came to an end with this production.

It becomes clear that Shankar was constantly searching for new ways of expressing various configurations of embodiment. The dancing body for him needed to be the experiential/experimental space of assimilation and representation. They were theatrical and mimetic bodies, everyday/natural bodies, stylised/aestheticised bodies, gendered and amorphous bodies, privileged and well-fed bodies, unfed and labouring bodies, urban/upper caste and marginal bodies from different parts of rural India. Use of mixed media maximised the possibilities of sharing

Shankar's scopic imaginations with the public, beyond the screen, proscenium or shadow plays.

Shankar's experiments of the three choreographic productions taken up in this chapter are much ahead of their time in the Indian context. Ashish Rajadhyaksha asks an important question in the context of the technologies of production that becomes an important address in this chapter. He asks 'The question of how the (often primitive) technologies of reproduction could be mobilised in the way they were, needs to be asked from the other end as well: what does such symbolic production mean and how does it work within the broad scope of high-nationalist productions in early twentieth century India?' (2009: 144).

Shankar's experimentations with regular proscenium based choreographies, shadow performances, and dance on camera signifies a journey from what Rajadhyaksha calls 'primitive' to what may be designated as avant-garde in the context of choreography in Indian dance in the pre-independence times. Same dances and similar scenes, dresses, and movements resurface in his choreographies, his scenic imaginations, and in *Kalpana* in more than one scene, especially while showing everyday life in the form of festivals, processions, community dances, and ritual celebrations. In all the three different experimental productions, Shankar's choreographies appear to be benefitting from his knowledge of the changing techniques of symbolic communication, more than the dance movements themselves. The idea of using symbols in different manners and creating languages of appropriate communication that could then be used for telling a story seem to have intrigued and challenged Shankar to the extent that he took chances beyond his means throughout his life.

Modernity as a New Form of Subjectivity or a Duty Towards the Nation

Randy Martin's idea of mobilisation is what becomes important in this context to understand the changing forms of subjectivity that Shankar seemed to have discovered within himself. Randy Martin argued:

> Mobilisation is situated through dancing so as to indicate the practical dynamic between production and product. Here, production is what dancing assembles as a capacity for movement, and the product is not the aesthetic effect of the dance but the materialized identity accomplished through the performativity of movement. (Martin 1998: 4)

Shankar's work beginning with his first shadow play, his film *Kalpana*, and his multimedia production *Shankarscope* have been considered as results of his experimental mobilisation of his curiosity and interest in the use of different aural and visual technologies and performance processes. As he himself never tried to explain his inner urge or his subjectivity, there has been almost no discussion on the new ways in which Shankar himself was excited to mobilise expressive embodied subjectivity. The clarity of the path he sought also kept on evolving, making his mobilisational goals significantly different in these three phases. But it is important to note that his own subjectivity developed through his personal journey, making sense of the fascination, craving, and understandings of the mobilisational requirements from within himself and from outside.

In the first of the three experiments, a conversation between the proscenium and screen representation began to take place through the shadow play—with Shankar challenging himself through limiting the available ways of balletic representation and facial expressions. The second experiment with the medium of films may have been a result of the vast canvas he wanted to create in responding to the inner urgency to document his dream, his choreographic works, and the unfulfilled desire of creating an institution. This phase of mobilisation saw Shankar struggling with his political voice and images that were used specifically to build an idea of a diverse and secular India. *Shankarscope* seems to have been built on a different sort of mobilisation altogether. It was an amalgam of concluded and unfinished journeys in the past, of paths traversed and discarded. In a kaleidoscopic basket, a number of thoughts and dances of yester-years were put together with somewhat chaotic thoughts of the ongoing experiences. Randy Martin's observation, 'Hence, through mobilisation, bodies traverse a given terrain that by traversing, they constitute. Further, by constituting that immediate context for movement, bodies display as their identity the practical effects of dancing' (Randy Martin 1998: 4), thus, has provided a logic for stringing all the three technologies of these productions spread over thirty-one years of Shankar's life. Over these years—Shankar's ever-restless urge to mobilise his everyday realities seems to have been pushed to work with embodied creative possibilities. It is helpful to think of this restlessness as a product of his transcultural exposure. These experiments create a space for Shankar within the culture/history-specific modernity in India as his work leads to a range of performance process and products, which may be seen as 'diverse experimentations and life-projects where nothing remains static and stable' (Pathak 2006: 14).

References

Bhabha, Homi. 1990. "Introduction—Nation and Narration." In *Nation and Narration*, edited by Homi Bhabha, 1–7. London and New York: Routledge.

Bleeker, Maaike, ed. 2016. *Transmission in Motion: The Technologizing of Dance.* London: Routledge.

Brochure of USICC, Almora. 1941.

Brochure for Shankarscope, October 8, 1971.

Chatterjee, Partha. [1997] 1999. *The Nation and Its Fragments: Colonial and Postcolonial Histories (Reprint).* New Delhi: Oxford University Press.

Erdman, Joan L. 1997. "Reflecting Our Past; Reflecting on Our Future." *Proceedings, Society of Dance History Scholars, Twentieth Annual Conference*, 270–74. Riverside: University of California, Riverside.

Ernst, Wolfgang. 2013. *Digital Memory and the Archive: Electronic Mediations, Volume 39.* Minnesota: University of Minnesota Press.

Ghosh, Bishakha. 2019. *Shankarnama: Smritichitre Amala Shankar (Bengali).* Kolkata: Ananda Publishers.

Interview of Uday Shankar by Shambhu Mitra. https://www.youtube.com/watch?v=JHq-uBio5vE. Accessed on 25 January 2018.

Khokar, Mohan. 2001. "Shankar's Repertoire." *Nartanam* 1 (4, October–December): 43–64.

Khullar, Sonal. 2018. "Almora Dreams: Art and Life at the Uday Shankar India Cultural Centre, 1939–44." *Marg* 69 (4): 14–31.

Layak, Suman. 2016. "The Charmed Life of Legendary Cameraman Mahendra Kumar." *The Economic Times*, October 23, 4.

Lutgendorf, Philip. 2017. "Two Dances and a Conference." *South Asian Popular Culture* 15 (2): 217–23.

Martin, Randy. 1998. *Critical Moves: Dance Studies in Theory and Politics.* Durham and London: Duke University Press.

Mehra, Girish N. 2007. *Nearer Heaven than Earth.* Delhi: Rupa & Co.

Pathak, Avijit. 2006. *Modernity, Globalization and Identity: Towards a Reflexive Quest.* Delhi: Aakar Books.

Rajadhyaksha, Ashish. 2009. *Indian Cinema in the Time of Celluloid: From Bollywood to the Emergency.* New Delhi; Bloomingdon: Tulika Books/Bloomington: Indiana University Press.

Raju. 1971. "From Kalpana to Shankarscope", October 24. Vol. 24. No. 23. Pp. 27–28. 1971. "From Kalpana to Shankarscope." *Shankar's Weekly*, Vol. 24, No. 23, 24 October: 27–28.

Sarkar Munsi, Urmimala. 2011. "Imag(in)ing the Nation: Uday Shanlar's Kalpana." In *Traversing Tradition: Celebrating Dance in India*, edited by Urmimala Sarkar Munsi and Stephanie Burridge, 124–50. Delhi: Routledge.

Sarkar, Sumit. 2015. *Modern Times: India 1880s–1950s, Environment, Economy, Culture.* Ranikhet: Permanent Black.

Segal, Zohra. 2010. *Close-Up: Memories of a life on Stage and Screen*. New Delhi: Women Unlimited (An Associate of Kali for Women).

Shankar, Rajendra. 2001. "Uday Shankar—Personal Reminiscences." *Nartanam* 1 (4, October–December): 12–34.

Shankar, Uday. 1998. "Fundamental Approach to Indian Dancing." *Nrityakalpa, Journal of West Bengal Dance Group Federation*, 8–11.

Archival and Audio-Visual Material

Dartington Hall Records. Dartington Hall Trust Archives files [Devon Heritage Centre, Great Moor House, Bittern Road, Sowton, Exeter, Devon, EX2 7NL]. https://www.dartington.org/?s=archives.

———. LKE/IN/19: Title—LKE India 19: Uday Shankar India Culture Centre, 1932–1973.

———. DWE/A/8: Title—Dance 2, Shankar and other Indian Dancers.

———. DS/UK/843: Title—India Culture Trust; 1937–.

———. DS/UK/836: Title—Admin History Uday Shankar India Culture Centre; 1938–.

———. MC/Chekhov/S4/39: Series 4.General Files: A. Uday Shankar Play bills.

———. USIC Centre Newsletters 1939—1944 (Fortnightly), Ranidhara, Almora, U.P. Editors: Rajendra Shankar and Vishnudas Shirali (Source: Dartington Archives, Devon Cultural Centre, UK).

Guha Aniruddha. 2012. A dream uncanned: Uday Shankar's 1948 film 'Kalpana' https://www.dnaindia.com/lifestyle/report-a-dream-uncanned-uday-shankar-s-1948-film-kalpana-1691196. Accessed on 09 September 2021.

Interview of Uday Shankar by Shambhu Mitra https://www.youtube.com/watch?v=JHq-uBio5vE. Accessed on 25 January, 2018.

Sangeet Natak Akademi Website: Moulana Azad's speech. https://www.sangeetnatak.gov.in/sna/introduction.php. Accessed on 20 March 2018.

Shankar, Uday. Dir. Kalpana. 160 Mins, Uday Shankar Production, Gemini Studios, Madras. India, January 1, 1948. digital copy at https://www.youtube.com/watch?v=S6hnsycStbY. Accessed on 30 October 2019, or https://www.facebook.com/NARTHAKI/videos/359372408830378. Accessed on 25 August 2021.

CHAPTER 6

The Illusive Legacy

It was not only movement, he was training the mind. He was making a thinking dancer. And he always said, you must think before you do it.

(Narendra Sharma 1998a: 86)

Your uncle always said that one dances the way one lives, and one lives the way one dances.

(Amala Shankar, in classes and rehearsals, USICC, Kolkata 1966–2015)

Shankar's Legacy: Acknowledgements, Pedagogy, and Legitimacy

In this chapter, the idea of legacy gets attention through three different key markers: acknowledgements, pedagogy, and legitimacy. All these markers have frequently been analysed in academic and biographical writings on Uday Shankar, and in addressing controversies, claims, and counter-claims. Thinking through these three ideas, this chapter frames Shankar in an increasingly smaller domain of shrinking relevance, eroding memory, and a near-absent transculturality of the remnants. The transcultural and translocational expanse of Shankar's fame and acceptance that was possible in the pre-independence time seems like a distant nostalgic

U. Sarkar Munsi, *Uday Shankar and His Transcultural Experimentations*, Transnational Theatre Histories,
https://doi.org/10.1007/978-3-030-93224-4_6

past now, impossible to access by any other dancer, even at a time when international communications have reached their peak. Khullar in her largely archive-based reading, aptly called USICC, Almora 'An incubator of modern art', acknowledging that 'the Centre played a unique role in the cultural history of India' (Khullar 2018: 20). Reflecting on Shankar's legacy a lived experience, I see the absence of a clear future path (in the absence of an institutionally legitimised curriculum propagated by Uday Shankar himself) and the histories of controversies regarding owning/inheriting the dance-knowledge propagated by him, as reasons that plague Shankar's legacy. This has resulted in several levels of erasure of Shankar's achievements. Almost no knowledge about him and his dance remains in the larger dance discourse in India for the current generation of young dancers to see, read, or experience.

Shankar and Institutional Acknowledgements

The relationship between Uday Shankar and The Sangeet Natak Akademi (SNA) remained fragile throughout the 24 years that Shankar lived after the Akademi was established. The Akademi's beginning years were marked by four national seminars—1955 on film in 1956 on drama, in 1957 on music and the fourth and last in 1958 on dance.

The Film Seminar,[1] was organised at the National Physical Laboratory in New Delhi. It was inaugurated by the then Prime Minister Jawaharlal Nehru. Shankar's film Kalpana received critical appreciation for being the only first-rate dance film. Shankar was invited to present his speech on 'Role of Dance in Cinema' in the Film seminar. He emphasised the need to go beyond the use of dance just as ornamentation—stating that most dances that are used in films are not intended for the camera at all.

The Dance Seminar of 1958[2] was planned by the General Council at its meeting held on 17 May 1957. Dr. P. V. Rajammanar was then the Chairman of the Akademi. Uday Shankar, Rukmini Devi Arundale, Hari Uppal and Dr. V. Raghavan were the members of the organising committee. In this seminar however, Shankar is not part of the speakers' list. Sachin Shankar (a student and troupe member from USICC spoke

[1] Film Seminar Report, edited by R. M. Ray (1956), was a publication based on the Film Seminar (1955) by Sangeet Natak Akademi.

[2] The papers of the Dance Seminar have been published in 2013. "Papers From the First Dance Seminar. 1958." *Sangeet Natak* XLVII (1–4) guset edited by Sunil Kothari.

on dance and creativity. Shankar's troupe was invited to perform as a part of the evening showcases.

Shankar was the first recipient of the Sangeet Natak Akademi Award in the category 'Creative dance/Choreography' in 1960. The Sangeet Natak Academy fellowship, officially known as Sangeet Natak Academy Ratna Sadasya, is an Indian honour for the performing arts presented by Sangeet Natak Academy. Each year 40 artists are selected for this award. In 1962 Shankar was the recipient in the category of Dance.

Shankar's somewhat symbolic inclusion in the University system was in the form of the introduction of the Uday Shankar Chair at the Rabindra Bharati University, where Dr. Sunil Kothari, a well-known dance critic, became the first Chair Professor.

Shankar Received Padma Vibhushan (the second highest Civilian honour in India), in 1971, in the category of Arts. In 1975 he received Deshikottam, the highest accolade awarded by Visva-Bharati University for his contribution to Indian society as an artist. Pandit Ravi Shankar organised Uday Utsav after Shankar's death in 1977, in Delhi in 1983 and His Birth Centenary celebration (2001) was curated by Sunil Kothari at the Indira Gandhi National Centre for the Arts (IGNCA) with an exhibition and showing of *Kalpana*. Sangeet Natak Akademi also celebrated his birth centenary in the years 2001–2002 in Delhi, Kolkata, Chennai, and Mumbai with seminars on Uday Shankar and his dance and numerous performances by Amala, his students, and followers.

Embodied Memory as Remnants and Legacy: The Present Scenario

The USICC, Kolkata, established by Uday and Amala Shankar[3] in 1965, my alma mater, shut down in 2015 and hardly anyone (including the people who became dancers by training under Amala Shankar in the school) mention or acknowledge it anymore.

Shankar's associates and students from USICC Almora, Simkie, Zohra Segal, Sachin Shankar, Narendra Sharma, Shanti Bardhan, Guru Dutt to name just a few, continued their association with dance and or films. Some of Uday Shankar's achievements live on in West Bengal through

[3] Amala Shankar was one hundred and two years old when she passed away. For her efforts as a dancer, choreographer, artist, prominent citizen of India, and her contribution to the community she has received several accolades and awards.

the work of his later associates and disciples post 1960, who were trained by him. Shankar's daughter Mamata Shankar (once my senior at USICC, Kolkata, and an accomplished dancer, an exciting choreographer, and a well-known actor) runs a large dance institution named Udayan Kala Kendra (with reference to the name of his dream academy from his film *Kalpana*). Since the early 1980s, she has worked hard to propagate a derivative form of Shankar's pedagogy, in her own institution and performing troupe, which are well known. Their achievements include teaching and choreographies in 'Uday Shankar style'[4] and reconstructing and restaging some of Shankar's older dances. Uday Shankar's daughter-in-law, Tanushree Shankar is also a dancer and began her independent journey as a dancer/choreographer/teacher, alongside her late husband Ananda Shankar, who was well known as one of the torch-bearers of the musical genre now known as World Music. She has been known for her openness towards collaborations between different evolving contemporary choreographic techniques from all over the world. She has worked recently on internationally funded projects conceptualised around the reconstruction of Shankar's work and the restaging of Shankar's dance choreographies. One of the important dancer/choreographers in this context is Bharat Sharma, Narendra Sharma's son, who has been endowed with his father's incisive understanding of the process involved in Shankar's pedagogy and a rare and critical understanding of Indian dance history. He has continued exploring Shankar's idea of 'creative dance' through his own explorations on pedagogy and choreography.

Shankar is assigned a somewhat marginal space in the dance history of India. It is almost impossible to teach Shankar's dance as a package, deliverable against an amount charged as fees as it does not just rest on a series of movement sequences that can be learnt as syllables. With increasing impatience towards long drawn learning processes, and the liking for the modular short-cuts and abstractions among the learners, this dance pedagogy does not suit the expectations of the parents of the large number of students who continue to learn dance in urban dance institutions. However, social media posts regularly claim Shankar's legacy, with photos to back the claim to fame. The claims to ownership of rights to perpetuate Shankar's dance go on, in Kolkata. In the rest of India, Uday Shankar is

[4] Shankar's dance pedagogy is a system, not a series of products, and hence, is useful only if the pedagogy empowers new dancers to think through the ongoing relationship with their bodies and the creativity that they generate as dance.

rarely remembered and only known to a few as brother of the famous sitarist, Ravi Shankar.

The Creative Process as Legacy/Legacy as a Creative Process

The USICC in Almora did not survive long enough for Shankar to demonstrate and establish a truly transculturally envisioned centre for dance and choreography. Narendra Sharma laments in his article, 'Indian Dance at Crossroads', the absence of a national school of choreography even today, when there was such a successful model present in the pre-independence times. He writes that while public and private resources were put to use to create institutions to teach classical dances and research traditional teaching methods of imitative knowledge transmission from the master teacher (guru) to the student (shishya). The problems with Shankar's legacy can be summed up with Sharma's questions, 'Why did we bypass what had already been achieved by Uday Shankar and Rabindranath Tagore in Santiniketan? Why did we minimise the need for a central institute of contemporary choreography right in those early days?' (Sharma 1998a: 34–35). Sharma's questions stem from the fact that most of the dance institutions established in the post-independence period rejected Shankar's modern efforts towards dance/art education and chose to teach according to the strictly traditional format of the guru–shishya parampara.[5]

A major uneasiness of the dancer is always regarding the ephemerality of the embodied knowledge. Unless documented, taught, and/or written about, dance seems to vanish into the blue with the dancing body. This is why pedagogy and grammatical structure become so important to all Indian classical forms, and even community dance forms have recognised that the only way for the form to survive is to create a structure for its transmission. Shankar realised the necessity of teaching the idea

[5] Kapila Vatsyayan describes guru-shishya parampara as the master–disciple tradition in the context of classical Indian classical dance and music. Revered by many classicists even today, this system has been often critiqued as a prescriptive and often exploitative feudal system of transfer of knowledge, whereby the guru or the master lays down the rules and the shishya or the disciple is bound by the unwritten bonds of servitude to submit to them, in order to qualify as a deserving receiver of knowledge imparted by the master.

of the process of creativity as the process of dance-making and choreography. Shankar's classes, as mentioned often by Narendra Sharma, Amala Shankar, Ravi Shankar, Rajendra Shankar, Zohra Segal, and many others, actively rejected the idea of imitation or 'copying' as knowledge. It is somewhat like learning a language, where memorising a sentence, and copying it over and over again may make one learn the line itself, but it would not teach the ability to create a new sentence. That is not because one is lacking in intellect but because one does not know the process of the construction of a meaningful assemblage of words that would help give shape to one's thoughts.

I remember some of the senior troupe members being told by Amala Shankar, 'you all are really good dancers, and you are doing well as teachers too, but you have still some things to learn about teaching the creative dance classes'. We were already senior teachers for her institution then and this observation puzzled us. Today, looking back, I realise what she had meant. Creativity is a never-ending endeavour. One learns from every class he or she teaches. There is no right or wrong and yet there are rules. Narendra Sharma's writing becomes one of the best texts in this context. Sharma writes about Uday Shankar:

> He used to take general class, technique class and improvisation class. In improvisation, he came up with new subjects every day. The subjects varied—for example, you are in a forest and it is dark, and suddenly there is a storm. What will your reaction be? One of the rare things in these classes was that there was always an orchestra available, because he had his own musicians in the troupe, and they attended this also. They had to improvise the music. There were a lot of instruments, he had one of the best collections of instruments. Being very versatile musicians, they would compose.... It was a thrill to be in improvisation class because you were free to do any movement. He had a way of doing improvisation. For example, he would draw ten different lines on a blackboard. He was a painter, you know. There was one flowing down like this, another shooting up like this, each line had a character. Now, he would say, look here, you don't see anything else but this particular line. Close your eyes and see it in your mind. That line. And start feeling the flow of the line and know the character of the line. (Sharma 'Making of' 1998b: 85)

Shankar's training had two parts: firstly, he gave a lot of importance to the techniques and for that there were three forms of classical dances that had to be learnt without any dilution; secondly, he taught students to experience moving by creating situations of intense engagement, recognition of patterns, and then by repeated work on those movements attempting to experiment with active realigning, changing, or replacing of those movement patterns. Often such endeavours needed the micro-management of effort, labour, imagination, and emotional realignment. Shankar's specific contribution was to teach each individual to create a specific 'somatic attentiveness' of one's own for being able to create an auto-ethnography of the processes of embodied reflections. Einav Katan would advise us on the same process by writing:

> The habitus, as the physical embodiment of former techniques, is a source within perceptual processes. Embodied reflection is an exchange between tacit knowledge, which is physically embodied, and the consciousness that new situations evoke. Accordingly, there is an exchange between consciousness and unconsciousness, as well as between direction and letting go (or letting undergo). (Katan 2016: 32)

The term, 'perpetual process' becomes one of the important tools of the form that Shankar named 'creative' dance. The process of dance-making remained continuous even after culminating in a product and therefore the movements, symbols, and designs remained open to changes, perpetually encouraging the conversation of the dancer and the dancing body with the patterns emerging from his/her everyday experiences. Shankar's pedagogy becomes evident from Narendra Sharma's interview. In his interview, 'Making of a Thinking Dancer' Sharma wrote about the organised routine and structure within Shankar's classes. 'It's not the dance as such, but the way of being in it, in a disciplined way' (Sharma, 'Making of' 1998b: 85). Sharma continues to explain the body training process in Shankar's classes as:

> The 'traditional techniques' he used only to enrich your body language. He said, don't play with the traditional techniques. You learn exactly what it is. But this is what I am giving to you to enrich your body language through the styles. He never believed in patchwork. One movement of Kathakali, one movement of this, no, no. If you have enriched your language, it automatically comes…
>
> For example, if I compose, I can never say from where the movements are coming. Because it is a part of the total whole, you know. You don't feel, I have used Manipuri, now to make it more forceful I'll use Kathakali,

> no, no. It automatically flows. And once you have a body language, you never know if you are drawing from modern dance or somewhere else. It blends into a total whole. (Sharma, 'Making of' 1998b: 85–86)

This process is completely in opposition to the learning process in classical dances where the grammatical base works as the unchangeable repository of a certain cluster of rigid movement principles. As Sharma has explained above, Shankar managed to develop a pedagogy that worked for him and also as a transferable knowledge system for the dancing body and the developing choreography as a visual and perceptive tool. Sharma insisted that Shankar did not teach movements, he trained the mind and the body to come together to create a dance and be the dancer. He described the class situation in the following words, 'Usually we used to sit in a semi-circle, and there was a very big drum. He used to sit down also and on the drum he used to just give a beat, to create an atmosphere, and everybody would close their eyes and think of that particular line. And then he would say, now start doing what you have felt about it (Sharma, 'Making of' 1998b: 86).

What becomes clear is that there is a transfer of agency and, therefore, through relegating of responsibility to the student, the master teacher transfers an idea and leaves the end of each movement open as a response from the student(s). Thus, each process of creation in dance is open to innovation, agency, responsibility, aesthetic choice, as well as an ability of the student to finally sculpt the movement to become her or his own, rather than being any unit of knowledge imitated and reproduced. Of course, Shankar encountered the repeated accusation of disrespecting the idea of authenticity, even though in his classes he emphasised the need to respect the methods of knowledge transfer in classical dances.

It would have been great had the USICC in Almora survived a little while longer, at least till there could be a formalisation of the pedagogic structure and the courses and a permanent patronage was assigned. It needed to survive so that Shankar would leave a number of next-generation dancers successfully claiming the legacy of the USICC as graduates of the batches that passed the course with him at the helm. It needed to survive so that the people of independent India could have understood and seen the results of the transcultural conversations that had been negotiated by Shankar. It also needed to survive so that the modern dance in India could have had a chance to grow a stronger root. After it was dismantled, for a while there was no school for Shankar to teach his creative process in.

For *Kalpana* he engaged a large number of new dancers trained in various dance styles including Kathakali and Manipuri, of who a few remained associated with him until his demise. After making Kalpana, he seemed to have lost faith in institutional training and preferred working with performers trained already in different classical and folk dance forms. They participated in his choreographic processes to learn his older choreographies, participated in his new performances, learnt his experimental stagecraft, and performed with him in India and abroad. Most of those dancers were not exclusively attached to Shankar but worked as professional performers for a number of choreographers at the same time. Shankar trained them for the national and international tours abroad, the last of which was in 1968 during which Shankar had to be hospitalised and the tour had to be cancelled midway. The dream of creating a pedagogic process and the wholistic development of personalities seem to have remained largely unfulfilled.

The questions and hegemonic dominance of the classical dances that Shankar's immediate students and all of us have had to face made our relationship with the legacy rather complex and often fragile. Many of the later generations of students never got to the stage where they could boldly argue their position vis-a-vis the classical dancers. Most of them still do not understand that their core strength lies in the way they understood the 'process' rather than reproducing the 'items' as 'finished products'. This is a lack, a serious one, in the pedagogical process within the legacy itself.

The word 'legacy' therefore becomes a painful remainder/reminder of what could have been claimed as Shankar's contribution, of a lost opportunity for claiming modern dance experimentations by his associates, students, and by independent India falling prey to unrelenting cultural politics. Shankar nearly disappeared from the official records in the first three decades of the existence of the Sangeet Natak Akademi.[6] The words and vision of Maulana Abul Kalam Azad, the then Union

[6] As per the Sangeet Natak Akademi website 'The Sangeet Natak Akademi India's national academy for music, dance, and drama is the first National Academy of the arts set up by the Republic of India. It was subjectivity created by a resolution of the (then) Ministry of Education, Government of India, dated 31 May 1952 notified in the Gazette of India of June 1952'. See https://www.sangeetnatak.gov.in/sna/introduction.php.

Minister for Education, were not inclusive of works of 'intruders' like Shankar,

> India's precious heritage of music, drama and dance is one which we must cherish and develop. We must do so not only for our own sake but also as our contribution to the cultural heritage of mankind. Nowhere is it truer than in the field of art that to sustain means to create. Traditions cannot be preserved but can only be created afresh. It will be the aim of this Akademi to preserve our traditions by offering them an institutional form... (Azad quoted in https://www.sangeetnatak.gov.in/sna/introduction.php)

What is peculiar is the fact that Shankar's more than fifty-year long career is not systematically documented. Many of the existing collections are partial, personal, and not appropriately curated and publicised. This remains a historical necessity, regardless of whether Shankar was criticised by the Indian critics or not. Ignored by his country except for some recognition conferring him a state honour as an important citizen, Shankar was largely left to his own resources to survive, dance, teach, and keep his translocational conversations alive.

The dismissive reactions by Shankar's critics actually managed to create a significant opposition to his performances among the cultural elite of India. But the spirit of embodied experimentations that brought together regional as well as neoclassical movement idioms together with the everyday lived experiences in his dance was later claimed by dancers such as Ram Gopal,[7] Manjushree Chaki Sircar,[8] Chandralekha,[9] and many others though Shankar's contribution remains largely unacknowledged in Indian dance history. In my opinion, denying Shankar a significant space, the country has lost a portion of its dance history.

On the other hand, the regurgitating of his choreographic creations or imitative reproductions of dances that can be seen in *Kalpana* actually led to a 'kinaesthetic loss', whereby Shankar's dance no longer seemed to have any use besides being reproduced in exact or 'as exact as possible' a

[7] See details in p. 78.

[8] Manjushree Chaki Sircar developed a dance form that drew on major neoclassical dance forms from India and also from regional practices such as Chhau and Thangta.

[9] Chandralekha, is known for her contribution in developing experimental choreographies using Bharatanatyam, Yoga and martial arts like Kalarippayattu. Her contribution remains a landmark in Indian modern/contemporary developments in dance in India.

manner. This copying and pasting process is actually doing a disservice to Shankar's creations as they are judged as decontextualised, aged, jaded, and simplistic by the current generation of critics.

Many a times, Shankar's film, *Kalpana*, is taken as proof of what he created, for evaluating his creativity through the dance that is left behind in the film bearing his signature. Thus, *Kalpana* is considered one of the most concrete legacies left behind by Uday Shankar. This film (see Chapter 5 for details) is seen as a path-breaker that influenced the dance scenario in the Bombay film industry. Part of this golden era in Bombay films was populated by several of Shankar's students and associates such as Guru Dutt, Simkie, Prabhat Ganguly, Zohra Sehgal, Sachin Shankar, Narendra Sharma, Shanti Bardhan, Simkie and many others who had moved to Bombay soon after the USICC at Almora closed down. Many of them found their calling in the films as dance and music directors and some like Guru Dutt became one of the best-known directors of that time. In several of the films of the same time, including *Dharti ka Lal* (director: Kkwaja Ahmad abbas, 1946), *Neecha Nagar* (director: Chetan Anand, 1946) *Awara* (director: Raj Kapoor, 1951), *Jagte Raho* (director: Shambhu Mitra, Amit Maitra, 1956), *Kagaz ke Phool* (director: Guru Dutt, 1959) one may find traces of Shankar's dance legacy.

Exploring the Potential of the Body as a 'Symbol of Society'[10]

Shankar had, through his choreographic journey, clearly worked on the use of dance bodies to highlight a certain format of the aesthetic of attitude, stance, and movement of human bodies. The differences in embodiment due to social privilege, marginality, work, gender, emotions, and specific circumstances of service and labour by hierarchically differentiated communities, were passed through an aesthetic lens to become a part of his choreographic vocabulary, through pushing the ability of improvisation for each and every dancer. A part of Shankar's important legacy is perhaps to establish for the next generation of dancers, the assimilation of the binary of the modern everyday movements vis-a-vis the imaginary iconographic representation of the sculptured bodies from

[10] Ramsay Burt in his book *The Male Dancer* discusses the reflection of society in the body and the embodied (Burt 1995: 15).

history simultaneously. For his own dance, Shankar's representation of differential masculinities took as reference the socially formulated presences of gender binaries in a patriarchal society as inevitable outcomes of a gender/class/caste/religion based segregations.

The argument about authenticity and legitimacy was used against Shankar in a bid to control his indirect challenge to the one-way transmission of embodied knowledge in dance through the guru–shishya parampara. Shankar's legacy, given space within dance pedagogy creates a space for a modern conversation around the rights to **contextual references, transmission of knowledge**, and **cultural legitimacy** beyond hierarchical and hereditary control. The **improvisational process** propagated by Shankar, thus, was to learn to look for cues such as images and motifs (alphabets, numbers, monuments, geometric shapes, and almost anything and everything that generated a kinaesthetic possibility in the dancing body), communicative gestures led by human emotions, and the patterns of movements of all living and non-living presences in daily lives. If anything, Shankar was opening up the possibilities of creating new ways of being inspired by one's surroundings. He was teaching his students to be able to imagine different ways of using those inspirations to create new movements, while deliberately refraining from the exact reproduction or even identifiable representation of the original inspiration.

As mentioned earlier in Chapter 4, Shankar saw as his pedagogical base, the use of dance as an individually nurtured expressive skill, a community expression and embodying of ensemble identity. A large part of Shankar's work continued by his students and his wife, Amala, has been to establish the importance of ensemble practice and coming together in dance through a process of pooling in of artistic labour as a group and not as an individual dancer. In the classes, the dancer was taught to register the smallest of impulses from the ensemble he/she shared her/his artistic space with. Dancing could be an individual act or a group act, needing two very different kinds of agency, effort, labour, and negotiations. The expression, 'group feeling' used by Zohra Segal, Narendra Sharma, and Amala Shankar is familiar to all the students who have been associated with the Shankars, signifying a challenge of the hyper-sensitive state of moving together as a group, anticipating, and almost knowing without watching what the group members would be doing next. The result is that each of the dancers in a group thinks of his/her dance as a contribution towards the building of 'their' dance together.

The Remnants

I would like to draw attention to an important letter written by Shankar. On November 5, 1975, Shankar wrote a typed note that had his signature but was not addressed to anybody in particular, which was published in the Souvenir Book (1975) of the USICC, Kolkata's annual programme, in its original form. He wrote:

> Over the Long 52 years starting from painting and then dancing, I had chances to witness folk and classical dances of all the nations of the world and found that they were all different from each other, even in India, we have so many different kind of dances, even though the human body is the same all over.
>
> I found out with my experiences of the past that the root of all the dances in the world is the body and the mind and the past cultural heritage of the nations.
>
> So I worked out a method of my own..... It starts with walking—just simple walking, and through this method of mine, some problems are created, and then one starts feeling that he has never known his own body before. As he goes on, after few months he realises that how wonderful his body is, and this body can create wonderful patterns; and for the first time he starts to know that he has limbs which are so beautiful when they work with the mind.
>
> This method helps to develop the sense of rhythm—creation of environment—organisation, discipline, imagination—calculation—concentration—observation—alertness—improvisation—inspiration—composition—planning the movement—sense of space—sense of group feeling—creating one's own movement—psychology of body movement to know one's body well before taking up any kind of dance—creating an image of dance form in the mind before taking up any action—civic sense—knowledge of culture and its effect on one's own life and above all the sense of self criticism.
>
> In 1940 I tried this out in my Almora Centre for 5 years and I had a tremendous success. But unfortunately, the centre was closed down during the 2nd World War on account of food and communication. Now I want to start this course for the first time in Calcutta. And for which, I need suitable halls to work in, with as many students as possible, and a residential flat for my living, nearby or attached to the halls. This Centre will be run by a non-profit-earning society which has already been registered under Societies Registration Act.
>
> Signed
> Uday Shankar, 05-11-75. (USICC Souvenir Book 1975)

Shankar was taken seriously ill during his tour of the United States of America in 1968–1969. He returned to India soon after and passed away on September 26, 1977. The above-mentioned note was as much a promissory one to himself as to the possible new patrons he was planning to approach for opening a formal dance school again in Kolkata. His vision remained unfulfilled as his health deteriorated, but this note remains the directive for what he actually may have seen as the crystallised form of his legacy.

The note is not a detailed one. But it certainly carries the essence of some of the structures of pedagogy and their functions that Shankar developed as his at the institution in Almora. This note was written during the tenth year of the USICC, Kolkata. There was a serious rift between Shankar and his wife soon after the school became successful in its own right. Shankar's last tour of America in 1968 was with some of his senior dancers. Shankar's path continued to be separated from his family and also from the USICC, Kolkata. This caused a lot of speculation in the dance community in Kolkata, and split the group of people associated with the Shankars into two oppositional camps. 'Dada wanted Baudi to continue with the school. When he decided to go his own way, he requested me to be with Baudi' said Guru P. Raghavan, one of the closest and longest associates of the Shankars, in his interview to me.[11] The Kathakali expert, Guru P. Raghavan, had joined Shankar during the making of *Kalpana* and continued to be with Amala Shankar at her school as one of the principal teachers of Kathakali. He assisted Amala Shankar with choreography for many of the later dance pieces of the USICC, Kolkata, and also helped in the recreation of Shankar's original choreographies. His Kathakali classes were rigid. They were torturous in the precision he wanted and demanded out of the students. His teaching of vocabularies of Kathakali, beginning with the grammar and progressing through years of teaching complete dances, created possibilities for us to explore movements that could use the stability of the Kathakali posture and the strong steps while exerting different positions of the upper body, hands, and facial muscles to push the boundaries of possibilities beyond the Kathakali movement structures. She sought his inputs in movement explorations, even though she would often push him to move beyond the rigid boundaries of the classical Kathakali grammar. Such collaborations between them were a lesson

[11] Interview of Guru P. Raghavan, Kolkata, 2003.

for us that could later be clearly identified as a bifurcation between the classical vocabulary and its innovative applications.

The other form that was taught in the beginning years of the USICC, Kolkata was Manipuri. Guru Tarun Singh from Manipur had joined the USICC Kolkata from its inception in 1965. Shankar's preference for the male as well as female dance forms from Manipur that later got categorised as the classical dance form named Manipuri is very clearly understood in the way he invited Guru Amobi Singh as a faculty at the USICC, Almora.

Shankar saw the possibility of developing a range of indigenous kinaesthetic motivations from each of these very different forms. These impulses and kinaesthetic designs/motivations are not the same as straightforward imitations of the dance movements, but are significant embodied knowledge that can enrich the body's possibilities of moving beyond its limited structural, functional, and skill-related boundaries. His genius and capability as a master choreographer, an instinctive teacher, and an expert conductor that becomes evident in the discussions in the previous chapters, obviously were not a part of the USICC, Kolkata's teaching schedule. Neither was Shankar a regular visitor to the school after I joined the school. From the early years of the Centre in Kolkata, the structure followed by the school was always validated through often mentioned and referred syllabuses and class structures experimented on and consolidated at Shankar's institution in Almora.

Choreography: A Special Focus Within Shankar's Pedagogy

In my opinion, there is a clear division between dance/movement training and the choreographic compositions in Shankar's teaching techniques. Whereas the units of dance were small solo or ensemble movement sequences, choreographic endeavours needed complex spatial and temporal arrangements that used the dance movements but created something more holistic and complex. In a way, choreography, for Shankar, clarified Andre Lepacki's following words:

> To conceive choreography as an apparatus is to see it as a mechanism that simultaneously distributes and organizes dance's relationship to perception and signification.... To see choreography as an apparatus—moreover, to see

> it as an apparatus that captures dance only to distribute its significations and mobilisations, its gestures and affects, within fields of light and fields of words that are strictly codified—is to delimit those hegemonic modes of aesthetically perceiving and theoretically accounting for dance's evolutions in time. The casting of dance as ephemeral, and the casting of that ephemerality as problematic, is already the temporal enframing of dance by the choreographic. (Lepecki, 'Choreography as' 2007: 120)

Many of Shankar's students from Almora (1939–1944) and later from Kolkata (1965–2015) have had different opinions regarding the scope, agency, and freedom this method of dance-making accorded to the people who have learnt the technique directly or indirectly. Narendra Sharma remained a dedicated follower of Shankar's pedagogy and continued teaching dance at the Modern School in Delhi creating a significant group of students who benefitted from his teachings. His choreographic works consistently foregrounded his conviction about the importance of the process in Shankar's creative style of dance. His interview mentions the choreographic processes explored in classes in Almora, 'If you don't have the technique to know the body, body language can never develop. You fall back on styles. Because they are a readymade language' (Sharma, 'Making of' 1998b: 86). It is evident that the form that is described and dismissed as a simplistic fusion of different dance styles, could actually supply endless possibilities to dancers. The ideas would become different with age, maturity, experience, exposure, aesthetic choice, and changing responses to the everyday encounters. The dance would therefore never stop being in flow, accommodating social awareness, politics of gender, aesthetic choices, sexuality, body type, and so on. It could also be a completely free exploration of a philosophy or an abstract idea. Regarding the pedagogy around the creative process at the USICC, Almora, Sharma writes:

> Each student had to do his own choreography: after every two months, sometimes one month, sometimes three months. His own work was presented formally on stage. The music was provided by the troupe. Of course, there was no lighting, only gas lamps. We did our own costumes, because he had a lot of costumes, and you could borrow from there. And your composition was assessed the next day. (Sharma, 'Making of' 1998b: 86)

In her repeated references, Smt. Amala Shankar talked about the much-admired improvisation classes at the USICC, Almora where she experienced the pedagogical process that Shankar had developed for training students. Her work at the USICC, Kolkata consolidates many of the ideas discussed earlier in the chapter.

Amala Shankar (1919–2020) and Us: Negotiating a Space Between Shankar's Legacy and Dance

Engulfed by the halo of the illustrious husband and the great dance maestro Uday Shankar and the world-renowned sitarist Pandit Ravi Shankar, Amala Shankar's capabilities as a dancer and a teacher has gone without much academic, analytic, or appreciative attention even though she continued to live, breathe, and dream dance all her life. For over the fifty years that I had known her as a teacher, as a mentor, and as a guide, she practised and taught dance with an overwhelming and often obsessive single-mindedness, sometimes even at the cost of being misunderstood by her near and dear ones. Shankar's pedagogy, dance creations, and aesthetics became Amala Shankar's universe. Till her demise on July 24, 2020, she remained one of the key persons through whom the pedagogic structure remained in practice and was transmitted to several generations of students. The USICC, Kolkata can be seen as a culmination of Amala Shankar's long association with Uday Shankar since 1931. At the age of eleven she was exposed to Shankar's performance and in the following two years she had toured Europe extensively with Shankar, and finally at the age of twenty-one, she joined his institution, the USICC at Almora and soon after became his wife. For me, a student of Amala Shankar's from the age of six, it has been a privilege to understand the complex self-imposed responsibility that Amala Shankar built in her mind for the continuation of her husband's legacy (Figs. 6.1 and 6.2).

Amala Shankar, my dance teacher, mentor, and an important influence in my life, who I first met in 1966, was born on the 27th of June, 1919. While this section of the book includes her contribution to the continuation of Shankar's legacy, it also aspires to create a space for analysing her work as an extension of Shankar's embodied experiments. I give myself a bit of freedom to critically access the partially processed memories and nostalgia that she shared with her students over the years that now make newer sense through my experience in dance studies research. By trying to access my own memory critically, I explore a less-charted territory regarding her pedagogical contribution in the process of the

Fig. 6.1 Uday, Amala and Ravi Shankar with USICC students during the shooting of a BBC documentary film (© Photo is from author's personal collection)

Fig. 6.2 A class with an invited faculty at USICC, Kolkata (© Photo is from author's personal collection)

continuity of Shankar's thoughts and ideas on corporeality and embodiment. She had assumed the responsibility of carrying on Shankar's work. I argue for her recognition as an innovative pedagogue and an able teacher, whose relationship with dance was born as a modern engagement and had maintained an ongoing conversation with the changing times.

There is almost no academic writing on Amala Shankar.[12] Her students have not written specifically about her, her dance, her efforts to rejuvenate Uday Shankar's dance academy, her pedagogic endeavours, and the huge number of students—both male and female—that she has nurtured over the fifty years that she ran the USICC. Until much later in her life she never claimed her space as a wonderful painter who has created a large number of beautiful paintings using her fingers instead of brushes to paint with water colour, imagining dancing figures including that the characters portrayed by Shankar, such as Buddha and Shiva, within her paintings of temples, palatial architectures, and caves. Hardly anyone knows that she created the slides for the shadow play for Uday Shankar's choreography, named *Buddha*, which she re-choreographed in 1992 as *Mahamanav*. In the staging of *Mahamanav* at the beginning of the 90s also, she reused the slides with the sceneries in the production.

Hardly anyone knows that Amala actually read Tagore's poem, *Samanya Kshati* (meaning 'an insignificant loss') to Shankar who did not read Bengali comfortably. This led to the choice of the poem by Shankar as a choreographic theme. Nobody acknowledges her role other than as a dancer in Uday Shankar's film *Kalpana*, where her contribution behind the camera was as significant as in front of it. Amala Shankar hesitated to claim her space in the dance world without using her position as Shankar's wife.[13] In the process, she was known as a beautiful dance partner of Shankar at best, but not for her role in keeping Shankar's dance process alive.

Amala Shankar was a study in contradictions. She mentioned how long her long journey from a small village in undivided Bengal to the world stage, humbly placing herself in the social milieu of a village in Bengal

[12] Journalistic articles mentioning her as 'the muse' in fact robs her of any agency that she might have had in the history of Indian dance. http://write2kill.in/feature/amala-shankar-the-muse.html, accessed on 25 March 2018.

[13] Well known for similar comments, Amala Shankar is quoted in Hindu to say 'I am not a dancer. My life is a dance', http://www.thehindu.com/todays-paper/tp-features/tp-sundaymagazine/On-life-with-a-legend/article15941136.ece, accessed on 25 March 2018.

where she was born and raised amongst numerous siblings. She took pride in being traditional, being educated, and encouraged her students to learn epic texts as well as histories. She took pride in 'knowing' the work that women in traditional families 'need' to know and the age-old 'Indian' values. She also ran a performing troupe that travelled the world for more than 30 years. But her connection to dance is seen as a way of survival and duty to art and Uday Shankar.

It was her refusal to engage with the ongoing debates on modernity that left me as a scholar, a bit helpless for a long time regarding the way she should be placed, vis-a-vis, the dance history in India. After her recent demise, I am left wondering if it becomes an imposition to read her work as innovative and pedagogical if she saw herself and her work in dance as a revivalist, who wanted to propagate the Uday Shankar style of dance? Do I have the right to read her complex negotiations with subservience to Uday Shankar's image as a gendered position that she accepted as a woman traditionally bound by the norms of a patriarchal society? Or do I venture, through a scholastic reading of her contributions into the complexities of trying to create a specific space for her as an independent pedagogue who may have started from what her husband left as a legacy, but went much further in advancing the pedagogy of modern dance in a systematic manner?

Smt. Amala Shankar saw her life with Shankar as something ordained by the Gods. She handled being with him and without him, through personal ups and downs, without making her personal story available for any of us to gossip over. And we all were witness to her capable handling of the dance institution and the performing troupe of the USICC, Kolkata with professional and passionate engagement. In her numerous conversations with me through the period of intense rehearsals, tours, and performances, she repeatedly said that through her personal and professional life as Shankar's wife and dance partner, she had learnt to foreground Uday Shankar, the world-famous dancer, over Uday, her husband. Consciously or unconsciously, submitting to a largely patriarchal frame of evaluation that placed Amala Shankar, first as a student and then as a wife and the dance partner of the world-famous dancer, Amala Shankar remained ensconced in the shadows of Uday Shankar and identified herself as a woman whose life and dance were totally and completely shaped and directed by Shankar's ideas and creative genius. She never claimed her position as an independent dancer and choreographer, and the dance community certainly did not give her that position until much later in her life after Shankar's death in 1977. Even then she was acknowledged as someone who has made Shankar's legacy visible by carrying on with teaching his dances. It is only as a teacher, post-1965 (when she established the USICC in Kolkata with Uday Shankar and became known as its Director-in-Charge) that she asserted herself and her work within the Kolkata dance circle through her role as a teacher of Uday Shankar's dance technique, and carried on her work as a choreographer and as a re-creator of many of Shankar's choreographies as well.

The USICC in Kolkata, a popular and respected dance institution, closed down in 2015 due to Amala Shankar's inability to continue teaching. It has trained thousands of students and its performance troupe has travelled all over the world bringing huge visibility to Shankar's style of dance and the choreographies of Uday and Amala Shankar. But like many other performers, perpetually insecure regarding their position and largely unsure of how and when to create a legacy beyond their own lives, Amala Shankar failed to create a structure of visible continuity, whereby her pedagogic excellence would continue through an organised institutional structure, failing to enable teachers she herself trained and employed in her institution for over five decades.

The USICC is no more. It died twice, once in Almora when the path-breaking institution established by Uday Shankar shut down leaving its students confused and without any support, and the second time in Kolkata where the diminishing popularity of the institution as well as Amala Shankar's health conditions made it essential to shut the doors of the institution again, this time probably for ever. The USICC has made it possible for many of its alumni to become spectacular leaders and professionals all over the world and for many of them, Amala Shankar remains much more than a dance teacher. She continues to be acknowledged for the aesthetic, social, and gendered choices that these women make, the way they represent themselves, and the way they see and experience their lives. This in itself is no small feat.

The claiming and reclaiming of his heritage became a major issue even before Amala Shankar passed away at the age of one hundred and two in 2020. Marital discord during the last ten years of the Shankar's life had been the reason for several legal complications. As his wife, Amala had not been able to claim her familial rights to some extent and to the material part of legacy such as Shankar's costumes, recordings, props, and most importantly his film *Kalpana*. *Kalpana* has been rescued and thankfully even with the ongoing court cases copies of it is now available for people to see.

My vulnerability knows no bounds as I want to acknowledge and write about Amala Shankar's contribution as part of Shankar's legacy. Like Uday Shankar, Amala Shankar was also unable to provide her students any right to claim their space in the fold of this form as practitioners. But I realise that she who fought for her rights to be recognised as the only dancer who has inherited the tradition had her own vulnerability as she created a line of continuity for herself, unable to open up the legacy beyond herself. In a way, ironically, it may be what Shankar had wanted to leave behind, a global nostalgia about his dance and a pedagogy which hopes to excite the process of creativity through a rough but tested pedagogy. I, therefore, make myself more vulnerable as I promise not to claim any legacy through the art of imitating and regurgitating. As many students of Amala Shankar, I can claim to be a dancer whose creative imagination took off under Amala Shankar's tutelage through the process of observation, improvisation, and concentration, a set of three related skills that she sharpened as part of her teaching method around Shankar's dance.

Uday Shankar's Legacy? Amala Shankar's Legacy? A Sum of Both?

Mashima repeatedly said to us, 'your uncle (Shankar) was the genius, he should have been recognised in a more significant way and deserved the fame that dancers of his calibre get in many other cultures. But he did not live long and he also died dissatisfied, without really being rewarded appropriately for the way he worked as one of the prominent cultural ambassadors of colonised India. In comparison, I have lived long, and have revelled in the glory of his achievements and got recognition for what I became largely because of him'.[14] This comment itself reveals the extent to which she herself disregarded her own achievements.

A review of the history of the ninety years she spent associated to dance makes it clear that after coming to know Uday Shankar and his dance, Amala remained largely bound by the dance vocabulary that she used to cage herself in, in all her talks, interviews, writings, and claims. It is

[14] Amala Shankar's words, repeated on accasions while she reminisced about Uday Shankar are remembered by her students and associated.

impossible to allot her the agency that she never even wanted to claim for herself. In her role as a wife/dance partner/student/assistant, Amala Shankar never actively stood independently or separately on her own. She created her own space, but was always comfortable projecting herself as someone who carried on Shankar's work and not by standing out as a separate entity. She herself has always seen her relationship with Shankar as a dual one, where he was Uday the husband and Uday Shankar the dancer. One cannot but acknowledge her reservations about staking a claim as an independent dancer. She started as an eager admirer, following his work with almost obsessive patience and rigour, absorbing each and every nuance of the movements that Shankar effortlessly and organically created during the years that she spent in his company, first as a junior member of the company and gradually progressing and becoming a senior and an important dancer, and finally becoming his wife. Therefore, methodologically it became my only option to write about her only through her dance, infusing what she claimed she was with how her work defines her within the spectre of Uday Shankar's legacy.

At the same time, though, a rather uncomfortable question surfaces time and again in this context. It stems from certain conversations that Amala Shankar often had with her students regarding a series of life-changing coincidences and accidental connections that made Uday and Amala Shankar choose the path that they did and the legacy that got created out of their journeys. The first of such coincidences was Pavlova's interest in engaging Uday Shankar in creating two 'Indian' choreographic compositions, knowing fully well that he had no idea about Indian dance or any training in any form of dance at all, was an arbitrarily made choice. The second of the coincidences, according to Amala, was her travelling across the world with her father for the Paris Exposition and meeting Uday Shankar, Nyota Inyoka, and so many other luminaries, in spite of her upbringing in a village in Bangladesh, when, in spite of her lack of proper training, she was chosen by the dancer, Nyota Inyoka, to dance the Indian dance at the Paris Exposition.

Looking through the archives and making historiographical connections, these coincidental and arbitrary but timely and convenient arrangements clearly establish the troublesome and casual attitude of the dance entrepreneurs regarding the quality and depth of Indian dance and especially the dance technique and expertise that was expected out of either Uday or Amala Shankar in order to qualify as a dancer. While western ballet already had the rigid technique and high standards so no untrained dancer could be allowed to perform without training, everybody seemed to be ‘performing’ Indian dance. The body projection of the actual training, the flow, the languor, and the vigour that was considered ‘Oriental’ and more specifically ‘Indian’, could be adequate to produce an image of the Indian body in dance rather than learning the actual movements. More emphasis was on the dress and the hand gestures, vague but having some ‘Oriental’ reference that seemed sufficient to create an exotic representation. It was important for the dance to be named appropriately on some identifiably ‘Oriental’ theme. This casual attitude towards ‘Indian’ dance that they both had experienced in all their transcultural conversations may have been one of the reasons for the passionate wish for defining and claiming specific ‘Indian’ness in dance. In fact, they both seemed to have realised the importance to be nationally defined and rooted in order to have control over any transcultural negotiations. These teachers who we have later seen to be strict and rigorous regarding learning processes and the length of training that they insisted was essential for any dancer to be allowed on stage, were the same people who in the beginning of their dance journey actually devised, quite literally, their ‘Indian’ performances.

What Legacy?

I continue this section on Shankar’s legacy by sharing a few experiences of mine at the USICC, Kolkata. In retrospect, I understand Shankar’s dance through them. They have shaped the thoughts on creativity and innovation of the students in the institution. Amala Shankar taught us to be curious about all that is the dance in our country. She opened doors for us to appreciate the traditional lives filled with social, cultural, and ritual practices in India. She gave us the tools to investigate, accept, and appreciate practices from all over the world. The USICC, Kokata also structured many of us as individuals, as well as social beings. Hence, these memories are important to share, in order to explore Shankar’s legacy, even if this reminiscing quality pushes this section of the writing away from an otherwise academic framework.

One of the most unique and different characteristics of the USICC, Kolkata was that it was a dance institution that opened its doors to very young children. The school had a junior and a senior section. The junior section admitted students from the age of five. Samik Bandyopadhyay's interview with Amala Shankar in 1965 (Bengali year 1372)[15] on USICC was first published in the Bengali Periodical, *Porichoy*. Interestingly, it was an interview in the year that the USICC opened its Kolkata branch on the Rabindra Sarobar Stadium premises. Amala's aspirations are recorded in it. In the beginning few lines of the interview, Samik Bandyopadhyay described a class:

> Amala Shankar is teaching the class herself. The method of teaching is unique. Even the youngest of students are creating the hand gestures and steps according to their wish and imagination. In their class, the older students started walking in circle and created their own rhythm was walking together. The percussion instrument started following the same rhythm. The dancers add hand movements, and then gestures (*mudra*) and then neck movements to the rhythmic walk. Adding of small elements to the walk, creates a cycle of rhythmic movement sequence that is repeated.... The dancers learn to be conscious of the audience and at the same time can be unaffected by their presence while concentrating in their work of bringing their mind and body together in the class. (Bandyopadhyay 2020: 43 [translation mine])

The souvenir of the USICC, Kolkata of 1968 has a short article by Amala Shankar, where she introduced the Centre's second public programme titled '*Arghya*' (A Divine Offering). She talked about beginning the Centre with only three thousand Rupees and two rooms at the Rabindra Sarobar premises and with only twenty-five students. She acknowledged that 'Today the Centre has on its roll one hundred and twenty five students, some five times the numbers there were at the start... I am not ashamed of the tears that mist my eyes when an infant bursts into her first dance steps or a little girl of yesterday displays the grace of a polished dancer' (Amala Shankar, Souvenir of the USICC, 1968).

The First Set of Memories: Life to Dance and Back

The USICC as an institution and Amala Shankar as an extraordinary teacher guided many of us through dance training, of course, but also played a pivotal role in helping us in learning the ways of

[15] Samik Bandyopadhyay's interview of Amala Shankar provides a glimpse of her thoughts at the time of opening of the Uday Shankar India Culture Centre in Kolkata.

life through intense and prolonged lessons in socialisation, ethics, and over and above everything else, the role of aesthetics in everyday life. After I was admitted as a junior first-year student at the USICC in 1966, I continued to be associated with it as a student first and then a performer in the performance troupe and then gradually became a faculty/administrator/member of the managing committee till I moved to Delhi in 2004. I also never dissociated with the centre till it closed down formally. Through this time, in an ever-evolving and complicated manner, I have tried to locate Amala Shankar's work in relation to Shankar's legacy and that process has not been easy.

The Teaching Process and Pedagogic Structure

Amala Shankar repeatedly said that she did not want to create dancers out of her students, but actually wanted us to be good human beings. She also often assured the parents of her wards that a student who can observe, imagine, and remember well in dance classes is also bound to do well in his/her studies. The classes encouraged independent as well as group participation. The first day's class was a surprise and I have never forgotten it. It was a major shift from the conventional dance institution I was enrolled in for a little while, before joining USICC. The learning process in the older school was simply about the act of imitating the movements shown by the teacher or her/his assistants, without any creative initiative expected or allowed of us.

The USICC was an impressive change. The classes were about finding motifs from everyday life and turning them into non-verbal movements. They were also about transforming those movements under assisted procedural applications into specific structured repeatable sequences, ready to be called 'dance'. The training was special. We had to attend three classical dance classes (Manipuri, Kathakali, and Bharatanatyam), as well as one class on the Uday Shankar style of creative dance. The class on creative style was conducted by Amala Shankar herself. Recognising and linking music and rhythm to moods and emotions created for each exercise of the class was a part of the dance lessons. The musicians improvised and played the Indian musical instruments, the sarod, the flute, and the tabla. We danced to the music or the music followed our movements. We were instructed about picking the motifs and inspirations from everyday life to imagine creating a repeatable sequence. All movements were supposed to have a clear beginning and an end. No gesture or posture could be left half way and if they were, suggestions were given to improve them. Classes had us experimenting with walking on different rhythms; expressing through movements, simple words, such as 'no', 'give', 'go'; imitating the postures of someone sitting or standing in a particular way, or making movements with English or Bengali alphabets or numbers. It was as if I was looking at the world though dance and everything around me had started dancing!

The training was rigorous as well, full of disappointments and highs connected to simple facts like standing in the first line or the second one or being a part of a performance or not. In our minds we already were socialised to measure our success or failure in the accepted manner, always registering when someone was chosen to be in the first line or for a particular role or for a 'more visible' position and so on. Looking back, I understand what a monumental task it must have been for our teacher to address issues of personal aspirations and competitions that one is used to in the education system. In this institution one learnt to accept evaluation as a normal part of one's life and in fact constantly be self-reflexive so that it became easy to volunteer to step back and let someone else go forward. It was a learning and unlearning time, which many of the students and parents could not take and those who stuck on actually won a huge game of self-discipline as well as learning to acknowledge the importance of a collective. Dancing well individually was of no importance unless one was able to perform with a group and as a part of the group to contribute towards building the collective practice and image. What marks the Shankar style dancers coming out of Amala Shankar's school is what we learnt, how we learnt it, and what we loved to dance. We were taught dances of Shankar as recreated classics and they seemed ageless dances to the accompaniment of music composed by distinguished musicians. We were making movements every day in class from abstract ideas and human postures. We were also creating dance compositions.

Though criticised time and again for the dilution and the synthesis of styles, the USICC continued to teach multiple classical styles. Initially it was only Kathakali, Bharatanatyam, and Manipuri from 1965, and much later Kathak and Odissi, replaced Bharatanatyam and Manipuri. The creative style (also beginning to be specifically identified as the Uday Shankar style in the performance brochures/Souvenirs of 1968/1969 of the USICC) of dance remained the school's signature entry-point into the arena of Indian Modern Dance. The process remained grounded in the pedagogy established by Uday Shankar at his dance academy in Almora.

Unlike Shankar's adult students, the students at Kolkata were young children, teenagers, young adults, and adults. The process could not be as immersive as classes were eld only twice a week and had to be undertaken alongside other academic pressure, but the rigour was uncompromised. The classical dances provided a range of embodied knowledge and skills that extended the possibilities for exploration of the bodies. The strong belief was that the body of a new learner needed to be challenged and pushed into breaking movement stereotypes. The learner was encouraged to understand the connection between rhythms and moving, as they constantly interacted with live music that allowed them to experience the freedom as well as the challenge of becoming a part of a body-music conversation. The classes were focused on prioritising and teaching different processes of creating dance movements and choreography rather than teaching dance compositions as finished products. This was in complete opposition to the classical dance classes where dance grammars were being taught to achieve extreme precision.

Innumerable trips with the dance troupe of the USICC, both within and outside India since then, have really made me acknowledge how much there was to learn beyond dance. For many of us, the dance skills may have been instrumental in including us in the troupe, but the rest of the learning, especially the importance of being there for the troupe and not only for ourselves; to be interested in seeing new things and new sights; meeting new people and enjoying new cultures; and trying to absorb the sights, sounds, and wonders all around, gave us the strength to enjoy and endure many things in our everyday lives. Lessons in dance were accompanied by life-changing learnings: Travelling to new geographies, near and far, within and outside India, and taking care of one's own things; learning to share space, clothes, food, laughter, and dance; learning to take care of costumes, ornaments, and props; understanding that the show must go on; looking out of the train window and registering different colours of the soil, designs of the roofs, and being told the reasons for such differences in life in our country. I can go on, but instead there is one example that would clarify how the dance school became much more than where one learnt to dance. In 1974, the USICC was invited to perform on the occasion of the Indian Republic Day in Sikkim. This was the year before Sikkim was accessed as Indian territory. Five of us travelled with Mashima to Bagdogra from Kolkata on a small plane. This was my first airplane ride, I was in the 9th standard. Mashima asked me to come and sit beside her on the plane. I was on the window seat and the whole way she kept drawing my attention to the landscape that was visible from the window, while she identified important rivers, peaks, making my trip memorable in more ways than one. In the process, I started visualising India's aerial picture which became my first experience with a live map. My wonder at the unfolding sceneries of India has remained with me, now translating as her interest in my overall growth. This growth had nothing to do with the task she had promised to undertake as my dance teacher. This was far beyond her responsibilities.

'New' Movement?

Somatic and kinetic possibilities may be unlimited, but capabilities are finite in so far as human physical capacity, musculature, physiology, and skills can permit. Dance practice like sports or yoga challenges the body to reach beyond what it is used to doing and pushes the dancer to reach beyond the limits of the possible. The class for innovation and movement creation, therefore, pushed students to think of a new vocabulary, resulting in 'new' movements in dance that were created out of new triggers and therefore were 'out of the box', either in terms of grammar or imagination.

By way of the possible innovations for creating something new, the available physical and imaginative capacities most often served as the base for the dance technique mobilised by the dancers. At the USICC, the task of the teacher/facilitator often was to channelise the capacities available in the students, to constantly push them to explore all possible capabilities. In other words, the students were encouraged to go against the habitual reproduction of capabilities. The aim of the teacher in such improvisational experiments was to give the instructions to push for innovative ideas of generating 'new' movements. In a way, this worked best when the hierarchical structure of the teacher-student was dissolved temporarily so that the student felt at ease even to go against all pre-existing aesthetic boundaries set by the teacher to explore the 'new' in a manner that has never been practised in that class before.

Triggers for imagination could be images drawn in stick figures by Mashima during classes. They could be letters or numbers in English or Bengali. They could also be live bodies of the musicians who were part of every class or any other guest visiting the school. We were asked to take inspiration from the sitting or standing postures of the live bodies in the classroom and create movements. Sometimes the writing of a letter with hands, steps, or different parts of the body would generate the movement; sometimes the student would actually finish in a posture that resembled the image he/she was inspired by. Imagine a class of twenty to twenty-five students, where every student created a new dance movement inspired by the images or other bodies. Movement-making was a game, a dare, and also a very minutely observed, assessed, as well as critiqued method of skill development, introduced very early in the pedagogy for developing the understanding of the process rather than just the imitative cloning that happens at the beginning of classical dance classes. We were often asked by Mashima, 'It is easy to strive to be better than someone. What if you did not have anyone to compete with? Is it only competition that drives you? Then you must ask yourself, what you love best—competing and being better than someone? Or is it dancing that you cannot live without'.

Embodiment was often experiential. I have learned to direct a spray of water at friends by playfully hitting the water with the wrist of my hands at the confluence of three rivers—the Ganges, Yamuna, and Saraswati, while having a bath in the sacred meeting place for the rivers known popularly as 'Prayag' in Allahabad. We have been asked to work out dance movements from backstroke or freestyle, while bathing in the river, and then create movement sequences on stage based on the fluidity that we experienced in the river. We have been made to walk with a long skirt on, kicking imperceptibly at the border of the skirt with our toes, to create an extra movement of the skirt. Six or eight of us students have been asked to hold a long wet mop in a straight line on the floor, while standing at an equal distance from each other, so that when we walked forward, bent at the waist together, flattening our hands to hold the mop on the ground, we would practise walking together in a line and we would clean the rehearsal space as well. Such awareness of movements generated from everyday life made the effort of creating stylised movements a conscious journey. A class for creative innovative dance practice intrinsically involved structured and unstructured processes of moving, remembering the move, and being able to repeat and refine it as well. Introducing the students to the stages of creating movements, thus, had a logic that has never been mentioned by Amala Shankar herself or anyone else till now. Looking back and analysing the process, I identify a five-point consciousness that is instituted through the teaching process.

1. **Body awareness**: Knowing one's own body along with generating a mind–body connection through breathing, becoming conscious of the fingers, toes, spine, shoulder position, stomach, knees. This kinaesthetic awareness and possibilities thereof were essential to creating movement awareness.
2. **Observation and imagination**: Keen and concentrated observation of movements by cohorts and other moving objects as well as exploring the extent of movement possibilities that each body part is capable of, were ways in which one was encouraged to expand the embodied modes of imagination.
3. **Improvisation/Innovation and kinetic communication**: One of the main training was for innovative ways of being in a kinetic communication with other bodies, setting out specific criteria for moving together with others. This required a different set of skills and awareness than those required for solo dancing.
4. **Developing concentration through the use of a combination of different kinetic and memory-based exercises**: Challenging the students to constantly multi-task with different tools such as improvisation, observation, imitation, mirroring, assimilating verbal instructions, and practising concentration in different permutation and the combination was the challenge that students got used to in the creative dance classes.
5. **Thinking of a class as a laboratory space**: From early years all participants had to observe the movement(s) created by a particular individual or a group and then reproduce it as perfectly as possible. Great attention was paid to the creative process, the product, and the way each student observed and was able to get the actual essence of the movement in what they were imitating as a product.

The 'Walking' Exercise: A Preliminary Tool for the Processual Development of Movements

As is evident in Amala Shankar's interview by Bandyopadhyay, walking continued to be a class for senior students, inherited from the USICC curriculum in Almora. One excellent example of the training for layered consciousness in dancing is that of the 'walking to dancing' exercise that was a regular part of the exercises in senior (age sixteen onward) classes.[16] Starting without any rhythm, the students were asked to start walking to form a circle, while trying to arrive at a common pace and matching steps. Walking straight with an everyday gait the group started concentrating on walking on a common rhythm while listening to the instructions given by Mashima without stopping. The bifurcation of the mind that counted the rhythm in 1, 2, 3, 4, while continuing to follow increasingly complex additional movements that Mashima challenged the students with started with simpler exercises like walking and clapping on a particular rhythm to increasingly complex steps and breaking of rhythmic patterns in claps followed by hand movements added to the pattern meant that there was a need to concentrate on different requirements introduced to activate layers of capabilities. Over and above this she would talk to us, asking us what we had for breakfast, or who dropped us at the class that day, challenging us to continue with the moving and dancing while having an everyday conversation. In short, the classes were about consciously encountering mobility/ability and creating a logic of moving. It also enabled self-documenting and brought together observation, innovation, and skill within the otherwise mundane process of walking. Through the basic and yet most essential and empowering human movement of walking, we as a group were being challenged to experience our own places and motions—always in the context of a space created by motions of other bodies. Walking to dancing in our classes focused on the creation of an identifiable space through the coming together of different bodies and a multiplicity of gaits, rhythms, and mental frames. Walking gave us the tool to come together and find our ways of owning that space by arriving at an alert but relaxed way of co-inhabiting. It also challenged us to think creatively on the move—negotiating rhythm, matching steps with co-walkers, while experiencing mobility and movement generation differentially.

[16] Narendra Sharma in his interview to me (Delhi, 2004) talked in detail about Uday Shankar's methods of training in Uday Shankar India Culture Centre in Almora where this method was introduced for the first time as a part of the pedagogic process.

Dancing to the Music

Rabin Das as music director, sarod player and an expert in a range of other string instruments, Soumen Dey as the flutist, Souren Ghosh as the tabla/drum player, Kabita Nandi as the vocalists are only a few names I mention out of a number of able accompanists for our classes and shows. All these men and women were of excellent calibre and professional standard. The classes were the time and space for innovative explorations for both the dancers and the musicians. In the coordinated work that our teachers did with the accompanists in structuring the communication between the music and the movement generation exercises, the music did not remain merely the accompaniment but became a part of our dancing process. Mashima's classes were aided by the accompaniment of live music, something that I recognise now as a luxury that hardly any dance school could afford even at that time. Every day was a surprise planned to energise our ideas of the possibilities of moving, expressing, and communicating. With the help of the musicians who constantly improvised on the musical instruments of drums, table, sarod, cymbals, and flute, Amala Shankar introduced us to the rhythmic structures and moods with a deliberate push towards understanding differences in (1) pace (laya); (2) rhythmic patterns (tala); (3) natural movements and the application of aesthetic extensions and layering of those movements; (4) understanding the moods of the music and communicating the same through the embodied practice and; (5) giving the students the freedom and power to improvise, while the musicians followed and improvised on their musical instrument to create the appropriate accompanying environment. Thus, learning was a true ensemble experience, creating a shared experience of corporeal connectivity.

The Shrinking 'World'—The Illusive Legacy

To dance as if there is no one watching you is how one is commonly encouraged to engage with the act of dancing. At the same time, a dancer is constantly afraid that she will have no audience.

Faced with the total or partial marginalisation of the Uday Shankar's dance form (at least in the way he presented it to the world) the dance community that has invested in learning, teaching, and presenting the form has been grasping at any possible way of revitalising the form. As an anthropologist, it has always been important to me to be able to see why any dance form exists, dies, flourishes, or changes in order to suit the changing circumstances and needs of society. Thus, one of the principal questions for me is: what were the principal motivations for the form to emerge, for it to flourish, and what has changed for it to become redundant slowly over the years?

'Uday was greeted everywhere like a matinee idol, "Shankar" was soon the world's third best-known Indian, after Gandhi and Tagore' (Craske 2020: 46–47).[17] In the West, Uday Shankar and his glorious stage presentation (and not necessarily the form) is part of a transcultural history framed by the two World Wars. Shankar loved the audience in the West and they loved him back. He was the world traveller, offering uncomplicated glimpses of the Orient through his presentations. Dartington Hall and some other very special educational institutions recognised the extant possibilities of his dance form. Because of its claim of 'Indian'ness and an inherent ethnocentrism, the form had a global audience but had a limitation that stopped it from becoming a global form or leaving a global legacy. According to Craske, Ravi Shankar 'credited Uday with helping to devise a style of music for creative dance that was, like the dance itself "entirely new but basically Indian"' (Craske 2020: 38). The second World War had hampered Shankar's frequent visits to the lands of his ardent fans for a while. Though he continued his world tours in the post-war years, the priorities shifted to more rooted teaching and performing within India.

Amala Shankar's motivation was different from Shankar's and she worked hard to get the USICC Kolkata, the second edition of the Uday Shankar India Culture Centre started. Her work had taken a trans-generational turn. She loved working with new learners, to reiterate her and society's faith in a form that for her signified the work of a genius. At the USICC Kolkata, she had begun the process of new germination of dance in the new bodies. She also kept up the transcultural conversations across distant geographies. She invited famous choreographers from across the world to our school and we were taken to all performances of international artists from all over the world. Guests, both foreigners and Indians, were frequent visitors at the dance school. Frequent tours

[17] A chapter in Ravi Shankar's biography, 'Dancing comes first' (Craske 2020: 37–55) is dedicated to the beginning of Ravi Shankar's artistic journey as a dancer. It throws light on the way Uday Shankar's legacy also needs to be complicated by his pre and post-USICC negotiations.

lasting a month or more at a time took us to different continents across the world. But there was almost no government support for her institution. Smt. Shankar gave a good fight but ultimately gave up and left the space open for yet other versions of Shankar's creativity to take root.

As Shankar's legacy in dance remains elusive, there is a struggle to manipulate certain parts of the facts as a strategy for claiming whatever legacy one can. Many associates and inheritors of Uday Shankar's form feel sad, troubled, and even lost today. For them, the road ahead is obscured, and there is also no way to return to the heyday of the form. I also see a peaceful and joyous strength in many of the past students who carry a part of that archive in their bodies. This book is also for all such people within and across borders, who identify with the legacy in their thoughts and in the pedagogical flow of the knowledge of movement creation and generation.

References

Bandyopadhyay, Samik. 2020. "Amala Shankar: Proshongo Nrityakala (Bengali)." In *Samik Bandyopadhyay Sakkhatkar songroho*, edited by Moloy Rakshit, 43–44. Kolkata: Lalmati.

Burt, Ramsay. 1995. *The Male Dancer: Bodies, Spectacle and Sexuality*. London and New York: Routledge.

Craske, Oliver. 2020. *Indian Sun: The life and Music of Ravi Shankar*. London: Faber & Faber.

Katan, Einav. 2016. *Embodied Philosophy in Dance*. London: Palgrave Macmillan.

Khullar, Sonal. 2018. "Almora Dreams: Art and Life at the Uday Shankar India Cultural Centre, 1939–44." *Marg* 69 (4): 14–31.

Lepecki, André. 2007. (Summer). "Choreography as Apparatus of Capture." *TDR* 51 (2): 119–123.

Ray, R. M. 1956. Film Seminar Report. Delhi: Sangeet Natak Akademi.

Shankar, Uday. 1975. Letter dated 05-11-75 (Published in USICC Souvenir Book 1975).

Sharma, Narendra. 1998a. "Indian Dance at Cross-Roads." *Nrityakalpa (Bengali)* 2 (1, December): 34–36.

Sharma, Narendra. 1998b. "Making of a Thinking Dancer." *Seagull Theatre Quarterly*. 18 June: 80–91.

Index

U. Sarkar Munsi, *Uday Shankar and His Transcultural Experimentations*, Transnational Theatre Histories,
https://doi.org/10.1007/978-3-030-93224-4

D

Q

R

Printed by Printforce, United Kingdom